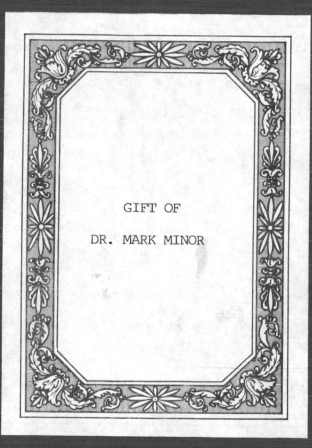

Rivermen

Rivermen

A Romantic Iconography of the River and the Source

FREDERIC S. COLWELL

89-1245

McGill-Queen's University Press
Kingston, Montreal, London

© McGill-Queen's University Press 1989
ISBN 0-7735-0711-6

Legal deposit third quarter 1989
Bibliothèque nationale du Québec

Printed in Canada on acid-free paper

This book has been published with the help of a
grant from the Canadian Federation for the
Humanities, using funds provided by the Social
Sciences and Humanities Research Council of
Canada.

Canadian Cataloguing in Publication Data

Colwell, Frederic S. (Frederic Stewart), 1933–
    Rivermen
    Includes bibliographical references and an index.
    ISBN 0-7735-0711-6
    1. English literature – History and criticism.
    2. Rivers in literature.   I. Title.
    PN56.R49C64 1989   820'.9'36   C89-090098-1

In memoriam
George Whalley

Contents

Acknowledgments

For permission to incorporate previously published materials, I wish to thank the editors of *ELH*, in which a version of the final chapter first appeared.

"The river," Wordsworth observed, "glideth at his own sweet will." Its progress is often a protracted, if not leisurely, affair. The course of this book has proved no exception. I wish to acknowledge readers of Romantic poetry whose researches were published after this inquiry was undertaken, who have confirmed me in my own and encouraged me in its pursuit. These are Christopher Wordsworth and John Beer, whose discussions of the river image are acknowledged elsewhere in my notes, and Geoffrey Hartman, who hinted in two sentences over two decades ago at the direction of my inquiry into the source and its guardian.

It is always with trepidation that one opens the book of another whom he has discovered to have recently piloted a similar course. It is, I think, a tribute to the amplitude of our subject that Wyman Herendeen's *From Landscape to Literature*, which charts the river from its upper reaches to the English Renaissance, plies channels quite different from my own.

I am grateful for the editorial advice of Kerry McSweeney and the skill and patience of Kathy Goodfriend, who prepared the typescript, and Bani Shorter, who showed me the difference between a shroud and a sail, and launched this undertaking.

Rivermen

Riverscapes: A Prologue

Water: for Thales, the first, for Pindar the best of all things. East and west acknowledged its primacy and power: "Water, thou art the source of all things and all existence" assert the *Purānas*.[1] Heraclitus witnessed his own city's losing struggle with the alluvial Meander and, from water, derived earth, the second of the elemental cornerstones of the created universe whose nature was flux and whose paradigm was the river. For Saint Francis water was the mirror of artless nature and a model for his own conduct: "Praised be my Lord for our sister water, who is very serviceable unto us and humble and precious and clean."[2] Mircea Eliade writes: "Water flows, it is 'living', it moves: it inspires, it heals, it prophesies. By their very nature, spring and river display power, life, perpetual renewal; they *are* and they are *alive*."[3]

Each river knows its birth, its passage from innocent purity to sullied experience, maturity, and death, but each also has its individual character and biography preserved in the myths recounting its origins and nature, myths which are not merely recollected from a fabulous past but continually reenacted as long as its springs feed its froward waters.

Civilization, we are told, was nurtured in the arms of the world's rivers. They drew man from forest and featureless plain with their uncertainties of weather and vagarious survival to fix his roots along the rivers' contours. There he might cultivate his agrarian, urban, and colonizing pursuits. But the presence of the same river that fostered his civilization and the identity it afforded him must have also served to undermine that sense of place and belonging, inviting him to ponder beyond the compass of his civilized complacency. Where did the river come from, and where did it go? Had not all things a beginning and an end? Somewhere the sea waited in unchartered immensity and the source lay hidden in the highlands of its birth.

The river draws us beyond the frontiers of our certainty to essay its wider and deeper mysteries where familiar demarcations no longer hold or are critically challenged and reconstituted. The river landscape is not simply geographical but profoundly psychological and metaphysical. It is, perhaps, no accident of history that western philosophy rose with the cities of the Meander plain. The river's passage to the sea rehearses and indeed may have inspired the entire range of philosophic inquiry: cosmogony and autogeny at the source, the problems of ontology, being and becoming, palpably rendered by its passage, the *telos* of the estuary.

The river was most commonly in the keeping of a god: it was his domain or even his person, but its source was the precinct of the female deities who attend birth, prophecy, and poetic inspiration, the threshold where dark procreative mystery rises into the light of our day. From its source to the waiting sea, the riverscape provides the fertile matrix where myth, the mother of all inquiry, is spontaneously generated.

Unlike the rhythms of Ocean, rivers have direction and purposive flow. The river's will is always its own, not laid down by man, for whom the river passage demands a surrender to its will, its currents and eddies. To move with the flow is to course with time and change; to stand astride or view it from a height offers the prophetic stance by which we contemplate its entire passage, its past, present, and the brightening waters or rippling shoals ahead.

But the passage upstream is the *opus contra naturam*, the journey toward beginnings from which time or the river would bear us away. Because of its challenges, scaling the highlands of the interior and bucking adverse currents, it is the direction seldom taken, the solitary struggle whose obstacles are challenged only by the intrepid, not those content to ruminate in the shade of the planes on the river banks, but those elected and driven by their own restless natures. For them the river and the river journey take on the character of the quest and its heroic landscape. The deeds of the hero and his history, like that of the river itself, are perennially relived in the chronicles of myth.

It is this interval land, the fertile juncture of myth and psychology, with its distinctive motifs, those of the quester or hero, the visionary, the mystery of beginnings and the creative impulse, and their expression in the familiar features and creatures of the riverscape that these essays propose to explore. This inquiry into our commerce with the river and its source, although concerned with the perennial and particularly the classical context of these features, will examine the psychic history of the literary riverscape at a late stage in its development: in the poetry of the early nineteenth century. The choice is not an arbitrary one. Just as mythopoesy begins with beginnings, its creation myths, so poetry has always been entranced by its own beginnings, the creative process that calls it into being. The English Romantic poets brought an unprecedented curiosity and self-consciousness to their trafficking with the poetic process, and their poetry has long been recognized as an instrument rather than a ratification of inquiry.

For the Romantic poet, such inquiry entailed "recognition" rather than pure invention or the validation of generally established principles: the recognition in his communion with external circumstance, most commonly with nature, of the operation of the receptive and creative functions of mind. For the Romantics, the river and its source provided the most compelling, frequent, and inevitable figurings of those processes and their implications. They are not merely serviceable metaphors deployed in order to articulate or exemplify preconceived notions of perception and mental process, but symbols in the deepest sense of that word, offering ingress to their workings as well as serving as their most apt expression. They are what Coleridge called "companionable forms," agents that establish and promote our most profound discourse with ourselves, offering a measure of self-knowledge otherwise inaccessible.

It is this radical reciprocity between mind and nature that links the Romantics so intimately with the mythmakers of the classical world and their mythologies, the feeder spring of so many Romantic mythologies. These readings of English Romantic poems are often placed within the context of classical myth and its literature, and I have on occasion argued the depth and breadth of the Romantic poets' familiarity with and commitment to classical tradition. By doing so, I do not intend to identify Romanticism as compliant heir to the Neoclassicism of a previous age, but to stress merely that Neoclassicism and Romanticism, with their highly individual characters, evince the enduring vitality of classical myth, or at least the efficacy of a continuing tradition of classical education.

We are no longer disposed to accept Classic and Romantic as antithetical terms in a dialectic of cultural opposites, but as divergent streams of different moment and character issuing from a common source. If Neoclassicism draws on their common element, the legacy of the classical world and its mythologies in order to establish an external resonance, a reassuringly secure sense of cultural context and continuity, the Romantic addresses himself to an ongoing process, the constitution of the same myths at their internal source, the psychological wellsprings which give rise and impetus to classical myth and indeed all mythologies.

In this respect it can be said that, despite its revolutionary credentials, Romanticism's concern with the psychological dimensions of

mythogenesis reveals it as more radically atavistic than the most conservative of Neoclassicisms. If in flood-time or its dry seasons, literature has always demonstrated an uncanny memory for its origins and
its subsequent coursing, Romantic poetry perhaps more than any other
literary tradition haunts and is haunted by the natal murmurs at those
well-springs.

It is not my intention to catalogue exhaustively instances of the river
motif throughout the major or lesser canons of Romantic and classical
literatures. The poems I have chosen for detailed discussion represent a
selection of significant works which develop the river and its features as
their structural scaffolding or dominant image. I have introduced lesser
poems either to indicate the prevalence of the motif or to establish its
context within an individual poet's works. These essays do not include
all of the poets currently identified as Romantic. I have omitted Byron,
whose use of the river and geographic names in general is largely and
splendidly rhetorical, and Blake, whose infrequent rivers are wholly
internalized, as well as a spate of river poems ranging from Coleridge's
derivative sonnet on the River Otter to Shelley's spirited fragment on
the Serchio.

Chapter one identifies the river as the most salient and compelling
feature of the physical and mental landscape of the paradigmatic
Romantic poem, *The Prelude*, in which the river is described by Wordsworth as progenitor and course of the poem as well as of its author.
Two series from Wordsworth's later career, *The River Duddon* and the
Ecclesiastical Sonnets, evidence the dominance of the river, but serve to
illustrate how and why this most commanding and resonant of figures
does not invariably buoy its author or his poem. *The Prelude*, *Duddon*,
and the *Ecclesiastical Sonnets* are preoccupied for the most part with
the river passage, its coursing. Chapter two turns to the river's source
and the fascination it holds for the mythological and religious imagination and, most important, the role it rehearses in its natural enactment
and embodiment of the creative impulse. The path traced by chapter
three is retrocessive, reversing the seriatim chronology employed in
chapter one in order to move from later examples of Wordsworth's
handling of the source to earlier ones and to amplify the complex of
poems associated with the figure of Lucy. Chapter three introduces the
role of the guardian or numen of the source. She takes on increasing
importance in the chapters to follow. Her association with the most
charismatic of Romantic watercourses, Alph, and a skein of anonymous Keatsian rivers is explored, as is the manner in which this initially
benign figure reveals an increasingly threatening aspect. The nature of
this transformation is examined in terms of Coleridge's personal

psychology and through Keats's access to contemporary speculation in classical and comparative mythology.

A brief biography of the literary and social destinies of the Regency nymph furnishes a further commentary on what happens when symbol is plucked from its psychological depths and shorn of literary and mythic contexts, and goes public, or is subjected to the indignities of domestication.

The heroic quest with its characteristic landscape and its confluence with the features of the riverscape, suggested in *The Prelude* and further developed in *Endymion*, frames the principal action of Shelley's *Alastor*, the subject of chapter eight. The final chapter examines Shelley's most accomplished feat of syncretic mythopoesy, *The Witch of Atlas*, in which the poet marshals, in the service of a personal vision all of these elements: the Nile, most fabled of geographic rivers, ancient and contemporary speculation concerning its source, the river journey, theogony, myth, and the undertow of satire.

"One Perpetual Progress": The Wordsworthian River

 THE PRELUDE

A traveller I am
And all my tale is of myself

And all the landscape, endlessly echoed
With waters running, falling, or asleep.

There is a sympathy in streams, –
"one calleth to another"

Before Wordsworth established the identity of *The Prelude* as a portico or antechapel to the Gothic fabric of his principal work, he referred to it in a letter to De Quincey less monumentally but more aptly as "tributary" to *The Recluse*. Wordsworthians who prefer their devotions in the chapel to the nave nonetheless find the designation unworthy if not misleading. The term "tributary" has the virtue of eschewing the architectural and the fixed (as well as the ecclesiastical) and conveys the sense of natural impulse and flow characteristics of the art of *The Prelude*.

Wordsworth described his narrative as his account of the growth of the poet's mind, his mind. Its subject is the poetic faculty, the imagination, and the presiding image throughout the poem is, I propose, the river. The river is not merely the most salient feature of the Cumbrian landscape, but of Wordsworth's England, France, Germany, and Switzerland, of the entire itinerary, both mental and geographical, of *The Prelude*.[1]

The quotations serving to introduce this chapter characterize *The Prelude* as an itinerant poem, the literary journey or quest. The itincrary of the poet, the landscape through which he must pass, is epitomized by its rivers and their courses. The first quotation secures the internalization of the quest motif in which the rivers of the second are expressive of mental process, while the final quotation anticipates the visionary disclosures toward which the whole poem tends, when all rivers and their voices are, under the aspect of eternity, one.

It is through the preeminent image of the river that *The Prelude* establishes its narrative as well as its psychological and metaphysical dimensions and secures their integrity. And as I have already argued, it is the river that is uniquely adapted to bear this freight and to occasion such inquiries on the part of its rivermen.

Wordsworth's earliest recollection of childhood in *The Prelude* is of his Cockermouth birthplace, more particularly of the River Derwent blending "his murmurs with my nurse's song" (1.273).[2] The passage is the point of departure for Wordsworth's entire narrative of the "Growth of a Poet's Mind," its preeminence clearly established by the 1799 two-part *Prelude* in which it appeared at the beginning of the earliest version of the poem.

The circumstances of Wordsworth's actual childhood were adapted, though less than perfectly, to the fictional role enacted by a young hero or wayfarer embarking on the perennial quest.[3] Some tinkering or self-dramatization was necessary to attune fact to myth. Heroes are generally born without parents, or of unknown parentage. They are left in the keeping of kindly, often aged foster parents who tend their childhood. The course of the hero's subsequent quest usually involves a search for one or both of the true parents, since the discovery of a true family or dynastic connection will define him and his proper role in life. The homecoming, the great circuiting of the mythic quest, is a return to oneself and the recognition of one's true nature. The outcome is as much psychological as situational. The actual missing parents may have become unnecessary or superfluous to the anagnorisis, but the hero is brought to his confrontation with what is more crucial: their living legacy, mother and father as they persist within him and continue to shape his destiny.

Although Wordsworth was not orphaned until he was thirteen, when the death of his father occurred, his mother having died five years earlier, he chose to banish both parents from his accounts of early childhood in the first book of *The Prelude*. The poet's father is indeed mentioned only once, and obliquely, in the entire selective reconstruction of the poet's youth, and the mother is not recalled until book five, and then in terms empty of any recognizable personal content.[4] There the poet's account of her is occasioned by "Behold the parent hen amid her brood," and Ann Wordsworth survives as an impersonal exemplar

of the virtues of barnyard maternity (5.246). It need hardly be emphasized that, psychologically, this represents a remarkable repression of
biological fact in favour of poetic fiction. *The Prelude* poet's lineage lies
elsewhere:

> Was it for this
> That one, the fairest of all rivers, loved
> To blend his murmurs with my nurse's song,
> And, from his alder shades and rocky falls,
> And from his fords and shallows, sent a voice
> That flowed along my dreams? For this, didst thou,
> O Derwent! travelling over the green plains
> Near my "sweet Birthplace," didst thou, beauteous stream,
> Make ceaseless music through the night and day
> Which with its steady cadence, tempering
> Our human waywardness, composed my thoughts
> To more than infant softness, giving me
> Among the fretful dwellings of mankind
> A knowledge, a dim earnest, of the calm
> That Nature breathes among the hills and groves.
> When, having left his mountains, to the towers
> Of Cockermouth that beauteous river came,
> Behind my father's house he passed, close by
> Along the margin of our terrace walk.   (1.271–89)

In the beginning there is the infant, the river, and the nurse, the fostering male and female blending their voices, filling the child's sight and
ears, his waking hours and his dreams with their reassuring undertone.
The memory, reaching back to infancy, is like Proust's "unremembered
state which brought with it no logical proof of its existence, but only
the sense that it was a happy, that it was a real state in whose presence
other states of consciousness melted and vanished."[5] It lies beyond the
registry of conscious experience: Derwent is "a voice that flowed along
my dreams" (1.275–6). Derwent addresses its song to "childish
thoughts," composing them "to more than infant softness," providing
the child with an intimation of the "calm that is Nature" which he
will consciously recognize in later years, as the nine-year-old boy
of Winander who approaches the threshold of awareness of his
patrimony.

> ... in that silence, while he hung
> Listening, a gentle shock of mind surprise
> Has carried far into his heart the voice

Of mountain torrents; or the visible scene
Would enter unawares into his mind,
With all its solemn imagery ... (5.406-11)

Derwent, as father, tempers infant waywardness and those troubled impulses belonging to the "fretful dwellings of mankind" which witness his calm progress through their midst. The river flows, like the Thames of "Westminster Bridge" and indeed all rivers, "at his own sweet will," mirroring the transience of human lives on his shores by receiving on his "smooth breast" the shattered towers of Cockermouth castle, the fretful present and passing bravery of human history.

The child's intercourse with Derwent gains in intensity as infant passivity yields to the vivacity of childhood. No longer limited to the river's soothing undertone, the relationship is more immediate than mere sight and sound provided, vivid and directly sensuous, with the child as a "naked savage" "scouring," "sporting," "plunging," and "basking," a joyous youthful immersion not only in the watery element but in the sun and the earth on its banks. The child, however, is not yet prepared to essay the coursing Derwent in midstream; his playground is its tributary millrace "severed from his stream," scaled to his intimate world and yet furnishing the momentum, the pace and energy congenial to the growing boy.

In book three, the River Derwent has become the Cam, presiding over that one-sided stage of growth when, for Wordsworth, the imagination slept within Granta's cloisters. The river current is no longer deep and free-flowing, and from the boy's first entry into Cambridge threatens to slacken in the ominous arrest of the backwater and its shallows. During the uneasy ambivalence of the young undergraduate's entry into his new life, the eddying river seems to threaten his very existence.

The place as we approached, seemed more and more
To have an eddy's force, and sucked us in
More eagerly at every step we took.
Onward we drove beneath the castle; down
By Magdalene Bridge we went and crossed the Cam ... (3.10-14)

These ominous beginnings give way to the siren call of undergraduate life, which was occasionally no more than an attenuation of unreflecting youth in Derwent's millrace.

... on the breast
Of Cam sailed boisterously, and let the stars
Come out, perhaps without one quiet thought. (3.256-8)

Energetic as such larks may have been, there is none of the stunning impact of the bronzing sun and childish savagery which plunged the child into Derwent's millrace or led him to sport naked in the thunderstorm. Nights on the Cam and studious nights before the burning taper reflect the alternate rhythms of subsequent experience and growth, but these give way to stagnation, a sapping of vitality, arrest. The life of the mind proffers its enchantments to the undergraduate, but these conceal shoals beneath their eddying. Wordsworth's instinctive fears on entering Cambridge are borne out. At first the demands of change seem innocuous enough and welcome, with the heady experience of independence and the newly acquired uniform which brings about the outward transformation into the young commoner's world.

> As if by word
> Of magic or some Fairy's power, at once
> Behold me rich in moneys, and attired
> In splendid clothes ... (3.33-6)

But the Spenserian echoes in this passage become more pronounced as the current of the new life slips into moral stagnation, and the undergraduate discovers himself among the enchanted drifting isles of *The Faerie Queen*. Book three, "Residence at Cambridge," provides the highest concentration of Miltonic and Spenserian allusion in *The Prelude*, as the undergraduate world responds to the cadences of those fellow scholars of Christ's and Pembroke.

> Rotted as by a charm, my life became
> A floating island, an amphibious thing,
> Unsound, of spongy texture, yet withal
> Not wanting a fair face of water-weeds
> And pleasant flowers. (3.339-43)

The contrast with the smooth-flowing Derwent and its millrace is heightened as the chartered and domesticated Cam reflects the straitened and shallowing river of the student's mind with its tamer pursuits:

> I did not love,
> Judging not ill perhaps, the timid course
> Of our scholastic studies; could have wished
> To see the river flow with ampler range
> And freer pace ... (1850, 3.496-500)

Willingly did I part from these, and turn
Out of their track, to travel with the shoal
Of more unthinking natures ... (3.516–18)

Derwent's internalized voice has become, like Cambridge's river, stilled.

Hushed, meanwhile,
Was the undersoul, locked up in such a calm,
That not a leaf of the great nature stirred. (3.539–41)

Circuiting in its sluggish eddies, time nonetheless passes, and delivers its submissive idler in due term from Cambridge to his native Cumbria.

The labouring time of autumn, winter, spring –
Nine months – rolled pleasingly away; the tenth
Returned me to my native hills again. (3.670–2)

The returning Wordsworth's first glimpse of Windermere is a potent rebirth, in stunning contrast to the crossing of Cam and his entry into Cambridge. As he mounts Kendal heights, the lake bursts upon him, not as lake, but as "a vast river" unconfined, an uncloistered universe "stretching in the sun."

Lakes, islands, promontories, gleaming bays,
A universe of Nature's fairest forms
Proudly revealed with instantaneous burst,
Magnificent, and beautiful, and gay.
I bounded down the hill shouting amain ... (1850, 4.8–12)

Its overwhelming impact for Wordsworth, as well as for the reader, derives partly from the panoramic scale of this rolling universe succeeding the precincts of Cambridge, but also from the fact that the sun has been absent for the duration of book three, the entire eight-month Cambridge term.[6] In Wordsworth's reckoning of his Cambridge days, no sun penetrates their fenny gloom or dispels the initial impression of his entry into the town on that "dreary morning" after crossing its wide plain "overhung with clouds." Academe has been resolutely shrouded within "stately," "dusky," or "primeval" groves, "coverts" by day and night. So was it with Coleridge's Cambridge,

Where deep in mud Cam rolls his slumbrous stream,
And bog and desolation reign supreme;
Where all Boeotia clouds the misty brain,
The owl mathesis pipes her loathsome strain.

("Fragment Found in a Lecture-Room," 1792)

So was it always, Wordsworth maintains: "Bucer, Erasmus, or
Melanchton, read / Before the doors or windows of their cells / By
moonshine through mere lack of taper light" (3.489–91), while they and
their scholarly heirs burrow blindly

... in forlorn and naked chambers cooped
And crowded, o'er their ponderous books they sate
Like caterpillars eating out their way
In silence ... (3.463–6)

Boisterous nights aside, Cam is a dusky, mute river under lowering
skies, failing light, or night. Wordsworth recorded in a Cambridge
journal of 1789 a brief respite during a foray from the fens into the more
congenial hill country around Dovedale: "The river in that part which
was streamy had a glittering splendour."[7] But here, as in Keats's labyrinthine groves of self-conscious reflection, there is little or no light.
While reading his Chaucer by Trumpington's millrace, shaded within
the confines of a hawthorn, Wordsworth summons that sun-filled April
world of youth. Cambridge provides an apt and companionable setting
for the scholarly mind and its twilight world:

Caverns there were within my mind which sun
Could never penetrate, yet did there not
Want store of leafy arbours where the light
Might enter in at will. (3.246–9)

Wordsworth later italicized *caverns* and *arbours*.

What fitful light there is is merely figurative, the leaven of
"Companionships, Friendships, acquaintances." The Cambridge light is
unnatural, at times as seductively artificial as Spenserian pageantry –

The surfaces of artificial life
And manners finely spun, the delicate race
Of colours, lurking, gleaming up and down
Through that state arras woven with silk and gold ... (3.590–3)

– and masks a Spenserian sting:

> This wily interchange of snaky hues,
> Willingly and unwillingly revealed,
> I had not learned to watch ... (3.594–6)

Wordsworth is ferried across Windermere by a "Charon of that flood," who bears him from the land of shades, the plains with their dusky groves and river, to the far shore, a world of hills and sunlit waters.[8] Home is now Hawkshead, the Colthouse cottage of Ann Tyson, the aged foster-mother who succeeded the infant's nurse at Cockermouth and who furthered her tutelage: "She guided me; / I willing, nay – nay wishing to be led" (4.56–7). Ann Tyson lives by river lore. Her domestic life plies its smooth course, and Wordsworth indulgently notes "Her clear though shallow stream of piety / That ran on Sabbath days a fresher course" (4.216–17).

At Colthouse he seeks out a familiar sunny seat in the garden "friendly to studious or festive hours" where it was his habit to read as a schoolboy. The stone table beneath a pine is far removed from the shaded groves at that more celebrated seat of learning. Here Wordsworth recognizes the emblem of his Cambridge days in Spring Wood Ghyll, a channelled brook ornamenting the cottage garden.

> And that unruly child of mountain birth,
> That froward brook, which, soon as he was boxed
> Within our garden, found himself at once,
> As if by trick insidious and unkind,
> Stripped of his voice and left to dimple down
> Without an effort and without a will
> A channel paved by the hand of man. (4.39–45)

He greets it as fellow traveller and kindred spirit. No millrace this, but an emblem of Cam, which in this sunshot setting throws into relief his days on that river. A Derwent tamed, stripped of its purposeful movement and nurturing voice, of all "effort" and "will," it mimics the enthralments of Cambridge, blinking in the bright light, idling, baffled, and merely decorative. Fancy speaks:

> "An emblem here behold of thy own life;
> In its late course of even days with all
> Their smooth enthralment"; but the heart was full,
> Too full for that reproach. (1850, 4.61–4)

Wordsworth turns from the baffled stream to ply other familiar rivers, those roads which had fascinated him from childhood and borne him toward encounters with faces which spoke "like a volume to me," books of human life supplanting the wormy tomes of Cambridge. "The lonely roads / Were open schools in which I daily read / With most delight the passions of mankind." But the Wordsworthian road is also a river, and the journey a passage. On such a ramble, the traveller himself takes on the untrammelled character of the river that has recovered its muffled voice: "And when in the public roads at eventide / I sauntered, like a river murmuring / And talking to itself when all things else are still" (4.109–11). The road to Far Sawry is transformed into a river and bears him to the encounter with a retired soldier who waits by a milestone.

> I slowly mounted up a steep ascent
> Where the road's wat'ry surface, to the ridge
> Of that sharp rising, glittered in the moon
> And seemed before my eyes another stream
> Creeping with silent lapse to join the brook
> That murmured in the valley. (4.370–5)

This, the first of many encounters on other roads, yields a moving affirmation of what the young Wordsworth had dimly recognized by the side of the baffled brook: the value of the living books to be read in the faces of humanity and of the soldier's untutored faith: "My trust is in the God of Heaven, / And in the eye of him who passes by." In London, when road and river have snarled in streets, lanes, and courts, the open faces belonging to the open road are replaced by the inscrutable pages of an unopened book.

> How often, in the overflowing streets,
> Have I gone forwards with the crowd, and said
> Unto myself, "The face of every one
> That passes by me is a mystery!" (7.595–8)

London's "endless streams of men, and moving things" is not without vitality, but its eddies are undirected and meaningless; "living amid the same perpetual flow / Of trivial objects" (7.702–3). Wordsworth later emended "flow" to "whirl" (1850).

It is book five with its subject matter "Books" that resolves the vexed argument of reading, or affirms reading as it might be or as it was conducted by the young Wordsworth. Behind this passage lie those other studious seats, the bosky seat of learning on the Cam and the sunny seat beside Ann Tyson's muffled Spring Wood Ghyll. Wordsworth returns in memory to earlier days at his father's house in Cockermouth, and to Derwent, the progenitor of all *Prelude* rivers. There the young boy reads by the sounding river, buffeted by the heat of the sun on warmed rocks. Flowing river and its song, earth and sun meet, when in that place and that time of life to read was to devour with the same earthy hungering for life that plunged the child into Derwent's untroubled living stream.

> For a whole day together, I have lain
> Down by thy side, O Derwent, murmuring stream,
> On the hot stones, and in the glaring sun,
> And there have read, devouring as I read,
> Defrauding the day's glory – desperate! (5.508–12)

Books and the pursuit of learning on the banks of Cam were a comparatively bloodless affair.

By book six Derwent has become Eamont, as Hawkshead replaced Cockermouth and Penrith succeeded Hawkshead, but the streamlet and rivers are, in effect, one. As at Cockermouth and Cambridge, there is a recurrent image of river and ruined castle, Brougham "Low standing by the margin of the stream" at the confluence of Eamont and Dove, whose site had been piously confused with the seat of Sidney's Arcadia; for the pledged poet, a literary past. Reunited, William and Dorothy climb the broken stairs and mount the turret's head, where, above the stream in the midday sun, they listen (6.230–2).

Wordsworth's summer journey of 1790 with Robert Jones, described in book six, takes the poet through the unfamiliar landscape of France caught up in the brief festive aftermath of revolution. Its riverine features, however, are familiar, as the travellers pursue the public roads "Eager as birds of prey, or as a ship / Upon the stretch, when winds are blowing fair," (6.435–6) and river-roads give way in turn to actual rivers: the Rhone swelled at Lyons by its tributary Saone.

> Upon the bosom of the gentle Saone
> We glided forward with the flowing stream:
> Swift Rhone! thou wert the wings on which we cut
> Between thy lofty rocks. (6.385–8)

On the road to Simplon the travellers make the obligatory visit to Mont Blanc and the Mer de glace, and gazing at the summit and its dumb cataracts "grieved / To have a soulless image on the eye / Which had usurped upon a living thought / That never more could be." The following day that transcendent image gives way to its "Five rivers broad and vast," which "make rich amends, / And reconciled us to realities" (6.460–1) as the morning light is filled with the familiar sounds and sights which line their plunging course and speak of life familiar and abundant. Wordsworth greets them with relief. This is the course of life, the riverine matter and progress of his song.

Again, it is a river which serves to direct or misdirect the travellers to the summit of vision on the Simplon crossing. Lost, the campanions cross and part company with a mountain torrent in order to ascend the Feerberg, only to discover that their proper course lies here, as in life, "with the current of that stream." Their guide through the echoing Gondoschluct is the young river, and "led by that stream" they descend from the height to where it is swelled by its tributary "into a lordly river broad and deep," majestic as Rhone or Derwent, and leading to the sheltering valleys and golden days on Lakes Maggiore and Como. Book six is preeminently the book of rivers, trafficking among Cam, the Dove and Eamont, the Saone and Rhone, the Guiers Vif and Guiers Mort near the Grand Chartreuse, the five rivers of Mont Blanc, and the Lagginbach and the Grosswasser swelling the Doveria on the Simplon – all of these, like Derwent at the juncture of Cockermouth, rivers at their confluence, enhanced, augmented.[9] In retrospect the river journeys serve Wordsworth as metaphor for his own mental journey and its destination:

> Finally, whate'er
> I saw, or heard, or felt, was but a stream
> That flowed into a kindred stream; a gale,
> Confederate with the current of the soul,
> To speed my voyage; every sound or sight,
> In its degree of power, administered
> To grandeur or to tenderness, – to the one
> Directly, but to tender thoughts by means
> Less often instantaneous in effect;
> Led me to these by paths that, in the main,
> Were more circuitous, but not less sure
> Duly to reach the point marked out by Heaven. (1850, 6.742–53)

In addition to the identifiable rivers which lace the landscape of *The Prelude* there are anonymous, generic rivers which are directly and unambiguously expressive of the processes of mind and its growth, or its testimony, the unfolding course of Wordsworth's poem. The opening lines of the 1805 *Prelude* preserve the river's status as the original poem's initiatory image by introducing the course of the poet liberated from London in terms suggestive of embarkation on the river or of the river itself.

> What dwelling shall receive me? in what vale
> Shall by my harbour? underneath what grove
> Shall I take up my home? and what sweet stream
> Shall with its murmurs lull me to my rest? (1.11-14)

> Or shall a twig or any floating thing
> Upon the river point me out my course? (1.31-2)

Six books later, in the recollection of that launching in the address to Coleridge, the metaphor is still compellingly alive:

> Five years are vanished since I first poured out,
> Saluted by that animating breeze
> Which met me issuing from the City's walls,
> A glad preamble to this Verse. (7.1-4)

as it is in the final book when Wordsworth revised it some thirty-four years later: "In London chiefly harboured, whence I roamed ..." (1850, 14.351).

The arrested impulse of the river among Cambridge's quads and cloisters constituted a listless eddy in the poet's progress, but London with its "overflowing streets," its "endless stream of men and moving things" bearing meaningless encounters, is a maelstrom: "that concourse of mankind / Where Pleasure whirls about incessantly" (1850, 7.69-70). The turbulence reaches its confounding climax in the brilliant vortex of sound, colour, and movement which is the epitome of the city, Bartholomew Fair.

The course of Wordsworth's days is measured by the ebb and flow of his creative powers, as well as the course of the poem which is their chronicle.

> As oftentimes a river, it might seem,
> Yielding in part to old remembrances,
> Part swayed by fear to tread an onward road
> That leads direct to the devouring sea,
> Turns and will measure back his course - far back
> Towards the very regions which he crossed
> In his first outset - so have we long time

Made motions retrograde, in like pursuit
Detained. But now we start afresh: I feel
An impulse to precipitate my verse. (9.1–10)

This trope on the river course of Wordsworth's narrative furnishes an appropriate beginning to the book dealing with his second period in France, when the poet took up residence at Orleans and Blois, filling his days with long walks with Michel Beaupuy on the banks of Loire and at the source of the Loiret, rapt in conversations which anticipate those with Coleridge beside "Rotha's stream, / Greta, or Derwent, or some nameless rill ..." (9.399–400).

Rivers baffled by shallows or circuiting through meanders, sinking into the earth and surfacing, rushing streams swelled by tributaries to a lordlier dimension and statelier pace, all serve as recurrent metaphors for the progress of the poetic sensibility and its chronicle.

But I was hurried forward by a stream,
And could not stop. (5.183–4)

... like a torrent bursting,
From a black thunder-cloud, down Scafell's side
To rush and disappear. But soon broke forth
(So willed the Muse) a less impetuous stream
That flowed awhile with unabating strength
Then stopped for years; not audible again
Before last primrose-time. (1850, 7.6–12)

The termination of my course
Is nearer now ... (13.372–3)

The final book of *The Prelude* provides the culmination of the river images, now completely subsumed as metaphors of the imagination and the imaginative life. The course of the river may have been troubled from the beginning by the fretful dwellings of mankind and its ways, but its journey from its source did not proceed unhelped by human agency. In the beginning was the nurse, then Ann Tyson, then Dorothy, who tended the nascent stream and fostered the "feeling intellect" which lies at the creative fountainhead:

For, spite of thy sweet influence and the touch
Of other kindred hands that opened out
The springs of tender thought in infancy ... (13.216–18)

Then Calvert, who "cleared a passage for me, and the stream / Flowed in the bent of Nature" (13.366–7). When the river, having won its maturity, flows at the full, it invariably echoes with the sound of that first sunlit river which filled infant ears.

> Where is the favoured being who hath held
> That course unchecked, unerring, and untired,
> In one perpetual progress smooth and bright? (1850, 14.133–5)

The river unchecked, perpetual, is as it was in the beginning, Derwent, smooth-flowing in refulgent light, echoing within the channels of memory as it first sounded in infant ears. The river of the Imagination, Wordsworth's great theme, has found its less deliberate but nonetheless determined course, arrested but undiminished in its windings, and augmented with each confluent experience; it reflects its surroundings like Derwent, Eamont, and even the sluggish Cam, and bears like the river roads of England and France "on its solemn breast / The works of man and face of human life." Its course is that of *The Prelude* itself.

> This faculty hath been the moving soul
> Of our long labour: we have traced the stream
> From darkness, and the very place of birth
> In its blind cavern, whence is faintly heard
> The sound of waters; followed it to light
> And open day; accompanied its course
> Among the ways of Nature, afterwards
> Lost sight of it bewildered and engulphed:
> Then given it greeting as it rose once more
> With strength, reflecting in its solemn breast
> The works of man and face of human life;
> And lastly, from its progress have we drawn
> The feeling of life endless ... (13.171–83)

Coleridge, on first hearing Wordsworth's recitation of the poem addressed to him, recognized at once the distinctive role of road, river, and stream in the imaginative life of the *Prelude* poet in his 1807 poem, "To William Wordsworth: Composed on the Night After His Recitation of a Poem on the Growth of an Individual Mind":

> ... on the lonely highroad, when the stars
> Were rising; or by secret mountain-streams,
> The guides and the companions of thy way! (24–6)

On Snowdon's summit, *The Prelude*'s climactic mount of vision, Derwent, Rotha, Cam, Saone, Rhone, and Loire, guides and companions of Wordsworth's years, together with the torrents on the visionary height of Simplon, forfeit under the aspect of eternity their particularity and identities, and that intricate skein of rivers becomes as was Derwent in the beginning, one: "Mounted the roar of waters, torrents, streams / Innumerable, roaring with one voice!" (13.58–9)

On the twin heights of Snowdon and Simplon, the natural landscape coalesces with that of the mind and bodies forth the great river of its heartland, the imagination. The assertion "I recognize thy glory" is the poet's conscious recognition and affirmation of that river coursing within from its beginnings on the shores of Derwent's fathering stream. It is the recognition of his true patrimony, thence his identity and his calling. *The Prelude*'s journey is complete, the wanderer's knowledge won. Because of that knowledge, the poet's task has only begun, and new beginnings must lie with the old points of embarkation, the river, the mind of man, and their common song.

> Then might we return
> And in the rivers and the groves behold
> Another face, might hear them from all sides
> Calling upon the more instructed mind
> To link their images with subtle skill
> Sometimes, and by elaborate research,
> With forms and definite appearances
> Of human life, presenting them sometimes
> To the involuntary sympathy
> Of our internal being, satisfied
> And soothed with a conception of delight
> Where meditation cannot come, which thought
> Could never heighten. (13.294–306)

༜༝ THE RIVER DUDDON

> The Bard who walks with Duddon for his guide
> Shall find such toys of fancy thickly set:
> Turn from the sight, enamoured Muse – we must;
> And, if thou canst, leave them without regret!

The sonnets constituting *The River Duddon* celebrate stations of the river's course from its source on Wrynose Fell across the plain of Donnerdale to the Irish Sea. The deployment of the series suggests *The*

Prelude turned inside out. The river pulse which courses through *The Prelude*, in which the poem's imagery and thematic concerns inhere, has become in the *Duddon* sonnets an outer form containing rather than informing its individual parts. The poem's form and subject and Wordsworth's laboriously detailed notes concerning Duddon's riverscape and its natives place it, as it were, in the mainstream of topographical, or, as Wordsworth himself identified the genre by citing Dyer and Crowe, "loco-descriptive" verse.[10] *The River Duddon* is a subtle and effective example of that genre in which the various geographic, moral, and temporal dimensions through which the river passes are skilfully and unobtrusively manipulated with a minimum of digression and obtrusive sentence.

Stewart Wilcox has provided an account of the progress of Wordsworth's river and its poem, its temporal and spatial passage from early dawn at the mountain source to gathering dusk at the estuary, its successive stages of growth as nursling, stripling, and youth, and its progress toward maturity and oblivion on Duddon Sands.[11] The river is apostrophized and personified throughout, but Wilcox has indicated that Wordsworth consistently stresses Duddon's role as a "companion" to his journey, that this "permits him to avoid identifying himself with the river."[12] This observation points to the watershed where Duddon and the *Prelude* rivers part company. The river, although it enacts its old role as guide for the poet, always occupies the foreground and remains for the most part external. This is not to suggest that it is reduced to the merely emblematic: its associations are numerous and varied and acquire considerable symbolic resonance, although such resonance generally excludes the personal, the mental and spiritual processes of the poet. The ruddy children who challenge its swollen waters are other children, the young lovers at its crossing are other lovers. They are noted as such and are neither the poet's muse nor inspiration. Duddon knows the river's unending business of being born, growing, and dying, much of the life, but not the mind, of man.

Duddon may remember its history, but it lacks a mythology, and Wordsworth is reluctant to furnish it with classical credentials. No Horace or Virgil hymns its advent; Bandusian spring or golden naiads with "their bright liquid mansions" find no place on the austere Wrynose Fell. Duddon's lineage is bleak and his nativity spare:

Child of the clouds! remote from every taint
Of sordid industry thy lot is cast;
Thine are the honours of the lofty waste;
Not seldom, when with heat the valleys faint,

Thy handmaid Frost with spangled tissue quaint
Thy cradle decks; – to chant thy birth, thou hast
No meaner Poet than the whistling Blast,
And Desolation is thy Patron-saint! (2.1–8)

The infant wanderer's parentage is suitably obscure. Only in myth, where it is not only possible but commonplace, can paternity be confidently ascribed to a procreant cloud. But the elemental powers of this lofty waste and its spring are composed in a curiously formal tableau rehearsing a Christian rather than pagan nativity. "How shall I paint them?" Wordsworth asks, and cradled Nursling, handmaid Frost, Saint Desolation, and the whistling Blast, their afflative laureate, assume the conventional postures of a somewhat contrived translation of holy child and mother, with attendant virgin martyr and evangelist. A "gleam/Of Brilliant moss, instinct with freshness rare" promises the greening world to follow, the dawning gift of life issuing from the bleak heart of winter, a common motif belonging to pictorial representations of the nativity.

Wordsworth's stylized composition with its personifications disposed against an elemental setting serves to establish the character and dialectic of the sonnets to follow, with their recurrent combination of the contrived and the natural, of rhetorical excess and a "plainer and more emphatic language." The loco-descriptive genre which Wordsworth plies in *The River Duddon* summons, along with its formal conventions, echoes of the poetic diction that as a younger poet he had curtly dismissed. The sonnets often suggest the sort of interleaving of fustian with genuine sentiment that Wordsworth culled in his rendering of Gray's "Sonnet on the Death of Richard West" in the "Preface to the *Lyrical Ballads*." Duddon's descent from its heights should not be dismissed as yet another instance of Wordsworth's decline from Parnassus, or of the proscription against poetic diction proposed by the "Preface to the *Lyrical Ballads*." These sonnets deploy with varying success an integration of language, imagery, and argument in the service of a comprehensive poem and its river subject.

The opening lines of Duddon 1 ("Not envying Latian shades") and their invocation of Horace's Bandusian spring, although decorously appropriate to the historic genre which Wordsworth himself had transformed as early as his 1798 meditation on the banks of the Wye, augur an anachronistic Neoclassicism heightened through allusions to "enamoured" and "loitering" muses and "scaly tribes," a Miltonic "sinuous lapse," the stagey apostrophe "Sad thoughts avaunt," and the ponderous "From her unworthy seat, the cloudy stall / Of Time, breaks forth triumphant Memory." The muse of past poets is indeed loitering, but Wordsworth's lapses can be seen as less fortuitous than deliberate, a poetic strategy rather than a failing. "The false beauties of the moderns," the poetic diction Coleridge disparaged as an "amphibious something, made up half of image and half of abstract meaning," rises to rhetorical heights unrivalled by Gronger or Cooper's hills surveying their freighted Towy or Thames:

> ... behold him from afar;
> In stately mien to sovereign Thames allied
> Spreading his bosom under Kentish downs,
> With commerce freighted, or triumphant war. (32.11–14)

Such posturings scarcely square with Wordsworth's avowal in his opening sonnet:

> Better to breathe at large on this clear height
> Than toil in needless sleep from dream to dream:
> Pure flow the verse, pure, vigorous, free, and bright,
> For Duddon, long-lived Duddon, is my theme! (1.11–14)

The "pure, vigorous, free, and bright" verse that the impetuous river enjoins upon its poet is sharply at odds not only with the features of topographical verse and its customary heightened diction but also with the episodic constraints of the sonnet form.

The architectural analogy Wordsworth invoked while describing *The Prelude* would seem more appropriate to the Duddon series. And yet he clearly wanted a sequential impulse as vigorous as the flow of his subject river, the same "tributary" character he attributed to *The Prelude* in the De Quincey letter. But his literary Duddon must course unimpeded through the intricate baffles and chambers of the sonnet stanza. Although two distinct voices are audible throughout the *Duddon* sonnets, Wordsworth probably insisted, as did his wife, Mary, that "they all together compose one poem."[13] Their discrete styles introduce a continuous antiphon between levels of poetic speech, between form and its subject, the sonnet with its carefully worked "scanty plot of ground" and its larger form, the unbroken biography of the river coursing from source to sea. This odic rhythm of progress through alternation is as unforced, varied, and irregular as the flow of Duddon and the rich chiaroscuro of its passage through light and shade.

Stanza seven with its overcharged octave "Change me, some God, into that breathing rose!" plays off a Petrarchan conceit and the sparrow borrowed from Catullus's Lesbia against a homier "unculled flowret of the glen" and the uncaged wren "That tunes on Duddon's banks her slender voice." Rose and sparrow are the cultivations of a literary hothouse, while the language of the sestet is as disarmingly modest as its flowret and wren. This dialogue of artifice and impulse informs features of the riverscape such as the juxtaposition of Duddon's girdling bridges and artfully contrived stepping stones with the unrestrained river:

> ... lo! what might seem a zone
> Chosen for ornament – stone matched with stone
> In studied symmetry, with interspace
> For the clear waters to pursue their race
> Without restraint. (9.4–8)

The stanza closes with the heightened contrast provided by a figure of "declining Manhood" contemplating the swift career of mortality over Duddon's "high-swoln Flood." It is followed by the sonnet "On the Same Subject," in which a youthful mid-river courtship is arrested in a mannered pastoral not unlike the pictorial rendering of Duddon's nativity. "The frolic Loves, who, from yon high rock, see / The struggle, clap their wings for victory!" Wordsworth's frolic loves applauding the lovers' tryst are translated from the conventions of pictorial pastoralism flourishing when sentiment ran high over legions of chubby *putti* cascading down canvases or peeping from each cloud and brake. Even allowing for vicissitudes of taste, the anecdote is an appalling miscalculation, intrusively mawkish rather than merely affected. Duddon's own unlettered pastoral is more effectively served in stanza six ("Flowers") in which the river is described in its youthful passage through a spring world of pairing birds, marauding bees, thyme, eyebright, and the wild strawberry, and in stanza nineteen where its own pairings are celebrated in the river's modest nuptials with a tributary stream.

The modulations of rhetoric and unaffected speech proceed apace, and the riverscape and the imagery it evokes support a fluent dialectic of freedom and restraint, light and darkness. Duddon's course marshals memories of a past at least as sombre as the river's present is bright: the evolving spiritual history of man from the "hideous usages, and rites accursed" of the primitive, to pagan antiquity as opposed to a more enlightened Christianity, past and present. A dark dell may have sheltered man, "first of his tribe"; the fairy chasm, "this sunless cleft," witnessed the secret revels of elfin baby-snatchers; a "deep chasm" with its "gloomy NICHE, capacious, blank, and cold" might have harboured the effigy of a forgotten river deity; the ruins of an embattled house "Flung from yon cliff a shadow large and cold." Predators from England's past, the Viking raven in its blasted yew and the Roman eagle assailing timorous flocks by night, are glimpsed as the river glides through covert gloom and abrupt light. These episodes are at the frontiers where Wordsworth's history and myth merge, where the cromlech known as Long Meg and her Daughters, witness to Druid rite and primeval terror, subsides into the earth from which it arose at the bidding of "Sacred Religion! 'mother of form and fear,' / Dread arbitress of mutual respect," who ordains an enlightened creed from the shadows of the old, and new pastors for tamer flocks.

The dark deeds of the river's human past are given proportion, diminished, and dismissed in the wake of Duddon's flood. Springtime, children, summery loves, and the generous heart of the Rev. Robert Walker of Seathwaite and the good shepherds praised by Chaucer, Herbert, and Goldsmith provide the bright intervals by which the darkest annals of generations are relieved. Duddon's waters coursing through their familiar channel embody the ceaseless change of abundant life, racing, pausing, gathering, cleansing: "Thy function was to heal and to restore, / To soothe and cleanse" in the "radiant progress toward the Deep."

Frozen in the studied forms and rhetoric of tradition, Wordsworth's deployment of mythic analogues occasionally evinces symptoms of mythopoeic hernia. There are, however, two notable exceptions to this discomfort: sonnet twenty-two, which essays a native Duddon myth shorn of formal antecedents, and sonnet twenty-six, which reveals the most personal tone and achieves perhaps the finest poetry of the series.

In the former, Wordsworth fashions his own Duddon legend. Since it does not appear in his exhaustive notes describing the region and its historic associations, it is almost certainly his own spontaneous invention and, as such, another version of a familiar Wordsworthian theme and setting drawn from a personal rather than traditional mythology. Its elements are drawn from the deeply personal matrix of images that shaped the Lucy poems: a hidden pool, a solitary flower, a maid and her untimely death. The maid's narrative is brief and its conclusion precipitant. A hidden pool reflects the image of a primrose growing on the talus with such fidelity that in order to "ravish" the "starry treasure," she is uncertain whether to climb the precipice and pluck it or to seek it out in the mirroring depths. Whatever her choice may have been is undisclosed; her end is not.

> – Upon the steep rock's breast
> The lonely Primrose yet renews its bloom,
> Untouched momento of her hapless doom! (22.12–14)

Wordsworth's small drama ends and, like Duddon, the primrose and its seasonal renewal bear testimony to the changing yet changeless order of nature, as did Greenhead Ghyll, Margaret's deserted well, and the springs of Dove with their singular violet and star.

Sonnet twenty-six, as de Selincourt established, is a survival of a poem transcribed before 1804 and addressed to Wordsworth's natal Derwent.[14] Perhaps it is because of its derivation from *The Prelude*'s fathering river that it summons the power of language and conception of those rivers which served Wordsworth's inner life as guide and inspiration, their "rough noise" and impetus sounding a resonant undertone to the "servile reins" which threatened to bridle the poetic voice.

> Return, Content! for fondly I pursued,
> Even when a child, the Streams – unheard, unseen;
> Through tangled woods, impending rocks between;
> ...
> Nor have I tracked their course for scanty gains;
> They taught me random cares and truant joys,
> That shield from mischief and preserve from stains
> Vague minds, while men are growing out of boys;
> Maturer Fancy owes to their rough noise
> Impetuous thoughts that brook not servile reins. (26.1–3, 9–14)

Truant joys and random cares are the mixed lot of the tracker of streams, the riverman. They are described as shaping "maturer fancy," for Wordsworth a not inconsiderable gain. As such, they are elements in the nurturing of the creative sensibility at least as efficacious as the spiritual tutelage of beauty and terror recorded in *The Prelude*. These joys and cares contrast with and probably complement the Wordsworthian wise passivity since they involve pursuit, the quest with its absorbing demand and struggle. Each of these *vias* was, of course, implicit in the argument of *The Prelude* and its autobiographical materials.

In terms of his life and activity, the poet's truant joys are above all associated with the runaway character of his inspiration and its wayward élan, while the servile reins of his craft are chief among his random cares – in this instance, the constraints of the sonnet form and the loco-descriptive genre which serves to marshal the sonnets into a larger whole with its distinguishing conventions of diction, decorum, and formal organization.

Wordsworth has invoked the essential poetic agon, the often recalcitrant symbiosis of what Blake called the Prolific and the Devourer. The history of poetics has recorded the variable ascendancy of one or the other, how they have been harnessed in ironic tension or impressed into service within a dialectic of concord and discord, how an uneasy alliance has been negotiated, or a stable (and moribund) confederacy achieved.

The Romantic pact was negotiated in terms of organic form in which the formal reins themselves are submissive and responsive to the wayward character of their charge. Such pacts are negotiated, not concluded, since it was necessary to preserve or cultivate the energetic confrontation rather than force a stasis or frozen arrest of its elements. "Expect poison from the standing water," Blake warned in his Proverbs of Hell, "the cistern contains, the fountain overflows." The natural fluxions Coleridge felt in Wordsworth's art, the ebb and flow between mind and its matter, past and present, the multiform and the transcendent, poetry and the prosaic, constitute the ground rhythms of his art, whether formalized in the odic pattern of opposition and integration or less artfully realized in the pulse of discourse.

Wordsworth's achievement in the *River Duddon* sonnets is less than flawless, but rather than faulting the work for its discordant voices, and dismissing the poem as a general failure of poetic powers, we should value it for what it undertakes and is. The younger Wordsworth was prepared to hazard the dangers of exploring the treacherous middle ground between bathos and genuine sentiment, and something of the daring of the author of "The Thorn" persists in the *Duddon* poems, the poet who deliberately cast in the guise of a prolix but contrived garrulity his profound insight into the nature and process of mythopoeic creation. The *River Duddon* as a vehicle for Wordsworth's sonnets is neither juggernaut nor dray, but the art with which he directs his serviceable reins still challenges, and is accomplished and assured.

 ECCLESIASTICAL SONNETS

> Enough – if eyes, that sought the fountain-head
> In vain, upon the growing Rill may gaze.

The *Ecclesiastical Sonnets* record Wordsworth's celebration of the course of the Christian faith and its mysteries and chart the progress of its "living waters" throughout English history. Consequently, the sonnets are arranged for the most part in simple chronological sequence beginning, *ab ovo*, with the sacred well of Christian faith and concluding with that far-off event when its undefiled waters approach the eternal city. As in *The Prelude*, the commanding metaphor is that of a river issuing from its source, but, unlike that personal history which was of necessity incomplete, the holy river is permitted to course to its estuary and beyond in its *eschaton* in the waiting sea.

Wordsworth begins his series by alluding to his popular *River Duddon* sonnets, and embarks again on a river journey which is this time projected almost exclusively in a historic dimension. As such, the *Ecclesiastical Sonnets* present a somewhat swollen tributary of Duddon's brief excursus on Christian piety. The *Ecclesiastical Sonnets* or *Sketches*, as they were named in 1822, were received with an acclamation which outstripped that of the *Duddon* poems, and acquired a reputation that did not wane until the latter part of the nineteenth century when *The Prelude* eclipsed both. Thereafter, the reputation of the *Ecclesiastical Sonnets* appears to have run as thin as the peculiarly English faith they celebrated.

> I, who accompanied with faithful pace
> Cerulean Duddon from its cloud-fed spring,
> And loved with spirit ruled by his to sing
> Of mountain-quiet and boon nature's grace;
> ...
> Now seek upon the heights of Time the source
> Of a HOLY RIVER ... (1:1.1–4, 9–10)

Although, like the *Prelude* river, Wordsworth's holy river ranges widely about continental Europe as well as England, its channel is primarily temporal rather than geographical, proceeding "from the heights," so that the coursing of time traces a downhill path, downhill all the way. Wordsworth skirts this uneasy implication, although it is likely that the sympathies of the author of "London, 1802" and chronicler of Anglo-Catholic history would have admitted the nature of its decline.

The ultimate source of the living waters lies with the cross, but its native English headwaters are established through those malleable legends which Wordsworth and his faith entertained concerning the founding of their church: Stillingfleet's version of Saint Paul in the west country and, more plausibly for Wordsworth at least, Saint Joseph of Arimathaea's foundation at Glastonbury, those who "call the Fountain forth by miracle / And with dread signs the nascent Stream invest." Saints Joseph and Paul, who "sojourned here to guard / The precious

Current they have taught to flow," usurp the role of the tutelary river god whom Wordsworth imagined within Duddon's vacant niche and in the sonnet on Gordale Chasm, "Teaching the docile waters how to turn / Or (if need be) impediment to spurn, / And force their passage to the salt-sea tides!"[15]

For Wordsworth, the native headwaters antedate the sources identified by pious English chroniclers, and flow from an antecedent religion of nature, a yet unbaptized stream under the guardianship of ancient Druids: "And still, 'mid yon thick woods, the primal truth / Glimmers through many a superstitious form." Later, in stanza twenty, the poet essays firmer and more familiar ground by locating the informing source of primal truth within human psychology rather than history, so that the birth of faith is a perennial rather than merely historical event, springing from man's confrontation with the bald fact of death.

> From this sad source have sprung
> Rites that console the Spirit, under grief
> Which ill can brook more rational belief. (1:20.5–7)

But Wordsworth's task is neither to gaze into the mystery of beginnings nor to do more than assert the bright eschaton at the river's mouth at the close of his poem. His subject is the visible course, the current of faith made manifest and revealed in human history: "Enough – if eyes, that sought the fountain-head / In Vain, upon the growing Rill may gaze" (1:5.13–14). The central river image is both explicit and casually subsumed in metaphors that range from the serviceable to the heavy-handed conceit:

> ... and mass is sung;
> And prayer, man's rational prerogative,
> Runs through blind channels of an unknown tongue. (2:33.12–14)

> The tears of man in various measure gush
> From various sources; gently overflow
> From blissful transport some – from clefts of woe
> Some with ungovernable impulse rush. (2:32.1–4)

– or to the more richly allusive account of nuns driven from their convents during the Dissolution:

> While through the Convent's gate to open view
> Softly she glides, another home to seek.
> Not Iris, issuing from her cloudy shrine,
> An Apparition more divinely bright!

Not more attractive to the dazzled sight
Those watery glories, on the stormy brine
Poured forth, while summer suns at distance shine,
And the green vales lie hushed in sober light! (2:22.7–14)

The rivers range from the generic stream carrying the freight of Christian piety to explicit rivers: Rhone, Po, Tiber, Ganges, Nile, Rhine, and Thames. Their impulse is always seaward, toward eternity, as with the brook which bears the desecrated ashes of the martyred Wycliffe.

... flung into the brook that travels near;
Forthwith that ancient Voice which Streams can hear

...

"As thou these ashes, Little Brook! will bear
Into the Avon, Avon to the tide,
Of Severn, Severn to the narrow seas,
Into main Ocean they, this deed accurst
An emblem yields to friends and enemies
How the bold Teacher's Doctrine, sanctified
By truth, shall spread, throughout the world dispersed." (2:17.4–5, 8–14)

As Wordsworth gathered the skein of his rivers in the high countries of *The Prelude* into the converging torrents of Simplon, into the single voice of all waters heard on Snowdon's summit, and into the five rivers sprung from the bleak image of Mont Blanc, here he essays the heights of the Jungfrau, supposing its glacier the feeder of the waters of the young Rhine.

The Virgin-Mountain, wearing like a Queen
A brilliant crown of everlasting snow,
Sheds ruin from her sides; and men below
Wonder that aught of aspect so serene
Can link with desolation. Smooth and green,
And seeming, at a little distance, slow,
The waters of the Rhine ... (2:43.1–7)

The Rhine waters gather momentum "Till madness seizes on the whole wide Flood" in their leap over the Schaffhausen escarpment, "Deafening the region in his ireful mood." Despite the anger of the tormented currents and their reckless plunge, their glacier source, rather than overwhelming in its transcedent "soulless image," is no more than

serenely regal. This potentially powerful image garnered from Wordsworth's tour of the Alps and preserved in *The Prelude* has been dutifully pressed into the service of a tamer faith, and its baptism only
serves to attenuate that power as the poet proceeds to labour his
sentence:

> Even such the contrast that, where'er we move,
> To the mind's eye Religion doth present;
> Now with her own deep quietness content;
> Then, like the mountain, thundering from above
> Against the ancient pine-trees of the grove
> ...
> ... O terrible excess
> Of headstrong will! Can this be Piety? (2:44.1–5, 9–10)

As in *The Prelude*, the river is frequently used as a means of charting
the course of Wordsworth's poem:

> As with the Stream our voyage we pursue ... (1:37.1)

> Down a swift stream, thus far, a bold design
> Have we pursued ...
> ...
> So have we hurried on with troubled pleasure:
> Henceforth, as on the bosom of a stream
> That slackens, and spreads wide a watery gleam,
> We, nothing loth a lingering course to measure,
> May gather up our thoughts, and mark at leisure
> How widely spread the interests of our theme. (3:12.1–2, 9–14)

These passages, however, are poetic editorializing, and their insistent
externality fails to augment the commanding resonance which ought to
energize Wordsworth's central river image. The course of his poem,
contrary to Wordsworth's protestations, is less than bold in execution
and in design, and the "interests of our theme" spread wide indeed. This
river of faith runs true to type, and, shorn of symbolic resonance,
belongs preeminently to an emblematic or typological tradition. The
rivers of *The Prelude* mediate between an intensely personal world and
one of external fact that is often recalcitrant, occasionally antagonistic.
But in that poem's great moments of visionary calm or grandeur, the
one is gathered into the other, effecting the profound reconciliation that
gives point and meaning to the poet's ongoing life. The *River Duddon*

sonnets unfold in response to the particular geographical and historical features of the Cumbrian river, investing them with immediacy, authenticity, and pulse. The *Ecclesiastical Sonnets*, however, are occasioned by an undeviating course ordained by the detached historical perspective directed by Wordsworth's faith. As such, they are resolutely public poems whose integrity lies in their allegorical relation to an externally constituted system of belief. Wordsworth's river of faith lacks those confluent streams that augment the swelling rivers of *The Prelude* and establish the poem as a personal odyssey, the process of becoming and of growth and overriding identity which the figures of the river and the river journey as literary metaphor so powerfully accommodate. The architectural elements of the individual *Ecclesiatical Sonnets* check the "tributary" impulse. The course of Wordsworth's river of faith is droughty, and the result is neither a single poem nor a sequence, but a collection.

This discussion of a late work inevitably suggests a minor postscript to the achievement of *The Prelude*, as well as the *Duddon* sonnets and their deployment of the river motif. It is perhaps unjust to tax a late work merely because it is so insistently different in kind. Those few of Wordsworth's critics who have taken on the poetry written after 1815 are uncomfortably aware that the faint, intermittent, and cautious praise they accord shards from the later poetry may damn the lot. Few, since de Selincourt's edition of the 1805 *Prelude*, resist the temptation to surface from the 1850 redaction as if from a wreck, offering one or two salvageable relics which miraculously attest that the later Wordsworth was, if sunk beneath waves of piety, senility, or propriety, intermittently capable of unsheathing a rare flash of untarnished brilliance. Abbie Potts's exhaustive study of the *Ecclesiastical Sonnets*, especially when compared with her study of *The Prelude*, failed to disguise the impression that her work on the sonnets was less than a labour of love, and that if *The Prelude* is antechapel to a ruinous cathedral, she was left with the unrewarding task of excavating its midden.[16]

The sonnets on mutability and King's College Chapel have generally been recognized as eminently salvageable examples of poetry of their kind, the late Wordsworthian public rhetoric which otherwise has proven an embarrassment to modern readers. Although I am unable to allay such impressions, I would like to consider two passages from the sequence of one hundred and two *Ecclesiastical Sonnets* that reveal the personal rather than the rhetorical voice. They seem strangely out of their element, perhaps because they are so strongly suggestive of a younger Wordsworth and his preoccupations.

While entertaining thoughts of the comforts of monkish seclusion, Wordsworth imagines or remembers a retired poolside retreat:

> ... to some dry nook
> Scooped out of living rock, and near a brook
> Hurled down a mountain-cove from stage to stage,
> Yet tempering, for my sight, its bustling rage
> In the soft heaven of a translucent pool;
> Thence creeping under sylvan arches cool,
> Fit haunt of shapes whose glorious equipage
> Would elevate my dreams. (1:22.2-9)

The place recalls the many pool- or springside retreats, consecrated places where the younger Wordsworth dreamed or communed with that inner self which opened the channels to imaginative experience. One of these reveries, undoubtedly dreamt in such a place, is recounted in the opening poem of part three, a dream which Wordsworth admitted to have been of his daughter Dora; he described it as composed spontaneously during a walk, while not a few of the others were laboriously worked and reworked.[17]

> I saw the figure of a lovely Maid
> Seated alone beneath a darksome tree,
> Whose fondly-overhanging canopy
> Set off her brightness with a pleasing shade.
> No Spirit was she; *that* my heart betrayed,
> For she was one I loved exceedingly;
> But while I gazed in tender reverie
> (Or was it sleep that with my Fancy played?)
> The bright corporeal presence – form and face –
> Remaining still distinct grew thin and rare,
> Like sunny mist; at length the golden hair,
> Shape, limbs, and heavenly features, keeping pace
> Each with the other in a lingering race
> Of dissolution, melted into air. (3:1.1-14)

This passage, unique among the august ceremonies of the *Ecclesiastical Sonnets*, recalls one of Wordsworth's rare personal anecdotes from *The River Duddon*. It is occasioned by "a whisper from the past" rather than a dream, and is a haunting evocation of his deceased cousin Mary Smith (née Wordsworth), whose luminous presence haunted such companionable places as Duddon's banks "when here I roved / With friends and kindred tenderly beloved."

> Her glistening tresses bound, yet light and free
> As golden locks of birch, that rise and fall

On gales that breathe too gently to recall
Aught of the fading year's inclemency! (*Duddon*, 21.11–14)

Memory and affection have disclosed her as a transfigured spirit of place, a natural presence. Dora Wordsworth and Mary Smith emerge as those evanescent figures who, for Wordsworth, tended the fountainhead and nurturing streams of his poetic imagination, those who "opened out" / The springs of tender thought." Their fostering role and its transforming presence at the headwaters is the subject of chapter three.

CHAPTER TWO

Sources

Paramount among mysteries are those associated with beginnings, with when and where life commences and the unsullied innocence which accompanies its youthful passage. "No objects of the natural world," Farnell writes in his *Cults of the Greek States*, "attracted the religious devotion of the primitive and later Greek so much as rivers and springs, and no other obtained so general a recognition in the cults of the Greek States."[1] In countries of fierce heats where droughty rivers are a seasonal feature, the rare unfailing spring or coursing waterway not only recalled but enacted the mystery of generation and nurture. Pausanias scrupulously recorded the fountains and springs affording relief to the traveller, noting their location, their virtues, and their presiding genii. Always sceptical concerning myth, the Roman Baedeker nevertheless appreciated the practical comforts of the spring to the wayfarer in a dry land. The modern Greek, Kitto's *In the Mountains of Greece* claims, is no less fastidious in his connoisseurship of the peculiar virtues of neighbouring springs and knowledgeable concerning their genesis and genealogy;[2] nor is the Roman of today, whose lore concerning the springs' urban cousins, the fountains of Rome, is as inexhaustible as their waters. This perennial fascination was not limited to countries subject to midsummer heats under the dog star; long before Rome carried her standards north to a damper Europe, it was shared beyond the Danube, the Rhine, and the English Channel.

Although rivers with their mythological associations appear in Greek poetry as early as that of Hesiod and Homer (the one cautioning against passing water in the headwaters of a stream, the other demonstrating the perils of offending river gods such as Scamander), the river poem as a literary genre first emerges in a fourth-century account of a journey by water from Bingen to Trier, the *Mosella* of Ausonius. Symmachus, his friend and editor, commended the work: "And yet your noble and stately verse has upset my preconceptions and made this stream for me greater than the Nile of Egypt, cooler than the Don of Scythia, and more famous than this Tiber we all know so well."[3] Ausonius describes the riverscape, praises its natural features as well as the river's utility as an artery of commerce, and invests the Moseltal with mythology familiar to a citizen of the city on the Tiber.

Nor does the scenery of this region please men alone; I can believe that here the rustic Satrys and the grey-eyed Nymphs meet together on the border of the stream, when the goat-footed Pans are seized with merry ribaldry, and splashing in the shallows, frighten the trembling sister-nymphs beneath the stream, while they thresh the water with unskilful strokes. Oft also, when she has stolen clusters from the inland hills, Panope, the river lady, with a troop of Oread friends, flees the wanton Fauns, gods of the countryside. And it is said that when the sun's fiery orb stops in the midst of his course, the Satyrs and the sister-Nymphs of the crystal depths meet here beside the stream and ply the dance in partnership, what time the fiercer heat affords them hours set free from mortal company. Then, wantonly frolicking amid their native waters, the Nymphs duck the Satyrs in the waves, and slip away right through the hands of those unskilful swimmers, as, baffled, they seek to grasp their slippery limbs and, instead of bodies, embrace yielding waves.[4]

Branches of Ausonius's *Mosella* can be traced through Claudian's *De Nilo* and Venantius Fortunatus's account of his own expedition on the Mosel some two hundred years later, *De navigio suo*. Nymphs and satyrs have been exorcised from the Bishop of Poitiers's river, and the trade he plied was episcopal rather than commercial, although some sixty years earlier a rout of dryads, hamadryads, naiads, satyrs, and Bacchus himself enjoyed ecclesiastical tolerance in a fifth-century account of the interval land between the Garonne and Dordogne by Sidonius Apollinaris, Bishop of Claremont-Ferrand.

Aubin, in his *Topographical Poetry in Eighteenth-Century England*, to which this account is indebted, describes in his chapter "Murmuring Waters" the englishing of the river poem, first undertaken in 1543 by John Leland.[5] Aubin lists some one hundred and thirty-six English river poems written between 1648 and 1850. Among the authors is a spate of "anons," writers such as John Taylor the Water Poet, whose fame too was writ in water, as well as Herrick, Vaughan, Warton, Wordsworth, Coleridge, Keats, Hunt, Shelley, and Byron with tributes to Thames, Isca, Isis, Wye and Duddon, Otter, Nile, Serchio, and Po. The English river poem essayed both the homy and the exotic, and often mingled its waters by importing the figures of nymph and satyr from Ausonius, adopting them throughout the Renaissance as stock personifications and maintaining them into the eighteenth and nineteenth centuries.

The rivers of antiquity were frequently accorded individual cults and worshipped by those living by them or dependent upon them. Achelous, Scamander, and Alpheus were invoked both as the rivers themselves and as the gods dwelling within their waters. Homer's Scamander converses with Achilles in human form, but later threatens to overwhelm him as the enraged torrent. River waters are often as treacherous as they are serviceable, and the Greeks nervously appeased even dry river beds by sacrifice before crossing them. Swollen rivers on the rampage, like a lusting Achelous or Alpheus, or Cachales the Roarer who plunges down Parnassus, were both menace and boon to the mortals and nymphs they favoured or ravished. Sir Walter Scott records in *The Lay of the Last Minstrel* the misfortune of Lady Drummlziel, who presented her husband on his return from the crusades with a stepson gotten on her by the River Tweed. The child was received into the family and named Tweedie.[6]

The Germans, Herodotus reports, addressed their prayers to the Rhine. The habitats of Sequana of the Seine, Verbeia of the Wharfe, Sabrina of the Severn, Peg O'Nell of the Ribble, and Peg Powler of the Tees course blithely and darkly, masking shallows and deeps, and commanded the respect of an antiquity more venerable than that of Greece or Rome, a veneration compounded of gratitude for their gifts and stark terror. As such, they beggared the enfeebled personifications of Father Thames, Nilus, or Tiber, senescent creations of more reasonable ages. The young Wordsworth was beset by qualms concerning the exercise of personification as inherited from the eighteenth century, and a Coleridge notebook entry draws the plight of a river deity and his *mysterium* when pressed into the service of commerce. Coleridge describes a convention gone heavy at the top:

The Frontispiece to the second Vol. of Brand's History of Newcastle is a head of the River God Tyne designed by Sir W. Chamber, which said River God has upon his head by way of head dress – a fishing net, 2 salmon with other fish, some ears of corn, a compleat collection of miner's tools, and to crown the whole a coal *fire* in a wicker basket. All these materials being so arrayed as to form the newest & most approvd head dress of a river God.[7]

Among the serviceable aspects of certain classical rivers were their mantic properties: the practice of divination known as hydromancy was usually conducted at the source. Homer describes the Greek expedition becalmed at Aulis turning in their bewilderment to a spring beneath sheltering plane trees.

At Aulis met, and we beside the fount
With perfect hecatombs the gods adored
Beneath the plane tree, from whose root a stream
Ran crystal-clear; there we beheld a sign
Wonderful in all eyes.[8]

At Dodona the oracular spring of Zeus of the Flowing Waters issued from the roots of the great oak. Book seven of the *Aeneid* tells of Latinus's consultation with the oracle of his father Faunus under the Alban Mount where a sacred spring released its sulphurous fumes. The spirit of the place is customarily pampered by sacrifice and consultation is conducted through visions or voices vouchsafed the sleeper at the springside. The method, whether followed for purposes of prophecy or of healing, was known to the ancients as incubation, and was and is still widely practised. Plutarch attests to the prophetic efficacy of running waters, and Pausanias cites the Cave of the Sphragitides on Mount Cithaeron where voices can be discerned in the reverie induced by their murmuring.[9] Coleridge describes an instance of hydromancy in his tale adapted from Drayton, the "Fable of the Madning Rain."

In the warmth of the approaching mid-day I was reposing in the vast cavern, out of which, from its northern portal, issued the river that winds throughout the vale, when a voice powerful, yet not from its loudness, suddenly hailed me. Guided by my ear I looked toward the supposed place for some Form, from which it had proceeded. I beheld nothing but the gleaming walls of the cavern.[10]

The voice spoke, as it did to Latinus, portending the future. The setting of fountain and cavern is as familiar to the Romantic poets as it was to the classical world. As Blake crustily observed, such sacred sites and practices were peremptorily institutionalized by the priesthood. The pythoness's lustrations in the Castalian spring, followed by draughts from the fountain of Cassotis, played their part by inducing her mantic frenzy. Oracles at Didyma seem to have drunk from sacred springs, and excavations of the adyton at Claros have confirmed the accounts of Iamblichus and Pausanius by freeing the still effulgent spring which inspired its oracle.[11]

At Dodona the voice issuing from its spring was that of the naiad Dione; the Sphragitides of Cithaeron too were *pegae* or spring dwellers. Among those offspring of Oceanus and Tethys, who spawned the rivers of the world, were the springs. In the classical world the spring dwellers were invariably feminine, as was their habitat, the *aqua femina*, as Varro calls it.[12] Like their brother rivers, they were often thought of as assuming human form and dwelling within the river, its grottoes, or its springs, but they were also intimately associated with the qualities of the water itself, with the spring they tended and its issue, so they appear as intermediate or liminal creatures sharing the nature of both. They can be glimpsed in the darting light of water welling out of the earth, and in the young changeable stream flashing through woodland light and shade, or their presence can be felt at the mysterious source they tend, dutifully clearing debris from its gentle urging. An inscription from *The Greek Anthology* praises the light-limbed graces whose role was identifiable with that of their sister nymphs: "The Graces bathed here, and to reward the bath they gave to the water the brightness of their limbs."[13] Among the most touching of these memorials are those preserved in the *Anthology*, inscriptions dedicating gardens, dells, springs, baths, and fountainheads to the naiads, hamadryads, and their half-sisters of the sea, the nereids.

Ye water Nymphs, children of Doris, water diligently this garden of Timocles, for to you, Maidens, doth the gardener Timocles bring ever in their season gifts from the garden.[14]

A garden by the sea:

How skilled was he who mingled the deep with the land, sea-weed with garden plants, the floods of the Nereids with the founts of the Naiads.[15]

Hermocreon records his thanks and his sacrifice:

Ye nymphs of the water, to whom Hermocreon set up these gifts when he had lighted on your delightful fountain, all hail! And may ye be ever full of pure drink, tread your lovely feet the floor of this your watery home.[16]

Only the inscriptions survive, remembering the pleasances and their guardians. The shades of the planes, the cultivation, have yielded to predatory time, grazing goats, and barren hills. All has passed but the miracle which first summoned the inscriptions: the springs still striking their brilliance in the harsh light, plying old or fresh channels toward the same destination, the waiting sea and the foaming embrace of their parent Ocean and nereid sisters.

Nymphs hold their roles in common, yet each has her particular identity and personality recognizable from her surroundings, her voice, her gait and motion, and her myth. Eliade's attitude toward these creatures is an attractive one:

They needed hardly to be created by the Hellenic imagination: rather they were there, in the water from the beginning of the world; all the Greeks had to give them was their human form and their name. They were created by the living, flowing water, by its magic, by the power emanating from it, by its babbling.[17]

Nymphs are discovered, recognized, rather than invented by self-conscious mythmakers. Their fascination cannot be solely a function of the place where they live with its particular magic, but of our apprehension of it and our response. "How much is written of Pigmies, Fairies, Nymphs, Syrens, Apparitions," Robert Kirk, the writer of *The Secret Commonwealth*, proposed in 1691, "which tho not the tenth Part true, yet could not spring of Nothing."[18] Our discovery involves recognizing a part of ourselves, through a deeply felt intuition of our own nature which is mirrored and articulated for us through these receptive natural images. The numinous or the mysterious, Walter Otto maintained in reply to Wilamowitz-Moellendorff's disarming postulate "the gods are there," can only be manifest to us psychologically and understood psychologically.[19] Opposed as they appear, the two views can be reconciled by the assertion that "the gods are *here*," and Romantic poetry itself showed a disinclination to distinguish how a metaphysical event is distinguished from a psychological one, to banish *psyche* from its psychology.

For all their watery qualities and the changeable character they suggest, nymphs are often of a reassuringly practical nature. As the *Kourotrophoi*, they mothered heroes and were associated with birth and child-rearing. They made excellent nannies and acquired superior credentials by serving the first families. Zeus was furtively raised by the deep-breasted mountain nymphs of Ida, and Dionysius by the *Nysiai*, the mountain nymphs of his homeland. Like the satyrs and silenoi who fancied them, the nymphs were rural deities and, apart from foster parenting, were usefully employed like good country girls in spinning and weaving. Like the muses, who were probably oreads or mountain nymphs, they were inordinately fond of country dance on the heights and about the springs they tended.

They were, however, not entirely unobjectionable. They were, and still are in modern Greece, kidnappers, spiriting away others' children to bring up as their own changelings; abductors, seizing hesitant young men whose lot it was to attract their attentions. They occasionally contract conventional marriages with mortals and are loving but unreliable. They are not to be crossed, nor their paths crossed at the inappropriate hour of noon.[20]

The veneration, consultation, and sacrificial rites associated with wells and springs are at least as old as neolithic times, outliving classical antiquity and surviving in western Europe beneath veneers of pious decency into our own century. Horace honoured his Bandusian spring, and in return for gifts of inspiration rivalling those of Castalia, Hippocrene, and Pieria, promised it a kid; Martial offered a sow.[21] The cult they observed was known to the Roman world as the Fontanalia, and was observed on 13 October when tribute was offered to the naiads of wells and fountains by ceremony and the casting of flowers or flowery crowns on the waters. The custom of "well-dressing" or "flowering" was common enough as late as the 1890s in Derbyshire, Staffordshire, North Lancashire, Westmoreland, and Shropshire, where the observance was moved to Holy Thursday or Ascension Day, coincident with the coming of spring. On this day the Fellows of New College, Oxford, according to Anthony à Wood, repaired to Bartholomew's Hospital, where "they place themselves round about the Well" and "warble forth melodiously a Song of three or four or five parts" before refreshing themselves with a draft and retiring to sermon. John Aubrey refers to Wood's account of a nymph translated to Oxford:

Near St. Clements at Oxford, was a Spring (stop't-up since the warres) where St. Edmond (Arch-Bishop of Canterbury) did sometime meet and converse with an Angel, or Nymph: as Numa Pompilius did with Egeria.[22]

Waking the well, the practice of drinking its waters, making offerings, and passing the night at the wellside on the eve of its patron saint, survived the middle ages as a memory of the ancient curative or oneiric practice of incubation. The observance was proscribed by Christian authorities as conducive to night-long licence.

The veneration of wells by day or night was ever a trouble to the church. Cults of wells and curative waters surviving under pious or fashionable auspices were prohibited by the second council of Arles in the fifth century, and the twenty-sixth canon of Saint Anselm in the twelfth century enjoined the faithful to "Let no one attribute reverence or sanctity to a dead body or a fountain, without the bishop's authority."[23] If pagan survivals were to be baptized in the new faith, and the living waters of the past plumbed for their legacy of Egyptian gold, the Helly or Holy Wells must be rigorously regulated. The ecclesiastical imprimatur was not uncommonly granted, and prayers for the blessing of the well found a place in liturgy.

Let us pray. Lord God omnipotent who hath summoned the abundance of water to flow through dark veins into the depths of this well, with your aid and through the duty of our office, ghostly doings and demonic snares having been cast out, this well may endure purified and cleansed through Christ our Lord.[24]

The nameless terrors that linger in dark, damp places had been officially displaced by the reconstituted waters of the new faith. Celtic deities and classical naiads were summarily baptized, their premises renovated and rededicated. The conversion was not difficult: the pagan Ausonius's evocation of a spring at Bordeaux might have been handily adapted as a hymn honouring the Virgin, who would divest the Celtic Divona of her regency over the living waters.

Hail, fountain of source unknown, holy, gracious, unfailing, crystal-clear, azure, deep, murmurous, shady, and unsullied! Hail guardian deity of our city, of whom we may drink health-giving draughts, named by the Celts Divona.[25]

In Sir James Frazer's day wells were still worshipped, and English wells continued to exercise the power of prophecy, although their pronouncements were never delivered in hexameters.[26] Water levels at Beckford's Fonthill in Wiltshire, Dudley's spring in Warwickshire, Langley in Kent, all forecast plenty or scarcity of corn or direr matters of "deathe, pestylence or grete batayle."[27] The Holy Well of Gulval was attentive to inquiries about the fate of friends.[28] Yorkshire was well watered by oracular wells, and the ebbing and flooding of Gibblesworth well was studied by Drayton in his *Polyolbion*, where its irregularities were attributed to a winded nymph pursued by a satyr and translated into the spring. The springs at Workinham, Surrey, rise "only upon the approach of some remarkable alteration in church or state."[29] At Gilsland,

In Cumberland there is a spring
And strange it is to tell,
That many of fortune it will make
If never a drop they sell.[30]

There are ways undreamt of by Hesiod of defiling a spring; some relinquished their prescience on being sluiced into the service of breweries or distilleries.

In the English Lake District, each Sunday in May witnessed successive ceremonies at four wells in the neighbourhood of Penrith. Saint Cuthbert's spring or holy well, also in Cumberland, had a naiad associated with it.[31] Wordsworth, who mourned the suppression of the great religious foundations of the English countryside, recorded in *The Prelude* his regret over the passing of more ancient rites familiar to him from his youth.

        ... and of youths,
Each with his maid, before the sun was up,
By annual custom, issuing forth in troops,
To drink the waters of some sainted well,
And hang it round with garlands. Love survives,
But for such purpose, flowers no longer grow:
The times, too sage, perhaps too proud, have dropped
These lighter graces; and the rural ways
And manners which my childhood looked upon
Were the unluxuriant produce of a life
Intent on little but substantial needs,
Yet rich in beauty, beauty that was felt. (1850, 8.152–63)

The poet would have sympathized with the historian of Cumberland who spoke with regret over the suppression of holy wells:

The good spirit of the well was sought out and supposed to teach its votaries the virtues of temperance, health, cleanliness, simplicity and love. Worse customs we might have, but few if any persons nowadays seek its blessings, and the old faith in its powers had died out.[32]

A moving tribute, it nonetheless suggests that the mercurial guardians of the ancient springs had sunk beneath a tide of whitewash and vapid Victorian sentimentality. But their bogyish nature survived in the treacherous nymphs or mermaids who haunted the Shropshire meres and other lonely, damp places, in Peg Powler who lusted after human life in the waters of the Tees, Jenny Greenteeth or Peg o' the Well, last or latest of the *pegae* or spring dwellers who frequented Lancashire streams and wells, snatching unwary children and dragging them, like Hylas or the Carian Hermaphroditus, into their immeasurable depth.

CHAPTER THREE

The Guardian and the Spring

 "THE TRIAD"

> From thence to search the mystic cause of things,
> And follow nature to her secret springs ...

> Never did a child stand by the side of a running stream,
> pondering within himself what power was the feeder of
> the perpetual current, from what never-wearied sources
> the body of water was supplied ...

The first of these passages was written by Wordsworth at the age of fourteen on the occasion of a school exercise; the second belongs to the "Essays upon Epitaphs" twenty-five years later.[1] Along with familiar lakes and meres, streams, becks, brooks, forces, rivers, and ghylls lace the landscape of Wordsworth's poetry, and it is in the nature of these that each must have a source, a course, and a mouth. This bounty of springs, well-heads, and natural fountains argues more than the obvious conclusion that Wordsworth's plashy Cumbria was a generously well-watered tract.

Allusions to tamer springs are commonplace among English poets who cherished the classical origins of their art, and even Wordsworth was not above embellishing a passage with a graceful genuflection to Horace's Bandusian well, to Castalia or Hippocrene, or the celebrated grotto sacred to the Egerian nymph at a civilized stroll from the gates of Rome. Horace's Sabine spring prattles in the imitative lines of Wordsworth's "An Evening Walk" in 1787, and as late as the "Musings near Aquapendente" in 1837.[2] It is the history of this spring, prattling so inauspiciously in its infancy in 1787, that this chapter will follow. These two Horatian allusions embrace some fifty years of Wordsworth's creative life, and within them can be traced the history of a living symbol at the heart of a poet's personal mythology. Because the spring embodied for Wordsworth the charisma he associated with the source of his own creative powers, it is intimately connected with those domestic figures whom Wordsworth recognized as having fostered those powers throughout his creative life: sister, wife, and daughter. The history of the spring is at one with Wordsworth's own; its command and resonance respond to the growth and decline of the poet who first summoned and later resigned it to the Horatian source from which it rose.

The Wordsworthian journey to the source offers none of the melodrama of John Armstrong's "sublime apostrophe to the great rivers of the earth," or the painter John Martin's *Sadak in Search of the Waters of Oblivion*, or Shelley's *Alastor*; it is more of an amble than an anabasis or strenuous heroic quest. The Wordsworthian source is a secluded, private, and generally secret place. To reach it requires some effort, but it lies almost, as it were, at hand. There is no eruption of demonic energy to overwhelm the seeker after sources; its emergence is epiphanic rather than apocalyptic, and it offers communion rather than terror. And yet the place is pervaded with the mystery of inexhaustible life welling from darkness into light, and we are invariably aware of an engaging presence, subtle, elusive, and pervasively feminine, whose charge it is. Although this presence has, I suspect, been felt by every reader of Wordsworth's poetry, she remains unacknowledged and unidentified. She is the elusive creature who dwells in grottoes and pools, the nymph or the naiad who tends the spring, the well-head, or the modest source of mighty rivers, and who, despite her retiring nature, appears with astonishing frequency in Wordsworth's poetry. This inquiry is addressed to the source and its shy ministrant, and their role in Wordsworth's personal and creative life. The route I propose to trace to her precincts is retrocessive, beginning with her appearance in the later poetry and moving back to its earlier and more compelling manifestations: upstream, as it were, to the source. The strategy is not eccentric. It has the advantage of avoiding a chronicle of artistic decline, and brings the hindsight of the subsequent to bear on the earlier work, the retrospective method implicit in all critical inquiry.

When Wordsworth banishes a rout of classical nymphs and their traditional haunts from his poem "The Triad" in 1828, stolidly preferring the "chaster coverts of a British Hill," he echoes the light-hearted dismissal which opened his prologue to *Peter Bell*: "There's something in a flying horse / There's something in a huge balloon." That "something" was hot air, cultural gas displacing the spirited courser of Hippocrene, an antiquarian mythology surviving its living context: *afflatus* turned flatulent.

I will not fetch a Naiad from a flood
Pure as herself – (song lacks not mightier power)
Nor leaf-crowned Dryad from a pathless wood,
Nor Sea-nymph glistening from her coral bower;
Mere Mortals, bodied forth in vision still,
Shall with Mount Ida's triple luster fill
The chaster coverts of a British hill. ("The Triad," 8–14)

Wordsworth's classical iconoclasm is evident at least two dozen years earlier:

... I would not do
Like Grecian Artists, give thee human cheeks,
Channels for tears; no Naiad shouldst thou be, –
Have neither limbs, feet, feathers, joints, nor hairs:
It seems the Eternal Soul is clothed in thee
With purer robes than those of flesh and blood ...
(*Miscellaneous Sonnets*, 31.7–12)

These passages recall the proscription against myth in the 1815 Preface to the *Lyrical Ballads*: "the anthropomorphitism of the Pagan religion subjected the minds of the greatest poets in those countries too much to the bondage of definite form; from which the Hebrews were preserved by their abhorrence of idolatry."[3] Inherited myth imposed a rigid anthropomorphism which diminished and confined the *mysterium tremendum* which the gods once commanded, and yet Wordsworth understood his own task as poet as proffering images of the "Eternal Soul" or "primal mystery."

Retiring and elusive as they may be, nymphs are made of stern stuff, whether proscribed or not. Plutarch, Lemprière calculates, allotted them a life span of above 9720 years, and they were not about to abandon Wordsworth, nor he them.[4] They have the cunning to withdraw into deeper shades or, as changelings, to alter their appearance. In "The Triad" Wordsworth substitutes for the nymphs three of his own company – Edith May Southey, his daughter Dora, and Sara Coleridge – and clothes them in the guise and borrowed splendour of the daughters of Zeus and the nereid Eurynome, the three graces or *charites* known as Aglaia, Euphrosyne, and Thalia. The poem domesticates and countrifies the elaborate conceit of a traditional court masque or entertainment. Its action, or, more properly, its progress, is enacted for an audience of two who provide its frame: a narrator-guide and a youth who, like Paris, witnesses the triple delight and will judge the fairest. Wordsworth tactfully withholds a judgment that might have precipitated a domestic Trojan War. The youth is promised that "one of the bright Three [may] become thy happy bride." This frail convention provided the original title of the poem, "The Promise," as well as the occasion for its pageantry. The youth in the implied role of Paris provides the link which tradition had forged between the three graces and Aphrodite, whom they served as embodiments of all joy, brightness, and beauty in the natural and human world.

Aglaia, whose name is synonymous with brightness, is rendered by Wordsworth as "Lucida." A classical grace might have laboured under the name of Edith May, but the Latinizing is significant, and Lucida assumes a role in the genealogy of Wordsworth's Lucy. The poet claimed to have sketched his three subjects from the life rather than from the myth, but they are, in fact, arresting creations who borrow whatever resonance they command from their mythic antecedents rather than nature.

Wordsworth identifies his three graces as "nymphs" throughout his poem, thus following the classical precedent which associated the *charites* with the muses, who were also fountain nymphs. The second of these, the youngest, Dora-Euphrosyne, is the joyous grace who clearly outshines her sisters and commands a disproportionate measure of her father's praise and genius:

> ... and lo! from pastimes virginal
> She hastens to the tents
> Of nature, and the lonely elements.
> Air sparkles round her with a dazzling sheen;
> But mark her glowing cheek, her vesture green! (94–8)

Her emblem is a lone flower, the anemone, and Wordsworth italicizes its singularity.

> But her humility is well content
> With *one* wild floweret (call it not forlorn)
> FLOWER OF THE WINDS beneath her bosom worn –
> Yet more for love than ornament. ("The Triad," 115–18)

The wind flower is appropriate to this lone dancer who is all grace and who flies "Swift as a Thracian Nymph o'er field and height" to the tents of nature and the lonely elements. She is both her father's daughter and his muse, and is also identified with the naiad at her station, the spring:

> A face o'er which a thousand shadows go!
> – She stops – is fastened to that rivulet's side;
> And there (while, with sedater mien,

O'er timid waters that have scarcely left
Their birthplace in the rocky cleft
She bends) ...
    ...
Fit countenance for the soul of primal truth ... (131–9)

Euphrosyne not only remembers her mythic progenitors, but she recalls as well her sibling or *alter ego*, Lucy: numinous, humble and retiring, dwelling by solitary springs among the untrodden ways, her emblem a single violet,

> ... and she shall lean her ear
> In many a secret place
> Where rivulets dance their wayward round,
> And beauty born of murmuring sound
> Shall pass into her face.   ("Three Years She Grew," 26–30)

"The Triad" of 1828 suggests, through its somewhat heavy-handed mythmaking, an earlier, subtler, and more profound mythic progenitor, the Lucy of the Goslar winter of 1798, and the course which I intend to trace through Wordsworth's poetry leads back to her, to Lucy at the source.

NAB WELL

"Composed when a Probability Existed of our Being Obliged to quit Rydal Mount as a Residence" was written two years before "The Triad" in 1826; its cumbersome working title recalls the domestic crisis which occasioned it.[5] When the poet and his family were threatened with being turned out of their beloved Rydal Mount, Wordsworth's recourse was as poetical as its was impractical. He turned to the spring at Rydal known prosaically as the "Nab Well" and wrote over two hundred lines of blank verse, his longest meditation on a spring. He relates that in this moment of crisis he was drawn instinctively, compelled it would seem, to the side of Nab Well: "Insensibly the foretaste of this parting / Hath ruled my steps, and seals me to thy side" ("Composed," 9–10).

There are many variants of the poem; Wordsworth took his subject far more seriously than subsequent readers. Mary Moorman relates that he told Crabb Robinson it was intended as an introduction to *The Recluse*, "containing a poetical view of water as an element in the composition of our globe."[6] Whatever its eminence in Wordsworth's *magnum opus* might have been, he was never satisfied with the results and the poem remained in manuscript.

Wordsworth's Rydal spring has the power of transforming the seasonal debris in its waters, so that felled branches and leaves beaded in its crystal waters seem to have fallen from silver trees. Snatched from that transforming element, their brilliance palls in the vulgar air.

> And oh! how much, of all that love creates
> Or beautifies, like changes undergoes,
> Suffers like loss when drawn out of the soul,
> Its silent laboratory! (60–3)

As poetic analogues, spring and soul keep a respectful distance: they fail to achieve the metaphoric identity which permits Wordsworth to internalize a natural landscape or to project an inner one. Neverthless, the poet does endow the well with a sense of the unfathomable mystery belonging to an entrance to the underworld.

> And the vault's hoary sides to which they clung,
> Imag'd in downward show; the flower, the herbs,
> *These* not of earthly texture, and the vault
> Not *there* diminutive, but through a scale
> Of Vision less and less distinct, descending
> To gloom impenetrable. (103–8)

Out of this same mystery a younger Wordsworth drew the opening quatrain of a sonnet of 1818 in which he describes a welling spring and its issue, and in a single stroke animated it with the shadowy presence of Persephone risen from Pluto's realm to bear her gift of renewed life to the barren world:

> Pure element of waters! whereso'er
> Thou dost forsake thy subterranean haunts,
> Green herbs, bright flowers, and berry-bearing plants,
> Rise into life and in thy train appear ... (*Miscellaneous Sonnets*, 33.1–4)

"The thought of parting," Wordsworth wrote of the Nab Well, "seals me to thy side," as surely and securely as Dora-Euphrosyne in "The Triad" is "fastened to that rivulet's side." A variant reading, B text of the Rydal poem, insists that the spring was frequented often and solely by the poet: "Such calm attraction have I found in thee, / My private treasure."[7] It is a prized and private place, and the intimacy of poet and spring very nearly seals their identities. The well is consistently characterized as feminine. Its constancy in drought and flood and its inexhaustible outpouring are elements of its peculiar witchery:

> ... for in spectacles unlook'd for,
> And transformations silently fulfill'd
> What witchcraft, meek Enchantress, equals thine? (27–9)

Among the springs' traditional enchantments is the gift of prophecy. Plutarch, among others, bore witness to their efficacy: "But the prophetic current and breath is most divine and holy, whether it issue by itself through the air or come in the company of running water."[8]

With this prophetic role in mind, Wordsworth executes a graceful transition from the Nab Well to the woodland "fountain of the Fairies" at Boischenu where Joan of Arc attended her militant voices, and where local folklore remembered Merlin's prophecy that one day a maid would leave that place to achieve untold glory. Thus Wordsworth encompases the entire mythic history of the source and its guardians. The fairies of Boischenu have preserved the seat and prophetic powers of the nymphs, and are in turn usurped by the votaresses of the new faith: the fairy fountain makes way for the well of the saints. In his sonnet "Nun's Well, Brigham," Wordsworth's nuns and the meditative life have in turn become as shadowy a memory as the nymphs, or at least a less substantial presence than their successors, the newly beneficed ruminative cows.

> A tender Spirit broods – the pensive Shade
> Of ritual honours to this Fountain paid
> By hooded Votaresses with saintly cheer ... (9–11)

Joan's voices are darker and more threatening than those which issued from the benign naiads, but in his description of the Maid at her well Wordsworth grasps what the ancients understood and Joan's inquisitors insisted, that the oracular voice issues as much from within as without. "We offer both sacrifices and prayers as the price for oracles," Plutarch wrote; "what possesses us to do so, if our souls carry within themselves the prophetic power, and it is some particular state of the air or its currents which stirs these to activity?"[9] This trafficking of soul and source is rendered with subtle power:

> A Voice
> Reached her with supernatural mandates charged
> More awful than the chambers of dark earth
> Have virtue to send forth. Upon the marge
> Of the benignant fountain, while she stood
> Gazing intently, the translucent lymph
> Darkened beneath the shadow of her thoughts
> As if swift clouds swept over it, or caught

War's tincture, mid the forest green and still,
Turned into blood before her heart-sick eye. (174–83)

Elsewhere in this poem, Wordsworth's mastery in evoking a mythic presence through the simplest of natural imagery is evident in the following reverie over Rydal spring:

How often I have marked a plumy fern
From the live rock with grace inimitable
Bending its apex tow'rd a paler self
Reflected all in perfect lineaments –
Shadow and substance kissing point to point
In mutual stillness; or if some faint breeze
Entering the cell gave restlessness to One,
The Other, glass'd in thy unruffled breast,
Partook of every motion, met, retired,
And met again ... (65–74)

Wordsworth plumbs the fountainhead where myth perennially gathers and rises. The tale of Narcissus is breathed into the image of the mirrored frond and is realized as much through a mute perfection of tone and the delicate lethargy of the passage as through the image itself. Forty years later Stéphane Mallarmé recast the same myth in strikingly similar terms in his "Hérodiade":

Triste fleur qui croit seul et n'a pas d'autres emoi
Que son ombre dans l'eau vue avec atonie.

Had Wordsworth left well enough alone, as he had in his 1818 evocation of Persephone, the Rydal poem might have troubled him less, and we might forget that it belongs to his poetic grand climacteric. The exposition which follows the passage, superfluous and fussily pedagogical, is a sad reminder of this.

                    ... such playful sympathy,
Such delicate caress as in the shape
Of this garden Plant had aptly recompens'd
For baffled lips and disappointed arms
And hopeless pangs, the Spirit of that Youth,
The fair Narcissus by some pitying God
Changed to a crimson Flower; when he, whose pride
Provoked a retribution too severe,
Had pin'd; upon his watery Duplicate
Wasting that love the Nymphs implored in vain. (74–83)

"Watery Duplicate" indeed. Such uncomfortable sinkings at least serve to affirm an antecedent height. Throughout his poem Wordsworth persistently undermines the best of his imagery in this manner. Much has been made of the two Wordsworthian voices conversing throughout his poetic career; although their tenor may have altered, they are distressingly audible here. One is that of a poet who, in Keats's words, summons with hands in breeches' pockets the fragments of a great and unobtrusive poetry, the other that of a tedious moralist who forces himself and his reader to dote on the all too palpable designs of his homily.

The elusive springside naiad also gives way to perfunctory allusions to the muses, their parentage, their haunts, and their role as the *maîtresses inspiratrices*: "their Hippocrene and grottoed fount of Castaly." *Post musam tristitia*, and Wordsworth turns to the Miltonics which served to tide him over the flats bared by the ebb of his creative powers. Synonymous with this decline is the manner in which Wordsworth's genius for shaping private symbol within his poetry yields to the ready-made or emblematic, when resonant personal myth becomes a public rhetoric. Under such circumstances myth serves as no more than a graceful allusion to a literary past, the sort of gesture an Augustan might frame had he not the wit to press the lost mana of myth into the service of the cankered muse. It is deplorably regressive, this turn in Wordsworth's career, as if the *Lyrical Ballads* and its preface were unwritten, and two generations of Romantic poetry lay stillborn in the womb of Blake's Enitharmon.

This transformation is underscored by the argument as well as by stylistic uncertainty in the Rydal poem. After paying lip service to the standard mythological accounts of the muses, Wordsworth offers his own version of their genesis. It is lamely euhemeristic: Apollo's nine were prosaically mortal, rustic mountain singers deified by deluded generations. Wordsworth's compulsion to explain away the peculiar power of myth does, in fact, limit mythological figures in their role and diminishes their stature, and we are left with little more than the merely decorative. We are forced to compare this strategy with the younger Wordsworth's treatment of an earlier mountain singer, the solitary reaper who attains in the span of her brief poem the lineaments of a profound mythic creation in the deepest sense, as an embodiment and unveiling of a mystery transcending the limits of her time and situation and her own particularity. Although the Rydal poem threatens to turn into a *paysage moralisé*, there are still saving gleams of Wordsworth's former powers, as if he were loath to freight a creature as fragile as his naiad and sink her from sight. Her presence still haunts and presides over his description of Nab Well when she is evoked as a felt mystery rather than merely delineated.

To turn and cleave to the Nab Well at a time when the permanence of the Wordsworth establishment at Rydal Mount was threatened suggests that the spring had become for Wordsworth a powerfully evocative place, a sustaining centre which ordered and fed the rhythms of their lives in that place, a well-head whose secret springs lay as deep within his own nature as within the hillside. Nab Well and the many sister springs which Wordsworth celebrated in his lifetime are more than reservoirs of serviceable myth and literary images from the past. It is the nature of the cistern, Blake insisted, to contain and stagnate, while the fountain overflows. The spring provided Wordsworth with a means of communion with a personal past, but it is also that place where myth continually renews and gathers at its inner source. Divorced from that deeply personal matrix, Wordsworth's myths and their creatures are not unlike the dead leaves and boughs drawn from Nab Well. Wrenched from that generative living context, they emerge as paltry desiccated things. But within the enchantress's waters, and subject to her witchery, they are no longer the detritus of past seasons, but silver boughs felled from silver trees.

SISTER, WIFE AND DAUGHTER: UNTRODDEN WAYS

Wordsworth's "Ode to Lycoris" (1817) and its sequel, "To the Same," were written for his sister Dorothy. The ode's title, which has attracted little attention, is baffling. De Selincourt proposes that Wordsworth drew the name from Virgil's tenth Eclogue, and because he liked it, used it, though it meant nothing to him.[10] If the subject is Dorothy, and the poem is addressed to her, it is indeed curious and less than gracious that rather than one of her more innocuous cognomens, Emma, Emmeline, or Louisa, Wordsworth chose the name of the strumpet actress who tormented the genius of the Roman elegist Cornelius Gallus and who was celebrated by Virgil in the last of his eclogues. Whatever Dorothy may have been to her brother, she was no Volumnia, the fickle camp-follower who jilted Gallus for another man in uniform. If indeed the name does derive from Virgil, a more apt candidate is the golden-haired naiad Lycorias who lived within the waters at the source of the River Peneus with Cyrene and her retinue of weaver nymphs. Wordsworth spoke elsewhere of his own Grasmere as a Vale of Tempe and as early as 1801 proposed Skiddaw as the English Parnassus pouring "forth streams more sweet than Castaly." Since the subject of his ode is mythology, Dorothy's identification as naiad is more appropriate than the Roman woman who was a once sordid reality. Wordsworth may have misremembered the name, which appears among the catalogue of

nymphs in the epyllion of Aristaeus the Arcadian beekeeper in the fifth
book of the Georgics.[11]

Lycoris appears to have provided Wordsworth with no more than his
title and a serviceable alias for the poem's apostrophes to Dorothy, but
in its campanion piece, "To the Same," Dorothy has shed her alias and
is found with her brother in the customary habitat of the nymphs, a
grotto. On a hot summer day, brother and sister climb a mountainside
and enter the cave's cool twilight. Initially the place is prosaically
linked to the "Egerian grot" and its tutelary nymph:

> such twilight to compose
> As Numa loved; when, in the Egerian grot,
> From the sage Nymph appearing at his wish,
> He gained whate'er a regal mind might ask,
> Or need, of counsel breathed through lips divine. ("To the Same," 27–31)

The poet and his sister sound the secrets of their private nymphaeum in
the voice of a trickling spring mouthing its cryptic messages from the
matrix of prophecy, the earth.

> ... let that dim cave
> Protect us, there deciphering as we may
> Diluvian records; or the sighs of Earth
> Interpreting; or counting for old Time
> His minutes, by reiterated drops,
> Audible tears, from some invisible source
> That deepens upon fancy – more and more
> Drawn toward the centre whence these sighs creep forth
> To awe the lightness of humanity. (32–40)

Again, Wordsworth deploys a purposive ambiguity and intimates a
source which lies as much within the suppliants as at the fountainhead
itself. Dorothy is not characterized as nymph, but there lies within her
an unfathomable calm whose waters only her brother may read.

> Or, shutting up thyself within thyself,
> There let me see thee sink into a mood
> Of gentler thought, protracted till thine eye
> Be calm as water when the winds are gone,
> And no one can tell whither. (41–5)

These lines derive from an early, discarded version of "Nutting" written
at Goslar, thus bridging the two poems of 1817 and the 1798 Lucy
poems from the Goslar period.[12]

The association of Dorothy with the well-spring is not without further precedent. She is, on occasion, not only linked with that image but implicitly identified with the naiad guardian at the source. Nor is she the only one cast in this role. Wordsworth on at least one occasion would place his affianced Mary Hutchinson in an idyllic setting near a spring, and would complete his domestic trinity by casting his daughter Dora in the same role.

Among the "Poems on the Naming of Places" is Wordsworth's tribute "To M.H.," his future wife, Mary Hutchinson, who briefly augmented rather than supplanted Dorothy's role as *inspiratrice*. Mary is assigned to a secluded poolside in Rydal Upper Park, "a small bed of water in the woods." The place is isolated, "a calm recess" sheltered from the restless eye of the profane traveller and shaded from travelling "sun / Or wind from any quarter." It is known only to those nurtured by that place: herds, herdsmen, and the poet whose life finds its roots there. It is likened to a well, a "spot made by Nature for herself," and for those who have access, it is a welling cup and a place of private nurture.

> ... even as from a well
> Or some stone-basin which the herdsman's hand,
> Had shaped for their refreshment; nor did sun,
> Or wind from any quarter, ever come,
> But as a blessing to this calm recess,
> ...
> The spot was made by Nature for herself;
> The travellers know it not, and 'twill remain
> Unknown to them; but it is beautiful ... ("To M.H.," 9 13, 15 17)

It is the familiar Wordsworthian *temenos*, the sanctuary or common ground where external fact is wedded with the inner image that embraces and sustains the creative life, as Mary Hutchinson, whose place it is, will enact that same role in his ongoing life.

> He would so love it, that in his death-hour
> Its image would survive among his thoughts:
> And therefore, my sweet MARY, this still Nook
> With all its beeches, we have named for You! (21–4)

Mary Hutchinson's role as her fiancé's muse was short-lived. Wives seldom, if ever, serve husbands, their own husbands, as muses. Something of Mary's forfeiture of her brief role can be read into "She Was a Phantom of Delight," in which she is demoted in three stanzas from a beguiling enchantress, an "apparition" or "spirit," and a "traveller

between life and death" to an exemplar of "the temperate will, /
Endurance, foresight, strength, and skill." Admirable qualities, but less
than inspirational, although the poet insists she is "yet a Spirit still, and
bright / With something of angelic light." The discarded mantle soon
passes to Wordsworth's daughter Dora:

> Thy nymph-like step swift-bounding o'er the lawn,
> Along the loose rocks, or the slippery verge
> Of foaming torrents. – From thy orisons
> Come forth; and, while the morning air is yet
> Transparent as the soul of innocent youth,
> Let me, thy happy guide, now point thy way,
> And now precede thee, winding to and fro ...
>
> ("A Little Onward Lend Thy Guiding Hand," 18–24)

The poem to Dora is strikingly anticipated by Wordsworth's "Louisa,"
written fifteen years earlier. The subject of this poem, published by
Wordsworth immediately preceding three of the Lucy poems, is usually
identified as Dorothy, an attribution which my own reading endorses.
Louisa-Dorothy enjoys the same nymph-like character later assigned to
Dora, and in the 1801 poem her identification with the course of the
vivacious young brook is intimate and energetic.

> I met Louisa in the shade,
> And, having seen that lovely Maid,
> Why should I fear to say
> That, nymph-like, she is fleet and strong,
> And down the rocks can leap along
> Like rivulets in May?
>
> And she hath smiles to earth unknown;
> Smiles, that with motion of their own
> Do spread, and sink, and rise;
> That come and go with endless play,
> And ever, as they pass away,
> Are hidden in her eyes.
>
> ...
>
> Take all that's mine "beneath the moon",
> If I with her but half a noon
> May sit beneath the walls
> Or some old cave, or mossy nook,

When up she winds along the brook
To hunt the waterfalls.[13]

The cave of stanza three anticipates the 1817 poem to Dorothy, "To the Same," while the superb second stanza, omitted from the editions of 1845 and 1849, links "Louisa" both with that poem and the progenitive lines in Wordsworth's earlier version of "Nutting."

A sonnet of 1801 flatly dismisses classical allusion for Dorothy (as Emma), who not only shares the qualities of an unpretending rill but is forever sealed by memory with that place and that moment as its presiding genius.

There is a little unpretending Rill
Of limpid water, humbler far than aught
That ever among Men or Naiads sought
Notice or name! – It quivers down the hill,
Furrowing its shallow way with dubious will;
Yet to my mind this scanty Stream is brought
Oftener than Ganges or the Nile; a thought
Of private recollection sweet and still!
Months perish with their moons; year treads on year;
But faithful Emma! thou with me canst say
That, while ten thousand pleasures disappear,
And flies their memory fast almost as they;
The immortal Spirit of one happy day
Lingers beside that Rill, in vision clear. (*Miscellaneous Sonnets*, 6.1–14)

"It Was an April Morning" was drawn from the same matrix a year earlier: a remote and inaccessible "wild nook," reached by climbing the lunging Easedale Beck, is again sealed with the image of Dorothy.

"Our thoughts at least are ours; and this wild nook,
My EMMA, I will dedicate to thee."
– Soon did the spot become my other home,
My dwelling, and my out-of-doors abode. (38–41)

Wordsworth's sister Dorothy presides at the still centre of the poet's creative life during these fertile years. She is the fountainhead itself or its guardian, the role which would be reenacted by Mary Hutchinson, and in her turn by their daughter Dora. Dorothy is intimately involved, moreover, with the genesis of the Lucy figure, but before examining her role in that context I should like to consider briefly Wordsworth's three Matthew poems and their affinities with the Lucy poems. They are framed by our certain knowledge of Matthew's death. Moreover, the second of these poems deals with the death of an "Emma" and Matthew's coming to terms with her death. Lastly, the images which command these three poems are a still pool, a naiad, and a fountain. The Matthew poems belong to the Goslar winter in which Wordsworth wrote the first three of his Lucy poems.

In "The Two April Mornings," an aging Matthew turns from the grave of his nine-year-old daughter and experiences an epiphanic encounter with an unknown creature who seems a radiant incarnation of his daughter Emma. "A blooming Girl, whose hair was wet / With points of morning dew," she is described by Matthew in the guise of the wet ones, the daughters of the fountain, the naiads, or the nereid daughters of Ocean:

> "No fountain from its rocky cave
> E'er tripped with foot so free;
> She seemed as happy as a wave
> That dances on the sea. ..." (49–52)

Matthew is consoled in his loss by his impulsive recognition that he can and must, in Blake's words, "kiss a joy as it flies," accept the death of his daughter as he does the brief passing of this numinous creature: "I looked at her, and looked again / And did not wish her mine." The poem "The Fountain," which immediately follows, gathers a greater poignancy when this last episode from Matthew's personal history is considered. The unchecked fountain whose flow has embraced Matthew's seventy-two years and witnessed his losses and his fleeting joys is associated with the fountain creature of "The Two April Mornings," the figure of the lost Emma, and his own youth: "for the same sound is in my ears / Which in those days I heard." The fountain knows no rest, and with its welling energy and its affirmation of life coming to be, of renewal and process, it is not only a permanent sustaining part of Matthew's awareness, it is Matthew himself, as it is representative of all those whose years are "pressed by heavy laws" of age and who yet can boast that "their old age / Is beautiful and free." Their conversation over, Matthew and his companion glide down with the same easy fluid motion of the fountain and its issuing waters.

> We rose up from the fountain-side;
> And down the smooth descent
> Of the green sheep-track did we glide;
> And through the wood we went ... (65–8)

It is the first Matthew poem, retrospective in nature, which establishes and frames the career of the old man. Matthew is in his grave, and this poem is as chilling and bald as "A Slumber Did My Spirit Seal." Matthew is reduced to an inanimate object, the gilt inscription of his name on the schoolhouse tablet. All motion and vivacity have ceased: fountain, stream, and Matthew himself are stilled in the numbing arrest of the closing image: "Poor Matthew, all his frolics o'er / Is silent as a standing pool ..." ("Matthew," 17–18).

BESIDE THE SPRINGS OF DOVE

> Now in the form of a nymph or other goddess who comes forth from the deepest bed of Sorgues and sits on the bank, now I have seen her treading the fresh grass like a living woman.   Petrarch, *Rime Sparse* 281

> She dwelt among the untrodden ways
> Beside the springs of Dove
> A Maid whom there were none to praise
> And very few to love.

The opening lines of Wordsworth's poem locate Lucy within a context which was less obvious to the readers of the *Lyrical Ballads* than to those familiar with the subsequent career of the spring and guardian figures in the later poetry. Probably it was less than obvious to Wordsworth himself, engaged with sounding his past for the first rendering of *The Prelude,* and with drawing Lucy out of the darkness of the winter season and his discontent. The isolation of the north-country brother and sister with little money and less German, confined within the walls of the recently half-gutted provincial town by the bitter Harz winter, must have imposed an introspection that the reclusive Wordsworth had never known. But there issued from the heart of this adversity a remarkable creativity, poetry fostered by the poet's intense communion with his personal past and preoccupied with the sources of its own creation.

The opening stanza, it is often noted, consists largely of negatives. Lucy's very grounds of existence are undermined from the outset, so that she is denied substance and granted only presence.[14] She may exist either in a mental world, or, at the other extreme, as a flesh-and-blood "dark lady" haunting an unwritten chapter in Wordsworth's biography, or indeed she may be the "boundary being" which Geoffrey Hartman has identified as both sprite and human.[15] Hartman's compromise is by far the most attractive of these alternatives, but it is possible to consider the matter as less problematic, and Wordsworth's Lucy has been vexed and rough-handled unnecessarily and far too long. When we are told that she has ceased to be, it is clear that whatever existence she once knew now lies solely within the memory of the narrator. One might insist that it is unlawful (compelling though it may be) to inquire further into whether Lucy enjoyed a prior life independent of the speaker's perspective, since whatever she might have been is sealed by the grave. The issue may be avoided by insisting that such inquiries lie beyond the scope of the poem, and rest with such unfruitful literary exercises as the identity of Shakespeare's W.H. or young Hamlet's syllabus at Wittenburg. Lucy's reality and meaning lie wholly within the heart and mind of the narrator and our access to him, his words, the poem. In a poem, however, as in myth, the event is never entirely a personal matter, since articulation, the transformation into literary expression, is the process through which the personal gathers to itself the transpersonal resonance of form, of myth, or of both. It is at this level that Lucy belongs to the sisterhood of those elemental creatures who command the secret springs, and her provenance is as much with them as with the personal source which lies, as it were, at the feeder spring of all mythologies.

The traditional nymph presides over a psychic as much as a physical event, fostering a birth or creation which either is projected upon external nature or for which external nature provides a receptive image serving to articulate its mystery. The source and the naiad have always served in this way. Theirs is the female precinct, and the naiads' role involves essentially feminine mysteries: birth, creation, and nurturing. In this role the naiad is surrogate or priestess for the great mystery itself, the unfathomable dark matrix which issues from the earth as the font of life. The fountain nymphs of Castalia, the muses and their naiad sisters, induced in mere mortals the transport of prophecy or of poetic inspiration. The graces or muses were the attendants of Aphrodite. The prodigality these creatures tend is expressed mythically in the many guises of the Great Mother, of Demeter and her daughter Persephone, the goddess called Natura, or Venus as genetrix.

The second stanza of Wordsworth's poem abandons negatives and characterizes Lucy through the more positive yet oblique statement offered by metaphor and simile, so that she is constellated rather than formulated in terms of external nature; first, by a single violet near the moss-covered stone within the spring. The retiring flower of modesty and chastity is appropriate to the "unknown" maid who commands the inviolate mystery of innocence at its unsullied source. The violet is translated to a comparable solitary setting in the sky, and the speaker insists upon its singularity ("when only one / Is shining in the sky"). He can refer only to the star which heralds both dusk and dawn, Venus. Lucy, beside her springs, presides over and encompasses the narrator's world as violet and star, ruling the chthonic and uranian mysteries of his earth and sky.

Lucy's secluded setting can be identified with the "one dear nook unvisited" of "Nutting" and its "virgin scene" with "violets of five seasons" which "reappear / And fade, unseen by any human eye," its "fairy water breaks" and green stones "fleeced with moss."[16] Wordsworth opens "Nutting" with "It seems a day (I speak of one from many singled out)" and the setting is, moreover, a place singled out from many of these familiar landscapes. Dorothy Wordsworth, Mary Hutchinson, and Dora knew such places; for M.H. "This spot was made by Nature for herself / The travellers know it not, and t'will remain / Unknown to them." The Wordsworthian *temenos* with its pervasive femininity is violated in "Nutting" by a growing boy who, as true son of Adam, will enact its apparent destruction. Because the element of shock in "Nutting" is powerfully sexual, a violation, the wilful mutilation of a sacred place and a private mystery, its impact is related to the brutal fact of Lucy's death.

De Selincourt quotes a manuscript version of "Nutting" in which, although the boy seems alone on his expedition, a guiding presence or presences are explicitly introduced: "They led me, and I followed in their steps," "They led me far / Those guardian spirits, into some dear nook / Unvisited."[17] Only a sense of their ministering presence remains in the final version.

The classical nymph has been described by Jung as an independent and fragmentary expression of a familiar aspect of the unconscious; Porphyry identified her with the soul.[18] Nymph, grace, or muse belongs to those figurations of that mystery with its feminine character. We become conscious of our unconscious desires and processes through their insistent dramatization in reverie or dream, or the projection of their features onto the external world, on objects, a landscape, or figure of the opposite sex who seems to articulate and accommodate them. In the beginning, this receptive figure was, for Wordsworth, his sister, as he saw her from early childhood, sensitive, responsive, and deeply understanding. There are innumerable moving tributes to Dorothy's patient fulfilment of this her appointed role, one which Wordsworth understood as fostering his own rapport with nature and his own inner nature, the sources of the creative powers which Dorothy elicited and commanded. Dorothy's role as mediatrix from her younger years is sensitively limned in "The Sparrow's Nest" of 1801:

Such heart was in her, being then
A little Prattler among men.
The Blessing of my later years
Was with me when a boy:
She gave me eyes, she gave me ears;
And humble cares, and delicate fears;
A heart, the fountain of sweet tears;
And love, and thought, and joy. (13–20)

Dorothy is the young prattler who bears the gift of heart and fountain, so that the whispered voice of brook, heart, and fountain are hers. Sonnet twenty-six of the *River Duddon* series provides a later allusion to identical gifts attributed, in Dorothy's absence, solely to the coursing stream.

    ... for fondly I pursued,
Even when a child, the Streams – unheard, unseen;
Through tangled woods, impending rocks between;
    ...
Nor have I tracked their course for scanty gains;
They taught me random cares and truant joys ... (26.1–3, 9–10)

Dorothy appears in similar guise in *The Prelude*, where she is as much a part of the inner life of the poet as those outward natural events which served to characterize her.

    Then it was –
Thanks to the bounteous Giver of all good! –
That the beloved Sister in whose sight
Those days were passed, now speaking in a voice
Of sudden admonition – like a brook
That did but *cross* a lonely road, and now
Is seen, heard, felt, and caught at every turn,
Companion never lost through many a league –
Maintained for me a saving intercourse
With my true self; for, though bedimmed and changed
Both as a clouded and a waning moon,
She whispered still that brightness would return,
She, in the midst of all, preserved me still
A Poet, made me seek beneath that name
And that alone, my office upon earth ... (1850, 11.333–48)

The closing passages of "Lines ... Composed a Few Miles above Tintern Abbey" and this passage from *The Prelude* are among the most sensitive and revealing of Wordsworth's celebrations of the intimacy of brother and sister. They recount the poet's reliance on Dorothy as both keeper and preserver of his personal past, and as the ministrant who fosters and tends within him that "saving intercourse with my own true self," the fertile but discontinuous rapport with the source of his own poetic powers. In the shooting lights of Dorothy's wild eyes, Wordsworth beholds his younger self on the banks of the River Wye; with the reassurance of her voice, a brook which "Is seen, heard, felt, and caught at every turn / Companion never lost through many a league," she summons him to that brightness she serves. Wordsworth's Lucy, as her name implies, dwells with light, the light into which the naiad shepherds her charge, the welling spring. "I am Lucia, suffer me to take him who is sleeping. So shall I help him on his way." So spoke the radiant-eyed lady who bore her charge, the sleeping Dante, toward the bright summit. The precise date of the composition of the Goslar Lucy poems has not been determined, nor that of the letter to Coleridge which contained them. They are usually assigned to the period from 6 October to 21 or 28 December 1798.[19] I would like to narrow those margins and propose that they were written on or shortly after 13 December, Saint Lucy's Eve, the feast of reborn light whose celebration once coincided with the mid-winter solstice.[20]

In the Lucy poems Wordsworth contemplates the extinction of that light belonging to the source and its radiant ministrant. In the *Prelude* passage I have quoted, that light is the moon, bedimmed, clouded, and waning. But it is Dorothy, her voice as constant as the sound of the young brook, who reassures the poet that the eclipsed brightness will come again to the full. Dorothy's ministering role at the source would pass into other hands, but of these, it was Dorothy, child and sister, who was first.

> Child of my parents! Sister of my soul!
> Thanks in sincerest verse have been elsewhere
> Poured out for all the early tenderness
> Which I from thee imbibed: and 'tis most true
> That later seasons and to Thee no less;
> For, spite of thy sweet influence and the touch
> Of kindred hands that opened out the springs
> Of genial thought in childhood ... (1850, 14.232–9)

Among those kindred hands whose office it was to open out the welling springs of genial thought were those of Mary Hutchinson. But Dorothy was not replaced by Wordsworth's wife, any more than Mary was by their daughter Dora, the gift of Wordsworth's middle years. One merges into the other almost imperceptibly, since they are the dramatis personae who reenact the same role central to the nurture of his creative life. The Lucy poems reveal neither Wordsworth's death wish for an overly dependent sister nor his fears for her mortality.[21] Lucy's death, when it occurs, is as natural and inevitable as the passing of the seasons, or of innocence. Even the classical nymphs were subject to mortality, and their passing rehearsed the fall from a world in its golden age to that brightness lost.

> ... the hiding places of my power
> Seem open, I approach, and then they close:
> I see by glimpses now, when age comes on
> May scarcely see at all ... (1850, 11.35–8)

There are many deaths to be faced in the creative life and the life of the spirit, where each death may serve as a threshold to a wider life, or may lead with shocking finality to that narrow chamber where the living symbol and myth which once held the power to animate and command the poet and his poetry have become a heap of dead images, their relation to the poet, the subject, and each other arbitrary. Blake provides an account of the sorry chronicle of the degeneration of myth and its subservience to the forms which supplant it, a universal history threatening every son of Adam: "The ancient Poets animated all sensible objects with Gods or Geniuses, calling them by the names and adorning them with the properties of woods, rivers, mountains, lakes, cities, nations, and whatever their enlarged & numerous senses could perceive." That brightness and its bright creatures having been forfeit or lost, Blake concludes: "Thus men forgot that all deities reside in the human breast."[22] Blake's account limns the course of Wordsworth's later career, when his poetry preserved only a glimmer of the bright creature eclipsed, a stilled voice diminished to what it was in the beginning, the prattle of another's Bandusian spring.

CHAPTER FOUR

Stations on the Sacred River: Maid, Woman, Bower, and Wilderness

🙟 PROSPECTS

For Coleridge's readers all roads lead ultimately to Xanadu; they are seldom as straight as those conducting to Rome. It is as if the scholarly meanders directed toward Coleridge's enclave of the imagination rehearse the labyrinthine argument of the first thirteen books of the *Biographia Literaria*, Daedalian antechambers to the oracular passages in which the author disburdens himself of the heart of his mystery. Travellers on Xanadu's road or river might well invoke the caveat of the author of the *Biographia* to "either pass over the following ... or read the whole connectedly."

I would prefer a heroic scouring of the Augean stable of Xanadu's scholarly accretions by a novel diversion of its sacred river, but I can offer no tidier prospects. I have attempted to keep in the company of Coleridge and his poetry by attending to the personal and poetic roots of his mythic topography and his dramatis personae, and to skirt as much as possible the thickets, presumed and actual, of his reading. Xanadu and its river are the goals of this inquiry, and if way-stations are of less consequence than the destination, they and their custodians nevertheless serve to further our passage and direct its course. In transit, I propose to examine variations on a familiar Coleridgean landscape with its presiding figure: the agreeable bowery setting with its river or fountainhead, and its companionable chatelaine. Like all deeply felt experiences, these personal moments translated into poetry find their resonance in myth and their literary ancestry, in this case in the pastoral and earthly paradises of tradition. Had Coleridge left matters at that, these places might be interchangeable with those of Wordsworth, tended by their benign and nurturing muses. But the sunny Coleridgean *locus amoenus* is complemented by a less agreeable and undomesticated counterpart, a waste or wilderness, the tenebrous *locus dirus* with its treacherous grounds and threatening genius. The great poems of the *annus mirabilis*, *The Rime of the Ancient Mariner*, *Christabel*, and "Kubla Khan," witness the polarization of this figure and her setting. Her presence can be recognized in Coleridge's relationship with the women in his life, and in dream, but most compelling and emphatic is her emergence and striking metamorphosis in the poet's successive reworkings of a single poem, "Lewti."

TREACHEROUS IMAGE: FROM MAID TO WOMAN

"Lewti" has been unmasked as one of Coleridge's unnatural children. In the 1940s Ernest de Selincourt demolished Lowes's speculations concerning the genesis of the poem by identifying its origin in the fragment "Beauty and Moonlight: An Ode" written by the young Wordsworth.[1] Coleridge took over Wordsworth's poem and made a number of manuscript revisions and amplifications before publishing it as his own. "Lewti" was withdrawn at the last minute from the first edition of *Lyrical Ballads* and replaced by "The Nightingale" because Coleridge had already printed it in the April *Morning Post* of the same year under a pseudonym. The identity of the author, however, was widely known, and to include "Lewti" in *Lyrical Ballads* would have compromised the anonymity of Wordsworth and Coleridge's collection.

Coleridge's attitude toward his foster child grew increasingly paternal. He would print "Lewti" in all editions of *Sibylline Leaves* as his own, and even in the privacy of his notebooks he seems to have regarded himself as the poem's sole author. Coleridge's pseudonym in the *Morning Post* version, "Nicias Erythraeus," however, hints at his covert attitude toward Wordsworth's authorship of the original. Coleridge frequently made use of inventive pen names which scarcely disguised his authorship, least of all among his friends, but which testify to his hesitation in allowing his poetry to go public. Walter Jackson Bate has called attention to the tone of apology with which Coleridge speaks of his poems or escorts them into print.[2] Coleridge's frequent use of "Punic Greek" pseudonyms leavened the serious business of committing himself to print and invested the proceedings with a certain nervous jocularity.

"Erythraeus" is derived from the Greek *Erythreia* (the red or blushing one) and designated the island in the western ocean, the domain of the setting sun where Hercules in the discharge of his tenth labour stole the oxen belonging to Geryon and his neatherd Eurytion. Coleridge may have used the name merely to allude to his seat in the west country, as he often did with "Bristolensis," but it is likely that he intended a reference to the mythic cattle rustler and the indebtedness which occasioned his blushing. "Nicias" speaks less equivocally of the provenance of "Lewti." He was the painter who tinted the marble works cut by Praxiteles, and it is reported by Pliny that, of all his works, the master sculptor valued most "those on which Nicias has set his marks."[3] It was as graceful and witty a genuflection to Wordsworth's authorship as Coleridge could afford. Nevertheless, Coleridge indeed set his seal on the poem: how and in what manner I propose to explore.

G. Louis Joughin's detailed study of "Lewti" in 1943 followed Lowes's false lead by attributing the original fragment to Coleridge and identifying the "Mary" of the poem as Coleridge's Mary Evans.[4] Lowes proposed that the source of the poem lay with Coleridge's readings in Bartram's *Travels*, and Joughin surmised that the Cora whose cancelled name briefly replaced Mary's in what is now known to be Coleridge's first reworking of Wordsworth's poem was a heroine drawn from contemporary exotic romances: Marmontel's tale of the Peruvian vestal, *The Incas*, or Sheridan's *Pizarro*, in which the Mrs Jordan to whom Coleridge sent a copy of the second edition of *Lyrical Ballads* acted the heroine Cora. This is entirely implausible, since "Cora" never survived the manuscript version, and Mrs Jordan would have seen in print only the unfamiliar title "Lewti." The Cora who replaced Wordsworth's Mary need not be subjected to biographical conjecture, since Coleridge probably intended to convey no more by the name than that which the Greek word *Kore* or "maiden" implied.

Lowes's and Joughin's conjectures fell blameless victims to de Selincourt's acuity as editor, but it is less excusable that Joughin's exhaustive examination of the structure, metre, rhythm, diction, tone, and imagery in "Lewti" ignores the transformation in the poem's subject in the course of its revisions. It is this radical transformation of the central female figure that makes "Lewti" unmistakably Coleridge's own.

The Mary of Wordsworth's "Beauty and Moonlight" is as mild and domesticated as her moon-over-Winander setting. "My Mary" secures the relationship in a confident manner that Coleridge's poem strenuously avoids. Wordsworth's lover seems complacent in his love, and there is no reason to believe that his Mary is other than compliant. His infatuation summons Mary's fancied image in all the features of the natural scene: her face in a moonlit rock swept by "tressy yews," her eye in the moon, her flashing smile (which Joughin analysed as a "dental image") in the waves breaking on the moonlit shore, her bosom in a brace of swans heaving on Winander's flood. Mary's image graces rather than haunts her Lake Country setting, and Wordsworth closes with a prayer to the gods to bear him speedily to his absent love.

Coleridge translates his love to precarious rocky heights with inse-
cure footpaths, and the cancelled version which transforms the maid
Cora into the Circassian Lewti (and temporarily describes her as a wild
Indian) replaces homy Windermere with the exotic Tamaha. In its various recensions "Lewti" logged considerable mileage: Windermere,
America, Peru, and Circassia. Lowes identified the name of Coleridge's
river as a misremembering from Bartram's *America*, the hooks and eyes
of association, as Lowes represents the imaginative process, oblivious
to niceties of geography.[5] Tamaha seems to belong to the same mythic
geography that generates Coleridge's river Alph, but landscapes of the
mind invariably reveal roots or counterparts in the external world. No
geographical river of that name exists, although the Circassian Lewti's
Transcaucasia or modern Georgia was ruled by a queen of the thir-
teenth century named Tamara. She was hopelessly loved by the
Georgian poet Rustavela, who dedicated an epic to his lady and died of
a broken heart in exile. History falls out of love with heartbreakers, and
Tamara's subsequent fate was to be portrayed by legend and by Ler-
montov as a heartless mistress who cast her discarded lovers from the
heights of her Caucasian stronghold. Coleridge's renovated mistress
may borrow some of her heartlessness from her association with the
Georgian queen. There is, moreover, a curious parallel in Coleridge's
derivation of Tamaha from Tamara with that of Abora from Amara.

Mary's image comforted her lover in Wordsworth's poem, but
Lewti's pursues and is a torment to a "dying man for love of thee," and
the stricken narrator desperately tries to banish her: "Image of Lewti!
from my mind / Depart; for Lewti is not kind." Coleridge's refrain identifies her as "treacherous image," and his final revision attempts to exor-
cise her: "Nay, treacherous image." Nevertheless, the same narrator
doggedly maintains a racking ambivalence by cherishing a less than
convincing hope for better treatment from his lady ("and yet, thou
didst not look unkind") and expresses in the closing lines a pathetic
wish which nearly revokes the entire poem: "Soothe, gentle image!
soothe my mind. / Tomorrow Lewti may be kind." The final line of the
last of Coleridge's revisions and his hesitant manuscript cancellation
not only indicate the lover's quandary but reveal Coleridge's own
unresolved ambivalence toward his subject: "Methinks thou lookest
not ~~kin~~ unkind!"[6]

Coleridge devotes two stanzas to the moon and cloud that Wordsworth compared in passing to Mary's eye, and fashions the familiar
Coleridgean image of the moon hidden beneath thin cloud. The cover is
briefly luminous in its light, but the moon's passing leaves it a poor
thing, gray and wan, "as white as my poor cheek will be." Veiled by its
"lawny shroud," the moon recalls the night world of *Christabel* with its

contracted moon beneath its cloud and its association with the shrunken eye of the menacing night creature Geraldine. Moreover, in its opening line, Coleridge's final version of "Lewti" introduces the hour: it is midnight, Geraldine's hour, rather than the innocuous twilight of Wordsworth's poem. Whatever might have happened on Windermere, clearly all is not well on the Tamaha, and Lewti's biography, from her genesis as Wordsworth's benign Mary to a comparatively neutral Cora, and then to Lewti whose name is a disturbing medley of the entrancing and lute-like with the lewd, chronicles an undeviating transformation into an enigmatic, demonic creature. She is capricious, treacherous, wilful, heartless, and irresistible, at least by her lover's and, we may assume, her poet's reckoning.

This singular metamorphosis of Lewti from guileless maid to demonic woman anticipates the counterpoint of the paired female figures that haunt the great imaginative poems of the *annus mirabilis*. Their antithetical natures are so sharply drawn that they appear deliberately contrived as a schematic means of framing or enacting a conflict fundamental to Coleridge's verse.

There are but two females identified in *The Rime of the Ancient Mariner*, and their presence can scarcely be overlooked in its resolutely masculine world: the blushing "red as a rose" bride singing with her maids within the garden bower of the narrative frame, and the whoring spectre woman with skin "as white as leprosy," indecorous whistle, and roving eye, adrift on the ocean wastes.[7] The bride exemplifies the world of community, of marriage with its promise of renewed life, the protected world of physical and spiritual health, while the sallow spectre woman is life denied, the terrible divorce between the inner and outer life, the nightmare, blood-chilling life-in-death. The figures are not peripheral to the action, they are deployed as geniuses presiding over the contrasting worlds of the *Mariner*, the nuptial frame and the voyage.

The opposition of Geraldine and Christabel constitutes rather than informs the action of their poem. Their polarity need not be recounted here; it can be summarized most succinctly by recourse to Coleridge's use of the designations "maid" and "woman." Both Christabel and Geraldine are presented as "ladies," a term designating no more than their station, but most often Christabel is "maid." Geraldine is seldom allowed that designation, and when she is, the circumstances are calculated to whet our suspicion. Geraldine refers to herself as a maid twice, and Sir Leoline does so on one occasion, while he is bewitched by the woman he believes to be the daughter of his estranged friend. It is on this same occasion that the narrator establishes with heavy irony that the she-wolf in lamb's clothing simulates a maidenly gesture solely for Leoline's benefit: "And Geraldine in maiden wise / Casting down her large bright eyes." The gesture deceives neither the narrator, who nervously invokes the protection of Jesu Maria, nor Christabel herself, who founders in helpless dismay. The distinction between Christabel and Geraldine, "the lovely maid and the lady tall," is carefully preserved throughout: "turning from his own sweet maid / Sir Leoline led forth the lady Geraldine." Geraldine is invoked as "lady" and "damsel," but most frequently, as Christabel never is, as "woman." The Abyssinian maid of "Kubla Khan" is unambiguously benign, and her influence beneficent. She celebrates with her symphony and song a remembered fulfilment or paradise. The woman who wails beneath the diminishing moon howls from absence or a terrifying loss. Geraldine, the whoring life-in-death, and the woman who wails for a demon lover are all as unabashedly erotic as their counterparts are asexual or sexually untried.

By actual count, Coleridge's maidens outnumber his women two to one. The concordance indicates that with few exceptions "woman" is used, if not simply as a designation of gender, for the most part pejoratively: "that foul woman of the North," "a woman's trick," "woman's wile," a "woman's scorn."[8] Coleridge, it should be noted, was disposed to idealize the females in his life, at least until reality could no longer support the dream of maidens.

It is not my intention to rehabilitate the character of Sarah Fricker from the wreckage of her marriage to Coleridge, but it is arguable that given the peculiar dynamic of her husband's emotional life, her chances of succeeding in the role of wife were doubtful. Coleridge's affections customarily expressed themselves in a curious penchant for pairs. Sarah's ascendency waxed and waned in the presence of her sister Edith, whose courtship with Coleridge's friend Southey prospered in a marriage that must have given emphasis to the Coleridges' failure. Dorothy, as Wordsworth's and Coleridge's sister-in-common, scarcely enhanced Sarah's waning image in her husband's eyes. Indeed, Dorothy's patronizing estimate of Sarah's worth as a "fiddle faddler ... wanting sensibility," acute as it may have been, must have exacerbated the role in which a not insensitive Sarah was cast and which she was forced to adopt. Sarah's reported unpleasantness and increasing shrewishness suggest the desperate defence of a woman whose sense of adequacy and integrity was under siege. Her idealized ascendency was alarmingly brief, and lapsed into her husband's more generalized celebrations of domestic rather than marital felicity. These so thoroughly excluded his wife that it would appear that young Hartley of "The Nightingale" and "Frost at Midnight" was a motherless child. Sarah's fortune was to decline in the strangely mechanical balance arm of her husband's affections as Dorothy Wordsworth and Sara Hutchinson were exalted.[9] Sarah's lot was to suffer under comparisons. Whether she was shaped to that end is impossible to determine; certainly she was cast in that unhappy role.

The brief domestic idyll having passed, the good-natured and commonsensical north-country woman Sara Hutchinson must have been perplexed to find herself elevated to the rarefied status of the maid Asra, whose anagram not only served to distinguish her from Sarah Coleridge but suggested an *alter ego* promising everything Sarah denied her husband. Whatever blame might be assigned to Coleridge in his later estrangement from the Dove Cottage circle might be attributed to his having idealized that household, with which his own Greta Hall provided a sorry contrast, beyond all reasonable expectations.

To suggest that the demonic females who haunt the *annus mirabilis* poems are Coleridge's projections of his disaffected wife is as absurdly reductive as identifying the wailing woman at the opening of "Kubla Khan" with Coleridge's wife and the tuneful maid at the close with Sara Hutchinson, a marital teeter-totter which even Coleridge found amusing. Coleridge's demonic women, the nightmare hags who troubled his dreams and were a part of the torment of opium withdrawal, appeared, in fact, as early as the Christ's-Hospitalized dreams of his school days. It is from this unconscious matrix rather than the discomforts of the marriage bed that the Geraldines, the spectre- and demon-women emerge, and it is likely that they, in their complementarity, were generated as a compulsive response to the one-sided idealizations with which the poet sought to people his waking life. That is to say that the dramatis personae of the waking life are assigned the roles of the unconscious drama or psychomachia whose operative mechanism is one of redress, the device by which a potentially neurotic imbalance (in this case an untenable idealism) is challenged by its complement. The language of unconscious process and motive is imaginal rather than discursive, mythic rather than conceptual, hence its persuasiveness and ineluctability. It cannot be met with simple argument. As such, the presence of these figures could scarcely be resisted, and they insinuate or assert themselves in the creative act itself, which, as Coleridge insisted, bridges conscious motive and unconscious impulse. They command the province of his poetry as they ruled the unconscious experience he projected on his relationships with others.

Such a process suggests not a further chapter in Coleridgean pathology but, on the contrary, a potentially salutary compensation bent on securing the emotional and intellectual equilibrium which the poet found essential to the maintenance of the creative life. Pathology threatens only while one is fleeing or burying such insistent promptings. They will, nonetheless, have their day and have their say. So common are these contrasting figures in Romantic poetry at large that we might sooner marvel at their absence than their presence, and it is solely in Wordsworth's poetry that they seem conspicuously lacking. The adverse elements of fear and terror in Wordsworthian nature and the tutelary role they play in informing the poetic sensibility are never personified; the homy nurse nature is no harridan, the abiding presences of river and mountain may be paternal in their embrace but are never the angry, jealous, or zealous father. The family drama, its actors and its agon, are absent from the Wordsworthian kingdom of springs, rivers, hills, and mountains, where it is only solitary man who is a trouble to the peace that dwells among them. Such places and their power to engender poetry, when they came to be personified, found their expression in the innocuous inmates of Dove Cottage and Rydal Mount's household Beulah: Dorothy, Mary, and Wordsworth's daughter, who in their turn served the poet as muse and held him in perpetual adoration. Rydal was to become a reliquary for its resident laureate, even during his lifetime.

One must look not to Wordsworth but to the second-generation Romantics to find a comparable company of dark ladies paired with bright maidens, those who slip through light and shade in a landscape of bower and fountain, and who tend there a source of power either creative or destructive in nature. Keats knew the friendly nymphs who fostered love and inspiration, but also the madness, they conveyed, and their fierce maiden leader with her train of deceiving elves. Shelley sketched the mischievous witchery commanding the source and the passage of his Nile, and the witch poesy whose eyrie overlooked the tumultuous birth of the five rivers of Mont Blanc, but also the malevolence "whose voice was venomed Melody" who "Sate by a well, under blue night shade bowers."

An announcement accompanied the first appearance of "Lewti" in the *Morning Post* of April 1798. It read in part:

Amidst images of war and woe, amidst scenes of carnage and horror, of devastation and dismay, it may afford the mind a temporary relief to wander to the magic haunts of the muses, to bowers and fountains which the despoiling powers of war have never visited, and where the lover pours forth his complaint, or receives the recompense of his constancy.[10]

The description would appear at first reading to be remarkably obtuse: there are neither fountains nor magical haunts of the muses within Lewti's bowers, and the lover's lack of recompense for his constancy might furnish ample grounds for complaint. But if "Lewti" fails to trace those fountainous bowers with their muses, nevertheless Coleridge himself knew such places intimately. The insight displayed by the note argues that Coleridge himself composed it. From those unconscious levels at which Coleridge reworked Wordsworth's reverie on Mary, there emerges a powerfully disturbing creature whose nature furnishes a dramatic contrast with the benign figures who tended the well-springs of Wordsworth's creative life. Coleridge would have preferred their amiable patronage, to carve his name on the rock at Sara's spring in the company of William, Dorothy, and Sara, and to traffic with milder muses, but muses are not chosen, they choose, and are as often wilful as they are willing.

 LOCUS AMOENUS AND THE GENIAL GENIUS

> Here is Moss, a soft seat, & a deep & ample shade
> "Inscription on a Jutting Stone"

> ego laudo ruris amoeni
> rivos et musco circumlita saxa nemusque.   Horace

Coleridge's translation of Wordsworth's setting to the high Caucasus of Lewti's Circassia introduces a mythic watershed of greater depth and amplitude than Wordsworth's unfabled Windermere. Shelly would explore these same heights in *Alastor*, "at the end of all the earth," as Kingsley described them, and we will return to them and their deployment in that poem. As one of the legendary sites of paradise and the source of its four great rivers, they belonged as much to the beginnings of all things as to the ends of the earth, the goal of all quests which seek to confront the mystery of beginnings.

In Coleridge's personal *paysage moralisé*, highlands seem to have been preferable to plains, and life's course, at least the protracted decline which the poet saw described by his own career, was imaged as a descent to the lowlands and to servitude. This is yet another Coleridgean rehearsal of the Fall, an account of our universal nostalgia for the high realm of beginnings from which we first set out.

We are born in the mountains, in the Alps – and when we hire ourselves out to the Prince of the lower lands, sooner or later we feel an incurable Homesickness. & every Tune that recalls our native heights brings on a relapse of the sickness.[11]

The passage is Coleridge's notebook rendering of Jean Paul's *Geist*. When he translated it in 1811, it must have sounded a responsive chord.

Coleridge associated the heights he had known in his own career with his emotional and creative heartland, and the landscape of the Quantocks and the Lake District served him in this respect more aptly than the gentle rolling landscape of his Devonshire birthplace. "Every Tune that recalls our native heights brings on a relapse of the sickness." This evocation of the universal nostalgia for our beginnings in terms of music lost and only partially recoverable echoes "Dejection: An Ode," where music and light are fused as the expression of a joy both personal and supernal, and where the failure of the current of feeling traces a declivity from our natural condition and birthright: "all melodies the echo of that Voice / All colours a suffusion from that light." These passages provide a context for the song of the Abyssinian maid of "Kubla Khan," who evokes a transcendent moment from the poet's personal past which he is unable to recover. But she also sings of Milton's Mount Abora," by some suppos'd / True Paradise under the *Ethiop* line / By *Nilus* head."[12]

Coleridge has secured the traditional association of the two Edens, that of personal childhood, and that of the childhood of man. The maid's Abyssinian homeland is mankind's; her place is at the fountainhead of paradise, and her song celebrates our lost felicity. Memories of the garden of childhood are augmented by the fleeting moments of joy we have known, and together these promise to reconstitute the Eden within. Moments and places such as these, reclaimed from the past or asserted by dream, are the green havens which the *Prelude* poet identifies as "spots of time," "moments ... scattered everywhere, taking their date / From our first childhood."[13] They are our bastions against the assault of the actual, sheltering and nourishing us, even serving to transform estrangement into paradises regained, the holy places of dream. Such moments and places have taken their date not simply from our own childhood, as Wordsworth proposes, but from mankind's, nor are they the exclusive paddock of Milton's genius (who himself was seduced by the "pleasing licence" of the feigned paradises of pagan myth) or the golden age which Dante and Chaucer refurbished as metaphors for Edenic innocence. The confluence of these themes can be traced in the fragmentary lines of a metrical experiment preserved in the notebooks. Coleridge unaccountably titled it "Nonsense."

O Sara! never rashly let me go
Beyond the precincts of this holy place.
When streams as pure as in Elysium flow
And flowerets view reflected grace.[14]

The natural history of the Coleridgean bower and its presiding genius, with its customary appointments of spring, pool or stream, leafy canopy, and mossy seat, reveals the confluence of personal, literary, and mythic tributaries which determine the flow and character of Coleridge's imaginative integration.

Lewti's bower emerged only in the final version of Coleridge's poem and, like many a Coleridgean bower, it is a sheltered or enclosed place, a personal *temenos* sanctified by the affections and transfigured by the imagination. Among others are the lime-tree bower at Nether Stowey, the jasmin- and myrtle-covered Clevedon cottage where these emblems of "innocence and love" remembered a brief conjugal idyll, the icicle-hung cottage of "Frost at Midnight" where marital is replaced by filial affection, and the fountain and ruined hut roofed with wild-rose which the poet recalls in "A Daydream," the record of a day passed with the beloved women, Sara and Mary. Although Sara is absent from an "Inscription for a Fountain on a Heath" she is, as George Whalley has shown, connected with this intensely personal place with its small basin canopied by the sycamore's "darksome boughs."[15] The flowery woodbine bower reflected in "the scarcely flowing river pool" of "The Keepsake" preserves the memory of "a maiden kiss" exchanged with Sara Hutchinson. The following entry from Dorothy's Grasmere journal testifies to the friends' enthusiasm for hidden bowers. It describes the "double bower" of Rydal which Coleridge identified in his notes of April 1802:

Coleridge went to search for something new. We saw him climbing up towards a rock. He called us, and we found him in a bower – the sweetest that was ever seen. The rock on one side is very high, and all covered with ivy, which hung loosely about, and bore bunches of brown berries. On the other side it was higher than my head ... We now first saw that the trees are planted in rows. Above this bower there is mountain-ash, common-ash, yew-tree, ivy, holly, hawthorn, mosses, and flowers, and a carpet of moss. Above, at the top of the rock, there is another spot – it is scarce a bower, a little parlour on [ly], not enclosed by walls, but shaped out for a resting-place by the rocks and the ground rising about it. It had a sweet moss carpet. We resolved to go and plant flowers in both these places tomorrow. We wished for Mary and Sara.[16]

That Coleridge, Wordsworth, and Dorothy express their desire to share the moment and the place with Mary and Sara speaks of the bond of mutual affection which linked their circle and regularly expressed itself in a deeply felt sense of place. Wordsworth's poems on the naming of places, and particularly Coleridge's habit of sealing his troth in the

poems linked to Asra with the abiding features of their landscape –
Sara's rock, Sara's seat, Sara's spring – nevertheless suggest, for all their
affectionate spontaneity, a somewhat self-conscious rehearsal of the
trystings of Angelica and Medoro of *Orlando Furioso*, whose love is
memorialized in every tree, rock, grotto, and fountain; an instance of
life imitating Coleridge's "darling Ariosto."

The retreats Coleridge and his companions found or established with
the thrill of discovery are, in truth, rediscovered, greeted with the
recognition accorded companionable places accommodating the green
recesses of memory and dream. The recurrent scene with its embowered
spring, reflecting pool, or gentle river is the cynosure within Coleridge's
emotional landscape embracing love and joy, the requisite pulse of
creative life. This is the *locus laetus*, the happy place beloved of Virgil,
or the *locus amoenus* which the Mantuan bequeathed as a rhetorical
topos to tradition. Curtius identifies it "as the principle motif of all
nature description from the Empire to the 16th century," a conservative
reckoning.[17] Virgil's commentator Servius associated *amoenus* with
amor, implying not only a lovely but a loving place, appropriate to the
pursuit of love.[18] Curtius describes the topos as a concoction of conventional ingredients: "It is a beautiful, shaded natural site. Its minimum
ingredients comprise a tree (or several trees) a meadow, and a spring or
brook. Birdsong and flowers may be added. The most elaborate examples also add a breeze."[19] If we recall that Lewti lies near the river
Tamaha, breeze, flowers, birdsong, and a bower at the heart of a
labyrinth complete the highly conventional formula.

> I know the place where Lewti lies,
> When silent night has closed her eyes:
> It is a breezy jasmine-bower,
> The nightingale sings o'er her head:
> Voice of the Night! had I the power
> That leafy labyrinth to thread ... (65–70)

The passage suggests a deliberate echo of *A Midsummer Night's
Dream*, where the labyrinth is supplied by the maze of mortal and
immortal confusion in the wood near Athens.

> I know a bank where the wild thyme blows,
> Where oxlips and the nodding violet grows,
> Quite over canopied with luscious woodbine,
> With sweet musk-roses and with eglantine:
> There sleep Titania sometime of the night
> Lull'd in these flowers with dances and delight ... (2.1.250–5)

Keats, by way of Shakespeare, shared this common plot of ground where even the flora is uniform. It is, as in the "Ode to a Nightingale," holy ground which harbours the promise or the memory of an ideal fulfilment. Keats's nightingale is embowered within its "melodious plot / Of beechen green and shadows numberless," where "haply the Queen-Moon is on her throne" at the heart of a leafy labyrinth of "verdurous glooms and winding mossy ways" appointed with violet, muskrose, and pastoral eglantine. The *locus* extends throughout the Keats canon in natural and artificial, romantic and ironic bowers, groves, elfin grots, bed and bridal chambers. But unlike Oberon, neither Keats nor Coleridge has the power to thread the labyrinth and master its deceiving elves.

These bowers, like Milton's "narrow room" of paradise, have their own harmonies. Lewti's bower, like Keats's melodious plot, echoes with the notes of the nightingale, whose tale is as horrific as its rendering is beautiful. The ambiguities lurking within the amenities of the bower, its promise of fulfilment and its threat of deprival or dissolution, are often sounded in its signature medley. Coleridge's transfigured lime-tree bower, no longer a prison, catches the homelier dissonances of the humble-bee song and the rook's creaking flight, but the Clevedon cot, embowered in its "valley of seclusion," boasts Eolian harmonies as bewitching and unsettling as Keats's evocation of the haunt of Cynthia and her retinue, his fairy child's song within her elfin grot, or the enchantment that lulled Titania to sleep beneath her woodbine canopy.

> Such a soft floating witchery of sound
> As twilight Elfins make, when they at eve
> Voyage on gentle gales from Fairy-Land,
> Where Melodies round honey-dropping flowers,
> Footless and wild, like birds of Paradise
> Nor pause, nor perch, hovering on untam'd wing!
>
> ("The Eolian Harp," 20–5)

When those untamed birds of paradise are followed home to roost in "Religious Musings," even in the midst of that poem's laboured rhetoric, the music of the spheres declares itself in an unaccustomed wild witchery of sound, and the harmonies of the biblical paradise, rather than complacently celestial, are an unbridled enchantment.

> When in some hour of solemn jubilee
> The massy gates of Paradise are thrown
> Wide open, and forth come in fragments wild
> Sweet echoes of unearthly melodies,
> And odours snatched from beds of Amaranth ... (345–9)

✣ *LOCUS DIRUS:* "THE PICTURE" AND THE WILDERNESS

"The Picture" seems an oddly contrived mating of a flight into the wilderness in order to forego the demands of love with a tale of a naiad drawn from the *Silvae* of Statius. It is a curiosity among Coleridge's poems in that it begins by rejecting the familiar setting of sheltering bower or *locus amoenus* for a bleaker landscape, a northern forest of Gothic glooms inamicable to love and resistant to its power to transform a natural site into a sanctuary for the affections. Its disaffected speaker seeks out his wilderness retreat, a hermitage rather than a trysting place, in a rigorously masculine landscape of gloomy natural vaults rather than embracing bowers.

Ernest Hartley Coleridge noted "that the conception of the 'Resolution' that failed was suggested by Gessner's prose idyll *'Der Feste Vorsatz,'*" and this attribution has been echoed by most of Coleridge's editor's.[20] Coleridge's indebtedness to Gessner, however, goes beyond matters of conception. Sixteen of the poem's one hundred and eighty-six lines are direct translation from Gessner, and much of its imagery and incident derives from the Swiss poet. The landscape of dark firs suggests a north German approximation of Gessner's Alpine setting, and Coleridge's description seems to owe much to notebook entries describing his walking tour of May 1799 in Germany. Coleridge versified portions of Gessner's prose idylls while in Germany, and in 1802, the year in which "The Picture" was written, was engaged with translating the Swiss writer's *Der erste Schiffer*, though he abandoned the work, as Godwin recalled, under "the influence of a double disgust, moral and poetical."[21] Coleridge wrote to Southey of Gessner's Theocritan eroticism: "I am a homebrewed English man, and tolerate downright grossness more patiently than this coy and distant dallying with the Appetites."[22] At this time the notebooks record that he was reading Statius, with whom he must have been familiar since schooldays.[23]

Kathleen Coburn identifies a notebook entry, probably of April 1802, as the only reference to "The Picture": "A Poem on the endeavour to emancipate the soul from day-dreams & note the different attempts and the vain ones."[24] The subject of the poem is, as its title announces, resolution, and as the notebook entry suggests, the chimeras which bring irresolution, a subject agonizingly close to Coleridge as man and poet. The day-dreams are of love, and, as in "Lewti," the more the speaker flees, the more relentlessly those images of love pursue him. He boasts at the outset to have "quelled the master-passion" and exults in a heady sense of freedom at the prospect of pursuing other paths. He is led or impelled by an inner guide, "a new joy, / Lovely as light, sudden as summer gust," imaged as a child or spring lamb, his own reborn adventurous youth which leads him to confront the bleak landscape compatible with his renunciation. The way is not handily won; he must "force" it, "climb," crush "with wild foot" the wortles beneath, and "toil" to achieve his goal through a strenuously brutal struggle.

There follows a series of parenthetical ruminations which occupy much of the poem and contribute to its apparent discontinuity, although they in fact further the poetic argument by demonstrating that resolution grounded on suppression or rigorous exclusion is actually irresolution, and that true resolve is won by attending to the language of the heart, to the unconscious desires which speak most palpably and irresistibly in the language of personification and myth. Coleridge writes in the eleventh of his *Essays on Method*:

... man sallies forth into nature – in nature, as in the shadows and reflections of a clear river, to discover the originals of the forms presented to him in his own intellect. Over these shadows, as if they were the substantial powers and presiding spirits of the stream, Narcissus like, he hangs delighted: till finding nowhere a representative of that free agency which yet is a *fact* of immediate consciousness sanctioned and made fearfully significant by his prophetic *conscience*, he learns at last what he *seeks* he has left behind, and but lengthens the distance as he prolongs the search.[25]

The mythic world is essentially an animate, personified world, not an inert external "other." It offers passionate engagement and is not merely observed or dispassionately analysed. Our commerce with myth is, before all things, an engagement with ourselves, particularly with what lies within us, for it is these suppressed or rejected materials that are most liable to be projected on others or external things. That is to say that we habitually attribute to others or even to recalcitrant objects what we are least prepared to confront within ourselves. To recognize that these apparent externals are not wholly other is to find and know ourselves through the external world – the process of recognition. Personification and mythmaking are our most profound ways of knowing, and "our feeling of the world," as Unamuno describes it, "upon which is based our understanding of it, is necessarily anthropomorphic and mythopoeic."[26] Its language is the language of experience rather than of analysis, imaginal rather than abstract.

The first digression in "The Picture" introduces a "gentle lunatic" "who of this busy human heart aweary, / Worships the spirit of unconscious life / In tree or wild flower." This is one alternative available to the fleeing narrator, who has rejected the worship exacted by the master passion, but it is offered as a false alternative for which he has no sympathy. This "fond wretch" worships a disincarnate ideal or a pantheist presence in an external world from which he is sundered: "He would far rather not be that he is; / But would be something that he knows not of, / In winds or waters, or among the rocks." The goal of such worship is a flight from self which proffers only dissolution. "The Picture" might have found its genesis in a critical insight into a younger Wordsworth, or Coleridge himself. In any case it confronts the same impasse that Shelley would decry in his portrayal of the Wordsworthian ideal in *Alastor*.

The narrator rediscovers the torments of the Desert Fathers. In spite of his having rigorously proscribed love and all elements of the feminine from the spare world he has consciously chosen, love stubbornly asserts itself in the external landscape and in that of his reverie. Fancy drifts toward snowy bosoms and maidenly brows during the very protestations which reject them, and a beleaguered Eros plucked from Gessner's idylls is grounded among the thorns and briars of an unlovely clime more congenial to mythologies of prickly fays, gnomes, and hedgehogs. Love as he is here depicted may be a ridiculously ineffectual plaything, but he is nonetheless personified, and as inescapable as the nymphs, oreads, and dryads who also appear. Coleridge's letter to Sotheby of September 1802, in which he censured the mythopoesy of the Greeks as creations of the fancy as opposed to the grander conceptions of the Hebrew imagination, must be understood within the context of the poet's activities at that time.

It must occur to every Reader that the Greeks in their religious poems address always the Numina Loci, the Genii, the Dryads, the Naiads &c &c – All natural Objects were *dead* – mere hollow Statues – but there was a Godkin or Goddessling *included* in each – In the Hebrew Poetry you find nothing of this poor Stuff – as poor in genuine Imagination, as it is mean in Intellect – At best, it is but Fancy, or the aggregating Faculty of the mind – not Imagination, or the *modifying*, and *co-adunating* Faculty.[27]

This dismissal of classical mythology was scarcely Coleridge's last considered word on the subject, and was written at a time when he was labouring with growing exasperation over the task of translating Gessner's pseudo-Theocritan pastorals. Coleridge's distaste for the entire subject was probably tainted by his impatience with Gessner's decorative and sentimental eroticism. But he was also aware that the business of transporting mythological figures to less congenial times and climes invariably results in grotesques such as "His little Godship, making him perforce / Creep through a thorn-bush on yon hedgehog's back." Coleridge and Wordsworth were both mightily engaged with capturing the *numina loci,* and understood that mythologies rise from pressures within, where they form or re-form, are animated or created. When myth is translated and cunningly rigged from a Lemprière or the genealogies of Hesiod or Boccaccio, the *numina* fades to the *prosaic,* that word whose Latin translation is *jejeunus* or *frigidus.*

The following passage from his translation of Schiller's *Piccolomini* is more representative of Coleridge's feelings on the subject. The italicized lines owe nothing to Schiller but the occasion, and are Coleridge's own interpolation.

> For fable is Love's world, his home, his birth-place;
> Delightedly dwells he 'mong fays and talismans,
> And spirits; and delightedly believes
> Divinities, being himself divine.
> *The intelligible forms of ancient poets,*
> *The fair humanities of old religion,*
> *The Power, the Beauty, and the Majesty,*
> *That had their haunts in dale, or piny mountain,*
> *Or forest by slow stream, or pebbly spring,*
> *Or chasms and wat'ry depths; all these have vanished.*
> *They live no longer in the faith of reason!*
> *But still the heart doth need a language, still*
> *Doth the old instinct bring back the old names* ... (2.4.119–31)

As if in response to the narrator's rigorous repression, a tale of love unfolds in "The Picture" with striking complementarity, as if it were a reply and a redress of his denial. It is the account of a young man's encounter with "the Naiad of the mirror," Coleridge's version of Statius's aetiological narrative "The Tree of Atedius Melior." Coleridge assumes the aetiology: Diana rescues her handmaid the nymph Phocis by warning her of the approach of Pan. The nymph dives into her watery retreat, and the frustrated god, with unaccustomed good grace, causes a plane tree growing on the banks to dip toward the pool, its genuflection sheltering Phocis from the heats of noonday. The young man of Coleridge's poem is haunted by the figure of a maid who rests "on the bare branch of half-uprooted tree, / That leans towards its mirror!" Her evanescence and her maddening indifference to his desires recall Lewti. The youth worships her image, the second mention of worship in Coleridge's poem, and although it is but "a watery idol," it is still an image, and an object preferable to that of the gentle pantheist for whom no image could suffice, and consequently for whom no dreams, no hope, no love was possible.

                    ... he now
With steadfast gaze and unoffending eye,
Worships the watery idol, dreaming hopes
Delicious to the soul, but fleeting vain
E'en as that phantom-world on which he gazed ... (81-5)

The indifferent "sportive tyrant" casts wild flowers upon her mirrored image, so that all is scattered and lost.

                    Then all the charm
Is broken – all that phantom-world so fair
Vanishes, and a thousand circlets spread,
And each mis-shapes the other. Stay awhile
Poor youth! who scarcely dar'st lift up thine eyes –
The stream will soon renew its smoothness, soon
The visions will return! And lo, he stays,
And soon the fragments dim of lovely forms
Come trembling back, unite, and now once more
The pool becomes a mirror ... (91-100)

The woodland scene regathers in its mirroring pool, but its cynosure is gone. Coleridge's lines gather into themselves other phantom-worlds and phantom creatures, Lewti, demon woman, and Abyssinian maid, and served Coleridge as his prefatory poem to "Kubla Khan," where a vision, if not of love, of the paradisal harmony predicated on love, is irrecoverably lost. That fleeting vision, too, lay under the aegis of a maid whose power it was to restore or withhold its promised fulfilment. Like Lewti, the "treacherous image" who promised and withheld, or Keats's deceiving elf, the naiad smiles winningly on her lover but a moment, then withdraws into her leafy labyrinth.

                    He turns, and she is gone!
Homeward she steals through many a woodland maze
Which he shall seek in vain. (104-6)

At first the telling of the tale spurs its narrator to a renewed avowal of his ascetic renunciation and the disclaimer that such tales scarcely belong to such unpropitious places. What he fails to recognize is that they are in fact the inevitable conciliatory offspring of just such unpropitious moments and places. Like the hero of *Alastor*, he resolves to trace the course of a wild and desert stream into the heart of darker glooms and further denial.

This be my chosen haunt – emancipate
From Passion's dreams, a freeman, and alone,
I rise and trace its devious course. O lead,
Lead me to darker shades and lonelier glooms. (118–21)

The path to denial, however, proves devious, and the physical landscape and the guiding stream respond to the awakened perception
fostered by the myth of the naiad. Divided momentarily by an inter-
vening islet, the stream is an admonitory image of the course of love
severed and reunited. In one of Coleridge's discarded variants the image
is unreservedly erotic:

They meet, they join
In deep embrace, and open to the sun
Lie calm and smooth. Such the delicious hour ... (*EHC*, 1:373,n)

The uncompromising landscape assumes feminine qualities. Having
traced the course of the desert stream to its source within the heart of
denial, the narrator discovers himself within a protective circular vale
where "Two crescent hills / Fold in behind each other." The melancholy
vaults of the northern wilderness have become a bower "Beneath a
weeping birch (most beautiful of forest trees, the Lady of the Woods),"
and at hand is a cataract where "a pendant ivy mass / Swings in its win-
now" as in Alfoxden glen. The eye, altering, alters all, and the wastes
are transformed into a Coleridgean Beulah, the bowers where love
flourishes and finds its fulfilment. A patch of heath pressed by Isabel-
Asra ("O blessed couch!") aligns the place with the familiar complex of
images: bower, reflecting stream or standing pool, the mossy seat
associated with Sara Hutchinson, an image more personal than Gessner's footprint in the sand. Here the narrator finds a scroll of birch
bark, the picture of the title, painted by Asra's hand. The way to his
flesh-and-blood love is as clear and as practicable as his new resolve.
There is no question as to where she may be found: the road lies
straight and she dwells within a coppice in her father's house. For all its
domesticity, love nevertheless preserves something of its sacred character: Asra is "divinest maid," and the work of her hand, the picture, is
her "relique."

Like the conversation poems, "The Picture" describes an unobtrusive
circular course and, like *The Rime of the Ancient Mariner* or "This
Lime-tree Bower My Prison," follows the route of denial to its nadir in
order to mount to a world animated by the power of joy and reconstituted by the imagination. The narrator, who at his setting out was

passively led by a nascent and childlike joy and submitted to its transforming power by attending to the language peculiar to the heart, is
delivered by the recognition of what lay within him in the beginning.
Having been led, he can, like the mariner, lead: "And I may be her
guide the long wood through."

Yet such comparisons are admittedly invidious. "The Picture" reveals
more direction, more method than is generally acknowledged, but, for
a poem whose subject is resolution, it has remarkably little fibre, no
realized tensions, not even the miraculous inevitability which distin-
guishes the meditative progress of the conversation poems, whose
unfolding comes, in Keats's words, "as naturally as the leaves to a tree."
Although Coleridge always insisted upon the primacy of the will in the
process of personal and imaginative integration, will is no more a factor
in the narrator's ultimate resolution than it is in the redemption of
the ancient mariner. The poem's conclusion, although not arbitrary, is
unconvincing, even maudlin. Isabel or Asra as divine maid casts no
shadow nor implies any, and Coleridge's poem, though formed in the
mould of his thought, skirts the province of his deepest feelings.
Between the two is no tension, hence no true resolution.

TRIBUTARIES OF THE ALPH

> Then thou art that Virgil, and that fountain
> That spreads so broad a river of speech.   Dante

> Unperishing youth!
> Thou streamest from forth
> The cleft of thy ceaseless nativity
> ...
> That the son of the rock, that the nursling of heaven
> May be born in a holy twilight!
> Coleridge, Imitated from Stolberg

Coleridge the talker, as Mme de Staël observed, spoke only in monologue. In this matter the author who, as Byron observed, "wrote in
octavos and talked folios" was a reliable witness. The fountain or river
images which came so readily to Coleridge's mind in his youth came as
readily to others during his later years. The unanimity with which the
flumen orationes, the formulaic praise of the author's copiousness and
eloquence, is invoked attests not only to acuity of observation but to
the vitality of the ancient topos. Washington Allston noted that on
their rambles in the Roman Campagna "the fountain of his mind was
never dry, but like the far reaching Aqueducts that once supplied this
mistress of the world its living stream, seemed especially to flow for

every classic ruin over which we wandered." Charles Cowden Clarke discerned in the poet's voice "a cataract filling and rushing over my penny vial capacity," and Cottle insisted that "few men ever poured forth torrents of more happily expressed language." Thomas Colly Grattan augmented that torrent: "His was a mild enthusiastic flow of language, a broad, deep stream carrying gently along all that it met with on its course, not a whirlpool that drags into its vortex and engulfs what it seizes on." Carlyle bore a tribute mean in all but its hyperbole; perhaps he ran afoul of Coleridge's refusal to be checked by interruption or objection. For Carlyle the mighty river debouched in a slough: "Besides it was talk not flowing anythither like a river, but spreading everywhither in extricable currents and regurgitations like a lake or sea ... so that, most times you felt logically lost; swamped near to drowning in this tide of ingenious vocables, spreading out boundless as if to submerge the world." Sir William Hamilton was more sympathetic: "For the full and rapid torrent of his eloquence of discourse soon absorbed all minor rivulets such as other men could supply." Even Carlyle grudgingly allowed that "in close colloquy it reemerged flowing within narrower banks," and Bryan Proctor affirmed its happy effusion: "Samuel Taylor Coleridge was like the Rhine, that exulting and abounding river."[28]

Claims for the prototype of Xanadu's river have ranged from the Arcadian Alpheus and the Blue Nile to Wookey Hole's Axe. The watersheds of the Nile and Alpheus lay beyond Coleridge's immediate experience, although not beyond the scope of his reading. He was probably aware that the limestone riverbeds of Greece, like those of Somerset, were known for their bewildering habit of swallowing and regurgitating their freight. The mysterious *katavothra* of the Peloponnese captured the imagination of the ancients and swelled rivers such as the Alpheus to mythic dimensions, while the swallets or sinkholes of Somerset snared only the occasional witless sheep. Coleridge's sources were not entirely bookish; he knew the Mendips and their vanishing rivers intimately, having walked the countryside with Southey in 1794 and again with Dorothy and William Wordsworth four years later.

As they did the young Wordsworth, springs, rivers, and their cataracts haunted Coleridge like a passion, even mute Welsh cataracts in the drouthy summer of 1794 when he could only imagine them in spate. "The rugged and stoney clifts are stupendous – and in winter must form Cataracts most astounding."[29] In 1802 he would scrupulously compare the character of three Lake District torrents: Scale Force, Lodore ("the Precipitation of the fallen Angels from Heaven: Flight and Confusion, & Distraction, but all harmonized into one majestic Thing by the genius of Milton"), and Buttermere Halse Fall, where "the mad water rushes thro its *sinuous* bed ... the war-Song of a Scandinavian Bard."[30] The notebook entries of July and August of the same year meticulously describe the lake and river systems of the district, identifying sources, charting courses and their flow and tributaries. The German notebooks, particularly those entries describing the Rauchenbach Valley, are rich in descriptions of caves, cataracts, and the waterbreaks which Coleridge skittishly dubbed "kittenracts."[31] The Wales tour with Hucks in 1794 records a striking incident of drinking from the cliff face, described as a sensual act of nurture and veneration of the waters moving within the rock: "It was scorchingly hot – I applied my mouth ever and anon to the side of the Rocks and sucked in draughts of Water cold as Ice, and clear as in fact Diamonds in their embryo. Dew!"[32] This vivid memory might well have served the author of *The Rime of the Ancient Mariner*. Still in flight from the heats of the Welsh summer, Coleridge tested the miraculous properties attributed to Saint Winnifred's holy well, by total immersion.

Coleridge's river poetry began as did Wordsworth's 1798 *Prelude* with his natal stream. The Otter sonnet of 1793 and "Lines on an Autumnal Evening" fail to agree whether the Devon brook is a "wild streamlet of the west" or plies a "current meek," suggesting an ear cocked to turn of phrase rather than an eye to nature. In the following year, "Lines to a Beautiful Spring in a Village" celebrates the Somer at Kirkhampton, a "useful stream" issuing from its mossy urn in the midst of the village, rather than welling from cavern depths mid pathless groves in the company of the "sad wood-nymph Solitude."[33] In lieu of wood-nymphs the poet allots Somer a local maiden filling her pitcher at its source, as well as sparkling noons and silver nights under a pensive moon.

Closer to home and the productions of Coleridge's *annus mirabilis* is the Quantock landscape about Nether Stowey, perhaps the only place in England other than the Lake District where the air is always alive with the sound of waters. Eight years after leaving Stowey, Coleridge would recall its waters in a fragment that must have been hastily abandoned when he recognized in it an unconscious echo of the opening of Wordsworth's reverie on the Wye.

> Eight springs have flown, since last I lay
> On southern Quantock's heathy hills
> Where quiet sounds from Hidden rills
> ... here and there like things astray.[34]

The domesticated Somer found a counterpart in the brook tumbling fresh from the Quantocks through village runnels, where it became

Coleridge's "dear gutter of Stowey," to flow across the fields and meet the sea at Combwich. A lesser stream branched from it to flow down Lime Street, where Coleridge noted "before our door a clear brook runs of very soft water; and in the back yard is a nice Well of fine Spring water."[35] With its rushing stream, its spring, and its orchard, and Tom Poole's adjoining walnuts and lime bower, the Stowey cottage was a Horatian retreat come true: "This is what I prayed for! A piece of land not so very large, where there would be a garden, and near the house a spring of everflowing water, and up above them a bit of forest." The lines are Horace's, not Coleridge's.[36] Otherwise, the house was cramped, draughty, and damp, a torment to Sarah and a goad to their marriage. The ineradicable smell of sulphur clung to the house as a result of Sarah's efforts to fumigate young Hartley, and must have charged the place with an infernal air.

The Alfoxden brook which ran through the dell beloved of Coleridge and the Wordsworths, which is described by William in his note to "Lines Written in Early Spring," has been identified in "This Lime-tree Bower My Prison," "The Nightingale," and "The Three Graves," and as the hidden brook of the *Ancient Mariner*.[37] It is the same stream mentioned in "To a Young Friend on His Proposing to Domesticate with the Author," in which Coleridge opines that its source is "bason'd in some unsunn'd cleft, / A beauteous spring, the rock's collected tears / Sleeps shelter'd there, scarce wrinkled by the gale!" (36–8) Coleridge would climb to that source in the company of Dorothy Wordsworth, who was addicted to seeking out hidden springs and recording her excursions in the Alfoxden journals. Coleridge's plan for his poem "The Brook," which, had it been written, might have rivalled in scale *The Prelude*, would have commenced with the source known as Lady's Fountain where Alfoxden Stream welled out of Danesborough Hill. Chapter ten of the *Biographia* and several notebook entries preserve the only relics of that venture.

I sought for a subject that should give equal room and freedom for description, incident and impassioned reflections on men, nature and society, yet supply in itself a natural connection to the parts, and unity to the whole. Such a subject I conceived myself to have found in a stream, traced from its source in the hills among the yellow-red moss and conical glass-shaped tufts of bent, to the first break or fall, where its drops become audible, and it begins to form a channel; thence to the peat and turf barn, itself built of the same dark squares as it sheltered; to the sheepfold; to the first cultivated plot of ground; to the lonely cottage and its bleak garden won from the heath; to the hamlet, the villages, the market-town, the manufactures and the sea-port. My walks, therefore, were almost daily on the top of Quantock and among its sloping coombs. With my pencil and memorandum-book in my hand I was *making studies*, as the artists call them, and often moulding my thoughts into verse, with the objects and imagery immediately before my senses.[38]

The project bore late fruit, as Wordsworth acknowledged, in his own *River Duddon* sonnets, but it may have influenced at a much earlier date his use of the river throughout *The Prelude*. It was this venture, as Coleridge explains, along with the friends' habit of tracing their rivers and streams from start to finish, or questioning the local Somersetmen on such matters, that precipitated the "Spy Nosey" affair. During a time of alarm over the threat of Napoleonic invasion, curiosity was not above suspicion. The Wordsworths' scouting activities were reported to the Home Secretary, and they were investigated by an underling for being "very attentive to the river near them," as well as for visits paid them by Citizen John Thelwall, Jacobin.

Wordsworth recalled in the Fenwick notes a perfect day when he, Coleridge, and Thelwall sat on the turf within Alfoxden Glen, savouring the spectacle of stream, waterfall, and the unsunn'd ash and the geniality of a companionable moment. Coleridge observed, "This is a place to reconcile one to all the jarrings and conflicts of the wide world." "Nay" said Thelwall, "to make one forget them altogether."[39] Coleridge could never forget or ignore the conflicts which were fundamental to his life and vision, and his words, spoken from a fleeting moment of equanimity and before the enchantment which is a river and its cataract, hint that even in such Arcadian moments, the jarrings, conflicts, and threats are not forgotten, only momently and miraculously reconciled. The scene speaks to us of Xanadu and its river.

A RIVERINE PARADISE AND ITS MAKER

> Where Alph the sacred river ran ... Cublai Can which is in our tongue Lord of Lords, the greatest Prince in peoples, Cities & Treasures, that ever was in the world.   Purchas

Alph and its riverscape provide the only salient natural features of Xanadu. The river traverses the walled gardens, whose sole unnatural feature, Kubla's pleasure dome, is exactingly sited in relation to it, its banks, its source, and its demise. Whatever significance the builder and his artifact may have for us is established by the singularity of their relation to the sacred river and its brief course.

The Avestan *pairi daeza*, from which the classical and modern forms of the word "paradise" derive, designates no more than an encircled place, a park or orchard. For the ancient Persian it meant a royal enclosure, most commonly an oasis in the desert wastes. Since "girdling" a square or rectangle is as ungainly as it is improbable, it may be assumed that Coleridge's Xanadu follows the circular shape of Purchas's and Milton's Paradise. A circular form of royal residence was common among the Medians, Parthians, and Sassanians, where a second wall formed a concentric circle, most notably in the round city of Mansur, or Baghdad. ("So twice five miles ... were girdled round.") These were essentially heavenly cities, forms of an *ouranopolis* or earthly image of the cosmic order.[40]

The topography of paradise varies from a random landscape, lowland rising gently to the hill or mount at its southern end from which issues its river, to the strictest symmetry, a mandala described by a central fount feeding four rivers extending toward the cardinal points. Were the demiurge a Neoclassical aesthetician, this quadrated circle would provide a fitting paddock for his creation. Coleridge's Xanadu boasts but one river, and the deployment of the landscape and its features scarcely suggests regularity.[41] The river seems as random as the country it traverses, and the disposition of its features, described in a disarmingly offhanded manner by "here were," "there were," and "enfolding," argues a disposition which is diverse and arbitrary.

A meander is a geological formation as well as the Phrygian river which is its paradigm, and in common usage the word describes a path turning almost back upon itself, flexions deeper and more labyrinthine than Hogarth's ogee line of beauty might produce. The Alph's meander is the lowland arrest of the impulse born in its highland, now winding, as Coleridge's "meandering" and "mazy" imply, tracing the labyrinthine path established by an alluvial river. Its course is directed by nature and is none of the great Khan's doing. Xanadu is the product of the calculation of neither a LeNôtre nor a Hogarth, ruled neither by line nor by "Pyramidall, Serpent-like and mutiplied by one two and three." The only "devizing" in Xanadu pertains to its unnatural features, the encircling walls and towers, and the pleasure dome subject to Kubla's fiat and lying at the heart of the mazy riverscape.

Paradises, like paragons of moral excellence, have always invited anxious scrutiny for evidence of flaws, and Kubla's Xanadu, as if it were a specimen of fine bone china, has been minutely assessed for the fault lines that might open, in Auden's phrase, "a lane to the land of the dead." A glance at a Coleridge concordance dispels notions that words such as "sinuous," "incense," and "dome" insinuate connotations of deviousness, seduction, or moral paralysis bred by oriental opulence.[42] As in Saint Patrick's Ireland, there are no serpents in Xanadu. The airs of paradise have been ever weighty with perfume as intoxicating as its harmonies, without any hint of overripeness or decadence. Purchas's paradise is furnished with "peares, pippins ... oranges, citrons, lemons and with cedars, palme trees with other trees and variety of hearbs and floures, to satisfie the sight, taste and sent."[43] Milton's envious Satan is assailed by the rich scents of paradise like the exotic offshore odours wafted to mariners from the eastern shores of Africa, and Coleridge's own version of paradise regained in "Religious Musings" celebrates "the odorous groves of earth reparadis'd."[44]

As with the Biblical garden, we have no certain impression of what, if anything, lies beyond the walls of Xanadu; nor can we plumb the unfathomable darkness which gives birth to its river or the measureless caverns and sunless sea that receive it. Unlike the walls defining its precincts, these are beyond our reckoning. Xanadu's double walls with their bastions can be compared to what Cassirer has called "the charmed circle of myth," or to the plot staked out by a work of art, which encompasses all that can be known with certainty and all that it is needful to know. Beyond this structured realm lies the domain of the unknown, the formless. Eliade has described the nature of what lies without: "outside this familiar space, there is the unknown and the dangerous region of the demons, the ghosts, the dead and of foreigners – in a word, chaos or night or death. The image of an uninhabited microcosm, surrounded by desert regions regarded as a chaos or a king-dom of the dead, has survived even in highly evolved civilizations such as those of China, Mesopotamia and Egypt."[45]

The *loci amoeni* of Coleridge's poems are for the most part geo-graphic entities, real places that can be located, and whose significance derives from their association with the personal events which transform them into symbols or evoke myths whose resonance transcends the personal. Xanadu, the Alph, and Abora, like Lewti's Tamaha, bear a tenuous relationship to geography; they are a synthesis of the literary, mythic, and geographic, and as such they exert greater fascination and establish a more compelling reality than an identifiable place, no matter how exotic, a relatively prosaic Alpheus or Mount Amara. "What we have here," Eliade writes, "is sacred, mythic geography, the only kind effectually real, as opposed to profane geography, the latter being 'Objective' and, as it were, abstract and non-essential ... the theoretical construction of a space and a world that we do not live in, and there-fore do not *know*."[46] Massive labours to identify Coleridge's sources prosaically and reductively, to sound the measureless caverns and chart the Alph, profane the sacred river with so ponderous a burden of criti-cal alluvia as to silt up its nurturing flow and deliver the pleasure gar-dens into the arid embrace of the waiting desert. It is essential for us to assert not so much the primacy of the ingredients of the visionary landscape as the imaginative integration of the informing centre which gathers and moulds what otherwise is merely irrelevant or discrete. Such "informing centres" lie with hidden sources scarcely recoverable from the general catalogues of the Bristol Lending or the British Libraries. For Coleridge they frequently disclosed themselves in dream or reverie, and his notebooks record at least three such encounters with an enclave within the desert or wilderness. They began as early as 1794.

A subject for a romance – finding out a desert city & dwelling there / – Asia –[47]

Three or four years later:

Some wilderness-plot, green & fountainous & unviolated by Man.[48]

By 1798 Coleridge had discovered the means of passage to the inviolate maiden-place. The toll exacted proved exorbitant.

Laudanum gave me repose, not sleep, but YOU I believe know how divine that repose is – what a spot of inchantment, a green spot of fountains, & flowers, & trees, in the very heart of a waste of Sands![49]

The entries speak of flight in order to secure peace and content in a place where, unlike the bowers of Coleridge's waking experience, no love is or can be. In fact, the desert city and wilderness plot are not populous places. They are deserted, uncompanionable, devoid of human life except for the dreamer himself, their creator and their lord. As in "The Picture" of 1802 they afford communion only with oneself.[50]

In a letter to Thelwall of October 1797, long recognized as containing several references to "Kubla Khan," Coleridge muses upon an isolation more splendid and complete than that of his dreams, the sort of perfected condition which finds expression only in myth:

& at other times I adopt the Brahman Creed & I say – It is better to sit than to stand, it is better to lie than to sit, it is better to sleep than to wake – but Death is the best of all – I should much wish, like the Indian Vishna, to float about along an infinite ocean cradled in the flower of the Lotos & wake once in a million years for a few minutes – just to know that I was going to sleep a million more.[51]

The passage is an amiable self-portrait of ruminative indolence, but it dramatizes in absolute terms the same tendency to withdraw to a guarded, isolated, and self-sustaining position: the Olympian serenity or nirvana of the contemplative ideal in which the genial Lord Vishnu, before the creation of mankind and the world of individuated forms, floats blissfully on his lotus raft over the measureless milk of the abyss.

The wilderness spot, the desert city, the lotus raft, and certainly Xanadu are all fine but eminently private places. As such, they are solitary counterparts of the companionable *loci amoeni* of Coleridge's personal geography, the springs and rivulets and bowers with canopied moss seats, the Alfoxden glens hallowed by the waking affections. This disjunction, between the offerings of the *ego nocturnus* and the *ego diurnus*, as Coleridge called the dreaming and waking selves, suggests a drive toward personal isolation profoundly at odds with the poet's faltering attempts to secure relationship with others, and a man who has not wilfully chosen loneliness, but whom loneliness has chosen for its own.

What is to be done in Xanadu, or in these dream fantasies, other than breathe their scented airs and contemplate their harmonies? Walled gardens flowing with the milk and honey of paradise suggest a return to the protective womb and maternal embrace, and although such reveries promise to sate all imaginable desires, they are one-sided and incomplete. Here all desire fades. They offer a regressively infantile world which will not go untried: if not by the demands of waking experience, then by the insistent complementarity of dream images which seek to redress the imbalance and force growth from arrest. The brightest light casts the darkest shadows, and that maternal, maidenly, and inviolate world is countered by the demonic wailing woman with her erotic cry, whose savage setting also finds its place within the precincts of paradise, even at the fountainhead of its vital principle. Coleridge's solitary Kubla, it would seem, has no handmaidens; Vishnu on his lotus raft has not yet his consort Lakshmi, Adam has not awakened to Eve, nor the Regent to Mrs Fitzherbert,[52] but before our general mother, tradition insists, was Lilith.

Paradise, like all pastoral worlds, assuming it is the creation of human hindsight rather than divine foresight, is an idealization of our mundane world and presupposes its existence. Somewhere beyond its walls are the unseasonable seasons, foul weather and deeds. Here the lion may couch with the lamb, there he dines on him. The peaceable kingdom always assumes its bellicose antitype.

Paradise is all too often characterized as "the place of perfect repose and inner harmony," as A.B. Giamatti describes it at the beginning of his study *The Earthly Paradise and the Renaissance Epic*.[53] But paradise is not nirvana, an insipid perfection offering only ennui. Such a retreat, even on weekends, would unman a mogul. For its brief tenure, paradise is a precarious attunement of the disruptive and threatening. We know that the walls and sentried gates of lapsarian paradise were meant to keep man out, but we are never entirely certain whether the unfallen enclave is a playpen contrived to restrain its inmates or a stronghold devised to exclude antagonists. In either case it is not very effective, possibly because threat lies within as well as without its walls. Paradises like Blake's insipid vale of Har are cisterns which contain, thus threatening stagnation and poison, while true paradises, if they are to flourish rather than languish, must be fed and animated with the mighty energies which they receive and attune in precarious equipoise. Paradise is a coiled spring, vibrant, volatile, alive, expectantly awaiting the single event for which it was created: its demise.

Yeats's diary of 1930 recounts a dream in which a young girl presses her ear to the bark of the tree of life to hear the music of paradise, and discovers that it is composed of the continuous clashing of swords.[54]

Kubla's pleasure dome lies at the heart of Xanadu. It can be argued that it occupies the geographical centre, midway as the crow flies, between the source of the river and its plunge into the caverns, where the commotions from the travail of its birth and its disappearance mingle in harmony. Certainly the dome, the miraculous artifact which comprehends and expresses all the natural antinomies within the garden, provides the imaginative centre and focus of Xanadu. The dome is to Xanadu what the tree of life or the tree of knowledge of good and evil is to other paradises. Moreover, it is not the walled garden and its precincts which the despairing poet at the poem's "close would recreate, but its cynosure, "that sunny dome, those caves of ice" and, presumably, the creative potency of its architect and resident miracle-maker.

Since dome and caves are twice invoked together, it can be concluded that one stands in relation to the other as attic to cellar, that they comprise a single structure, miraculous in that it "reveals itself in the balance or reconciliation of opposite or discordant qualities," warmth with chill, darkness with light, concavity with convexity, while its vault murmurs with the measured harmony from the alpha and omega of the sacred river. The pleasure dome is, as Coleridge understands the term, a work of art, synthesis of the natural polarities found in Xanadu. It is Xanadu's microcosm, and like all domed structures, a visible image of its universe. At the centre, the dome and its icy caves traverse the principal planes of existence – the sky, the mundane, and the underground – rearing from the shadowy realm of earth, the receiver of the dead and the source of renewed life, into the sun-filled air. The three realms are one within this miracle of man's devising, the axial creation whose stately image is reflected in the moving waters of the sacred river. It is, moreover, the seat of the great khan.

Kubla brings to Coleridge's poem little more than what is implied in

Purchas's account, the impression of illimitable power and magnificence commanded by a potentate of the east, "Lord of Lords, the greatest Prince in peoples Cities & Treasures, that ever was in the world." Although godlike in the exercise of his mighty creative fiat, Kubla is not God. Nor are the forces he commands ungodly, merely titanic energies summoned and directed, the human counterpart of the natural forces manifest at the source of the Alph. The figure of the great khan is necessary to Coleridge's poem, not because his are a match for these natural powers – they are clearly of a lesser order, since the Alph will outrun the course of Kubla's empire and its works – but because human creation in its own right is no paltry matter, and is given its due. Xanadu's scale and magnificence are the tangible expression of its architect's will, and yet for all its splendour, we are aware that this is the architecture of a finite mind. But the relation of the creative act within the finite mind to the great *fiat lux* of the cosmocrator is always central to Coleridge's theory of the imagination, and is secured in the poem by the introduction of the ruler and the quasi-divine role associated with the sacred king.

God knows all things, Coleridge maintains, because they proceed from him. The creative fiat within the Infinite I AM, as well as within the mind of a lesser finite creator, is epistemological as well as cosmogonic in nature. By creating, God knows himself, and so it is with his creative creatures. God cannot know chaos, only cosmos, that living order which is of himself, the conflicts and apparent oppositions reconciled within him, and expressed within his creation. In accordance with the role of sacred kingship, ruler and functionaries reenact and implement the divine plan by maintaining order, by upholding God and his Right, by ministering to the tensions and conflicts which threaten his kingdom and people from within and without. "The royal person," Rochedieu writes, "is a divine force living in man. But this divine force overflows, is superabundant. The king makes gifts to his subjects and equals, the king battles illness, he maintains the prosperity of the country."[55] The power the ruler exercises is not unnatural, but at one with the world of nature, so that the order he commands is a cosmological, not merely a political, disposition. The king is the visible image of the great cosmocrator, and his kingdom the image of the created universe. As such it must have a centre, the point where it all began, from which creation first issued, and, since creation's work is never done, from which it continues to manifest its potency. The life principle has a source, a divine fountainhead, and the maintenance of life and its promulgation, its fertility, involves a periodic return to this vivifying source, or a ceremonial communion with it through the functionaries who dispense and maintain its largesse. The place of power and the ruler together occupy the axial centre of their physical world, and although two navels are an anatomical or even a logical absurdity, they are not anomalous in the world of myth. Here the centre is not geographic in terms of the abstract division of functional space as defined by the mapmaker, but the metaphysical centre from which all directions derive their significance. These centres are not abstract but concrete; they provide the fundamental orientation which gives point and meaning to life and its activities, the norm or reality by which all action can be evaluated or adjudged as right of, left of, off, or "on" centre. Babylonian kings were known to their subjects as "the Axis and Pole of the World," and the cosmic dimension with its secure relation to the centre was no trifling abstraction for the Egyptian queen who lamented not only the ship of state set adrift, but how all life veers into the trivial or inconsequential when its standard is felled and its lodestar eclipsed.

The soldier's pole is fall'n: young boys and girls
Are level now with men. The odds is gone,
And there is nothing left remarkable
Beneath the visiting moon.   (*Antony and Cleopatra*, 4.15.65–8)

The source of the Alph is the generating centre from which natural creation bursts and flows. "That deep romantic chasm which slanted / Down the green hill athwart a cedarn cover" unleashes its confounding medley of the demonic, of the dark, threatening, and procreative mystery of sexuality, of violence and struggle bursting triumphantly into the light of the upper air. It is a stunning evocation of the irrepressible mystery of continuous creation, the fierce battle to escape the maternal earth and her realm, the expulsion of life from her dark womb with its convulsive thrust into the world of light, the whole uncontrollable mystery of birth.

Coleridge's description of the birth of the Alph commands all the prescribed elements of the sublime, and sounds its diapason to the tinkling counterpoint of springs and rills and the inspirational midwifery of their naiads or maids, the creative engagements of his waking life. As a portrayal of creation and its mystery, the place and the wailing woman, its genius, achieve expression which is richly ambivalent, a symbolism mature and complete with a resonance that beggars all efforts to characterize it by partial and shallow distinctions: birth, destruction, terror, beauty, good, or evil. Harold Bloom in *A Map of Misreading* follows the Freudian model by arguing that a poet's greatest energies are summoned as a consequence of his powers of repression, that his expression is charged or "daemonized" by these powers when he permits the expression of materials that he would in other circumstances consciously repress or rigorously proscribe. The result is a "high passion" or sublimity of expression.[56]

A Jungian account of the energies commanded by the archetype would be in substantial agreement with this, except that their articulation is not the result of the ego caught napping, a relaxation of the mechanism of repression, but the creative assertion for which the healthy organism was framed, the natural assimilation of unconscious content by conscious awareness, a phase in the growth or individuation of the self. In any case, these powerful realizations are the compelling and irresistible response to the *loci* and their geniuses consciously disposed elsewhere by their author. Coleridge laid his claim to those companionable places by carving his initials; those less genial would claim him as their own.

As an artifact, the dome centring Kubla's realm seems at best a delightful epiphany when contrasted with the natural apocalypse at the river's source. It is secular, as opposed to the natural elements it reconciles and expresses – the thrice-designated "sacred river" and the "holy" enchantment at its source. Monuments of unaging intellect, as Yeats recognized, provide at best a frail contrast with the sensual music of the natural order and its mighty imperatives, and Kubla's miracle of rare device, which is a place for prophecy, is at least a more commanding creation that Yeats's Byzantine gadgetry, the golden bird who sings "Of what is past, or passing, or to come" in order to rouse a drowsy emperor or amuse his court sycophants, a timepiece more Swiss than Byzantine in its ingenuity.[57]

Kubla's visionary capability and its modes are developed on at least two highly suggestive levels. The eminence and central location of his own creation, the pleasure dome, afford him the prophetic overview, the perspective *sub specie aeternitatis*. Midway between the alpha and omega of the paradigmatic river whose source is birth and whose course is the maze of life's unfolding passage, suspended within the miraculous equipoise of the creation whose still image hangs on its gliding waters, Kubla has achieved the contemplative disengagement which allows him to regard with equanimity the course of past, present, and future, the ancestral voices prophesying war. This is visionary indifference, the detached perspective from without, from which all engagement with events, with their demands and their myopic immediacy, recedes until only their formal tracery remains. It is the truth of abstraction, which, in spite of its allure for Coleridge, was at best partial, at worst superficial. But Kubla's voices are, after all, his voices, at least the voices of his own ancestors, and they declare themselves from within. The Romantic mode of cognition entails recognition, and for Coleridge the deepest levels of knowledge are ultimately self-knowledge. Again, it is Kubla's creation which grants him this perspective. The sounds from fountain and caves mingle in vatic harmony; Kubla hearkens to the voices of unconscious depths, the chthonic world beneath the sunny dome which rises from its embrace, just as the Alph rises from it and is received once again in darkness. Kubla communes with his own unconscious world in the cognitive act in which conscious and unconscious mingle. To translate these shadows into the measure and light of conscious awareness, into *logos*, is Kubla's office as ruler, to reenact the same natural process imaged in the rise of the Alph at its source. It is within the self that the voices of the past stir and speak in the language of present consciousness of those motives which will quicken future action.

Kubla's voices bring word of war, destruction, whereas the Abyssinian maid promises creation to the poet who could rekindle her harmonies. This contrast has troubled the khan's critics, who have understood it as further confirmation of the flawed nature of the creation of a tyrant whose works must come to a deservedly bad end. But it is the nature of all things as well as of mankind to come to a bad end, or at least an end. The heroic life meets its nemesis, the creative life drought, saints their martyrdom, and the most prosaic of creatures blind extinction. Even in Arcadia death waits, and paradises, like great loves, are embraced and lost. This much Kubla knows from his voices, and precisely because such truths are commonplace, they are commonly lost sight of, suppressed by the anxieties of those less favoured of the gods and overlooked by the hubris of those more pampered. The wars which Kubla recognizes are merely part of the human and cosmic condition, which knows no exception to the rule of death and renewal, dissolution and creation, even in the momentary stay effected by art and by the dream of paradise.

But the walled garden and its architect lie within the larger embrace of the perspective afforded by the poem's dramatic frame. Unlike the narrative of the ancient mariner, "Kubla Khan" does not make us aware of this until the closing section. This circumstance has occasioned distress, but ought not to, any more than when in "Lines Composed a Few Miles above Tintern Abbey" we discover belatedly that Wordsworth's monologue has a cast of two. The sequential progress of such poems is deflected by the introduction of circumstances which force a reconsideration of the foregoing materials within an altered context, a retrospective dissolution and reconstitution whose effect is suggested by the haunting image which Coleridge appropriated from "The Picture" and used as introduction to "Kubla Khan."

- all that phantom-world so fair
Vanishes, and a thousand circlets spread,
And each mis-shape the other.
...
And soon the fragments dim of lovely forms
Come trembling back, unite, and now once more
The pool becomes a mirror. (92–4, 98–100)

It is the final section of "Kubla Khan" that insists upon what is implicit in the vision of Xanadu: that, as most of the poem's readers have
observed, its subject is the creative act, its exercise and its failures. The
Abyssinian maid is the bright counterpart of the wailing woman inas-
much as the two constitute the opposed aspects, benign and threatening, of the female creatures who minister to the well-springs of creative
activity, figures haunting both Coleridge's dreams and his waking
hours, and who together or dividually command his poetry. In "Kubla
Khan" neither wins the soul of the enervated poet as her own, nor does
he win them. One stands at an ill-defined distance from the poem established by simile, the other seems no more than an *ignis fatuus*, a luminous memory from an indeterminate past. The poet is without muse.
Even the Mnemosyne who nourished Wordsworth's genius fails and
recovers nothing. For Coleridge she is 'Memory, a wan misery-Eyed
Female ... She fed on bitter fruit from the Tree of life."[58]

At the close of his reverie on the shores of the Wye, Wordsworth can
discern his own youth in the shooting lights of his sister's eyes, and the
past as reified through and in Dorothy is a living presence, guardian
and fountainhead of his art. But the poet of "Kubla Khan" is exiled,
estranged from paradises within and without, real or imagined, and
memory fails to rekindle its splendours.[59] Only the agonized series of
unfulfilled conditionals testifies to what might have been the gift of
visionary renewal. But these serve, as do the blessings heaped upon the
Lady of the Dejection Ode, only to heighten the tragic disparity
between her blessedness and the poet's loss, between what is left behind
and what might have been.

CHAPTER FIVE

The English Nymph: Her Literary and Social History

> Who then else should hymn the nymphs
> Who strew the ground with wild flowers?
> Who shade the founts with curtains green?
>
> Virgil, Ninth Eclogue

Like the rivers, which from the time of Ausonius were celebrated as arteries of commerce, nymphs were pressed into common service. During the Restoration and eighteenth century their fortunes in this respect were mixed. Often they served purely decorative purposes on the grounds of the English country house, framing a foreground or enhancing a background by extending the viewer's perspective in space and, as classical notations, in time. Beached amid shrubbery or penned within malodorous grottoes, they ruminate, surveying an alien landscape of drained sloughs and cultivated prospects. They appear no less frequently in the poetry of the age, where their impact is slight and their role often perfunctory. Such are the artfully disposed creatures of Ambrose Philips's or Pope's pastorals, and the nymphs afoot or adrift in "Windsor Forest," where the poet has tempered Pan's Mediterranean ardour for Syrinx by englishing her as Ladona, the river Laddon, tributary to the Thames and distant cousin to Arcadian Ladon.

The nymphs and their pristine springs were unaccountably sullied by Cowper in his poem "See Where the Thames," in which their union with Thames is a turbid mating:

> The nymphs of many a sable flood
> Deform with streaks of oozy mud
> The bosom of the Thames.[1]

Mythically anomalous, Cowper's conceit is at least morally congruent, as river and its nymphs are pressed into more sententious service:

Thus fares it with the human soul

...

But ah! a thousand anxious woes
Pollute the noble tide.[2]

Cowley's Latin poem *Plantarum* supplied the most populous convocation of dryads in English or Latin, augmenting their traditional classifications with fertile invention, so that native forests acquired dryads appropriate to various species of English flora, such as Philyra the lime-tree and Achras the crab. Cowley's poem resourcefully submits myth to the service of botany, history, and physiology.

John Dyer's account of the Towy riverscape in "Grongar Hill' was followed by his georgic on the less promising subject of sheep and the wool trade, *The Fleece*. Following a graceful tribute to the five sister springs of the Welsh Plynlimmon and their issue, Dyer's apostrophes to the rivers of England in book three are concerned principally with the progeny of wedded and canalized rivers and their technological and commercial prospects, so that the union of Trent, Severn, and "Thames' wave" might bear in mighty concert their tribute to "great Augusta's markt."

Matthew Prior invested the pursuit of the River Peneus's daughter Daphne by Apollo with a gritty Theocritan realism which divested the winded god of his *afflatus* and the myth of its elements of holy dread and sexual panic. The nymph, his quarry, weighs Phoebus's conciliatory proposition that if she will tread a little less hastily in her flight, so will he:

This care is for himself, as sure as Death
One mile has put the fellow out of Breath
He'll never do, I'll lead him t'other round
Washy he is, perhaps not over sound.[3]

The eternal pursuit has instructed the nymph in the powers of calculation. In this respect she is kin to Swift's thoroughly urban nymphs, the species Shelley and his circle would identify as poliads. Swift's Corinna, pride of Drury Land in "A Beautiful Young Nymph Going to Bed," is well used, stripped of her *numen*, and divested of glass eye, false eyebrows, wig, teeth, bosom and hip bolsters, before retiring to a well-earned sleep after a night of whoring. In "Strephon and Chloe" the watery element of the nymph has suffered a Swiftian defilement graver than Cowley's "streaks of oozy mud" or that which occasioned Hesiod's injunction against urinating in the headwaters of a stream.

Twelve Cups of Tea, (with Grief I speak)
Had now constrain'd the Nymph to leak.
This Point must needs be settled first;
The Bride must either void or burst.
Then, see the dire Effect of Pease,
Think what can give the Colick Ease,
The Nymph opprest before, behind,
As ships are toss't by Waves and Wind ...[4]

Perhaps the most learned tribute of the age is Mark Akenside's "Hymn to the Naiads," a celebration in the manner of Callimachus weighted with scholarly notes clarifying genealogies and other matters. Saintsbury commended its "icy elegance." Its sobriety is a function not only of its elevated style but of its argument, in which the nymphs and their sober element are commended and contrasted with the "unhallow'd rout" of Bacchus's wine-sodden horde, providing a singular instance in which the inspirational genius of the nymphs was enlisted in the cause of teetotalism. The "Hymn to the Naiads" with its Pindaric assertion that "water is best" nonetheless corroborates Horace's observation to Maecenas that "no poem can please for long – or endure – if written by water drinkers."[5]

In his preface to *The River Duddon*, Wordsworth invoked the authority of the ages as testimony to the imperishable nature of his subject:

The power of waters over the minds of Poets has been acknowledged from the earliest ages; – through the "Flumina amem sylvasque inglorius" of Virgil down to the sublime apostrophe to the great rivers of the earth, by Armstrong. ...[6]

The unlikely coupling of Dr John Armstrong, author of *The Art of Preserving Health: A Poem in Four Books*, with the Mantuan Swan testifies to the perishable nature of literary reputation: Armstrong's poem was esteemed by Wordsworth and his contemporaries. Written within a decade of Burke's *A Philosophical Inquiry into the Origin of Our Ideas of the Sublime and Beautiful*, Armstrong displayed a voluble enthusiasm for the sublimity of natural landscape, in particular the compelling mystery which attends the sources of the world's great rivers.

Now come, ye Naiads, to the fountains lead!
Now let me wander thro' your gelid reign!
I burn to view th'enthusiastic wilds
By mortal else untrod. I hear the din

Of waters thund'ring o'er the ruin'd cliffs.
With holy reverence I approach the rocks
Whence glide the streams renown'd in ancient song.
Here from the desart down the rumbling steep
First springs the Nile; here bursts the founding Po
In angry waves; Euphrates hence devolves
A mightly flood to water half the east;
And there, in Gothic solitude reclin'd
The cheerless Tanais pours his hoary urn.
What solemn twilight! What stupendous shades
Enwrap these infant floods! Thro' every nerve
A sacred horror thrills, a pleasing fear
Glides o'er my frame. The forest deepens round;
And more gigantic still, th'impending trees
Stretch their extrav'gant arms athwart the gloom.
Are these the confines of some fairy world?
A land of Genii? Say, beyond these wilds
What unknown nations? If indeed beyond
Aught habitable lies. And wither leads,
To what strange regions, or of bliss or pain,
That subterraneous way? Propitious maids!
Conduct me, while with fearful steps I tread
This trembling ground.[7]

Armstrong's tribute to the guardian nymphs and their "gelid reign" might have furnished the writer of the "Preface to the *Lyrical Ballads*" with a further example of the perfunctory personification whereby his literary forebears had reduced the charismatic figures of classical mythology to a glacial décor, but the poet warms to his subject as he proceeds to his highly charged evocation of the sacred mystery of beginnings, those precincts which proved irresistible to the Romantic imagination.

Armstrong can be numbered among those who, like Reynolds, would identify their enthusiasm for the sublime with the cult of Michelangelo and his "magnificently terrible chapel." A gathering torrent of praise for Michelangelo, culminating in Reynolds's final Discourse, eroded the reverence commanded by Raphael and the Virgilian serenity associated with the *beau idéal*. In 1771, under the pseudonym of Launcelot Temple, Armstrong championed the *terribilita* of the Homeric Michelangelo by celebrating the Sistine Chapel as "a prodigious display of sublime melancholy and dreadful imagination."[8] The fountainhead of art, like that of nature, had become a sublime, a terrifying, and a noisy place.

Armstrong's infant floods, with their "stupendous shades," "solemn twilight," "gothic solitudes," their *frisson* of "sacred horror" and "holy reverence," course from the deep romantic chasm which gave convulsive birth to Xanadu's sacred river and spawned a skein of mysterious Shelleyan rivers: "O stream! whose source is inaccessibly profound, / Whither do thy mysterious waters tend?" The mystique of the source finds its pictorial apotheosis in John Martin's *Sadok in Search of the Waters of Oblivion*, the heroic canvas which led Byron to inquire into its literary provenance as a possible subject for a poem. There was none. Martin claimed to have made it up, but not, as we have seen, of whole cloth.

THE REGENCY NYMPH

There is probably a higher incidence of nymphs per metric foot in the poetry of John Keats than in that of any other English Romantic, indeed of any English poet. One might even venture, more than in any classical Greek or Roman writer. Nymphs in their incarnations as naiads, nereids, or dryads are explicitly identified in at least seventeen different poems by Keats, and there are figures throughout much of the remaining poetry which can also be indentified as such. Occasionally their role is little more than decorative, part of the fauna peeking from every nook and brake in the congenial clime of the age of gold.

When George Keats faced financial ruin over an American steamboat venture, the worst imprecations his brother could heap on the offending continent blasted its dispiriting climate and dispirited rivers.

> That monstrous region, whose dull rivers pour,
> Ever from their sordid urns unto the shore,
> Unown'd of any weedy-haired gods;
> Whose winds, all zephyrless, hold scourging rods
> Iced in the great lakes, to afflict mankind;
> Whose rough-grown forests, frosted, black, and blind,
> Would fright a Dryad ...[9]

Aboard the *Maria Crowther* on the sea journey to Italy, Keats prepared for what might have been his last poem by reading Milton's *Comus*. Its subject was to have been Sabrina, the nymph of Severn.

The universal lament for the passing of Pan and his Arcadian rout had by no means diminished by the early nineteenth century, and Regency England harboured a healthy population of surviving émigrées. When the correspondence and the literary evidence of the inner and outer fringes of the Keats-Shelley circle are considered, it is apparent that concern with the nymph and nympholepsy, the worrisome discomfort she conferred, was obsessive and endemic.

The editors of *Shelley and His Circle* have indicated the distribution of the malaise and concluded that "the truth is that nymphs were at this period 'in the air' of the literary world."[10] This was indeed the case, and it was Leigh Hunt who singlehandedly effected their translation to that rarefied element. Hunt's poem *The Nymphs* has occasioned dispute over the possible existence of a literary competition among Keats, Hunt, and Shelley, resulting in *Endymion* and *The Revolt of Islam*. This was claimed by Medwin, and would suggest a somewhat improbable large-scale precursor to the Nile sonnet competition among the three poets on the night of 4 February 1818. It seems more likely that Medwin, ever a muddler, confused one competition with the other, although Hunt's biographer Edmund Blunden favoured his account.[11] Whether or not a competition existed, it is clear that each of the three poets knew and was interested in what the others were doing.

Blunden's claim that Hunt's poem is "sustained by a strong philosophical design," an estimate echoed by the editors of *Shelley and His Circle*, is less than convincing.[12] If so, the design boasts a subtlety which is scarcely evident in *The Nymphs* or elsewhere in Hunt's poetry. Hunt's contribution to the lore of the nymph seems to have been the annexation of the "nepheliad" or cloud-corralling nymph to the traditional classifications of nymphology. Blunden puckishly quotes Bessie Kent's grave approval of Hunt's innovation: "These beings were his addition to the classical mythology. The poet was the first and hitherto has been the only mortal, who has been honoured with the sight of the Nepheliads in person."[13]

Hunt begins his poem with an invocation, and his muse, who is yet untouched by "the blind feel of false philosophy," spreads unclipped wings and reveals to Hunt her sisters in lines which are an uncomfortably prescient parody of the closing passage of *Adonais*: "And from the clouds, like stars, bright eyes are beckoning to me."[14] Hunt proceeds to a Linnaean classification of the species. First are the dryads, who protect the blackbird from egg-plundering boys, the hare and deer from the hunter. (Had they custody of the Lake District, they might well have retarded the spiritual education of a young Wordsworth.) Hunt proceeds to hamadryads or tree-dwellers, who yield only to the axe, napeads, who nurse the retiring primrose, violet, and lily, shy limniads of the lakes, solicitous oreads, who succour the mountain goat and the occasional stray cow, and the ephydriad at her fountain.

> There lie they, lulled by little whiffling tones
> Of rills among the stones,

Or by the rounder murmur, glib and flush,
Of the escaping gush,
That laughs and tumbles, like a conscious thing
For joy of all its future travelling.[15]

Part one concludes with the naiads, who tend the coursing stream, and the nereids, who receive it in their ocean realm.

The second part of Hunt's poem is preoccupied with installing Hunt's own nepheliads in the pantheon. They steer a flotilla of saucy clouds which part and disclose glimpses of a foot or limb, "a sweeping back," "a smooth down-arching thigh," a "white raised bosom."[16] Bosoms, pale limbs, and poetry surface in Hunt's verse at the mere mention of a nymph, perhaps disclosing something of the nature of his abiding fascination with his subject. In his "Epistle to Byron" they surface to salute the voyaging pilgrim of eternity.

Phoebus looks forth with his long glance divine,
At which old Ocean's white and shapely Daughters
Crowd in the golden ferment of the waters,
And halcyons brood, and there's a glistering show
Of harps, midst bosoms and long arms of snow.[17]

If Keats's poetry was, as its author feared, writ in water, then Hunt's cloud-nepheliad land is fashioned from blancmange. Blunden saw Hunt's accomplishment impinging on the province of Shelley's genius, and Blunden is not alone in speculating on its influence on Shelley's "The Cloud." Any comparison, however, seems disproportionate and grotesque: the evanescent aerial forms which fill Shelley's poetry have nothing of the literalism or the confectionery eroticism of Hunt's marzipan pastoral.

Keats, however, was solicitious, and his amiable inquiries into the poem's progress indicate his familiarity with the composition. "How are the Nymphs? I suppose they have led you a fine dance ..." and he cites some of the more overworked phrases from Hunt's poem.[18] Shelley's encouragement and praise are recorded on two occasions in his letters. "When I read your Nymphs which is a poem original & intense, conceived with the clearest sense of ideal beauty & executed with the fullest & most flowing lyrical power, & yet diffused with the most intelligible outline of thought & language."[19] Perhaps Shelley's tolerance honours Hunt's friendship more than his poesy. In a letter earlier in the year Shelley made delicate reference to Hunt's celebrated and not infrequent poetic lapses: "The poem is not as faultless as it is beautiful."[20]

Shelley's own interest in the subject was characteristic of the atticizing cabal gathered around Marlow; their love of language and invention led them to pun endlessly and delightedly with those matters which commanded their love and respect, in particular their enthusiasm for the classics. Hunt was notorious for this, and Shelley's mixture of exasperation and indulgence with the inveterate punster is recorded in the *Letter to Maria Gisborne*:

> And there is he with his eternal puns,
> Which beat the dullest brain for smiles, like duns
> Thundering for money at a poet's door.[21]

Keats grew weary of the business and would find offensive the impulse to reduce everything of worth to mere verbal play: "Hunt does one harm by making fine things petty and beautiful things hateful."[22]

Peacock too, had contracted the fever, and planned a narrative poem on the subject of nympholepsy. Shelley's letter of August 1818 reveals their habit of mixing jest with earnestness in such matters.

> Pray, are you yet cured of your Nympholepsy? 'Tis a sweet disease; but one as obstinate and dangerous as any – even when the Nymph is a Poliad. Whether such be the case or not, I hope your nympholeptic tale is not abandoned. The subject, if treated with a due spice of Bacchic fury, and interwoven with the manners and feelings of those divine people, who in their errors, are the mirrors, as it were, in which all that is delicate and graceful contemplates itself, is perhaps equal to any. What a wonderful passage there is in Phaedrus – the beginning, I think, of one of the speeches of Socrates – in praise of poetic madness, and in definition of what poetry is, and how a man becomes a poet.[23]

The poliad or urban nymph was, as Dowden divined, a Shelleyan addendum to Hunt's classification. Peacock seems to have been stricken by several of the kind, the poliad in this instance being Marianne de St Croix. But Shelley also alludes to the nymph in her traditional role as instigator of the working of mantic possession or poetic inspiration. Forty years later Peacock would explain Shelley's sentiments in this passage in a memorial printed in *Frazer's Magazine*.[24]

Peacock's own spare prose outline of his poem gives no indication of whether he conceived it as a serious undertaking or merely as a diversion in the manner of Hunt.

> ... a joyous and festive youth, a leader of Bacchic rites, beloved by many girls but indifferent to them all in the desire of the love of higher beings. He becomes suddenly dispirited and melancholy ... The Nymph ... has built an altar to

Diana in a solitary grove and breathed on it a vow of chastity beneath the midnight moon. The prince has seen and loved her and been repulsed. The prince is seized with the nympholeptic madness ...[25]

Carl Dawson concludes from the similarity of this outline to Keats's *Endymion* that Peacock intended to use nympholepsy as a figuring of *pothos* or desire for the unattainable, the most infectious of Romantic aspirations and themes.[26] This seems likely, since the figures of Diana and her nymphs are associated throughout Keats's poetry, and not simply in *Endymion*, with the same theme. Peacock abandoned his project on learning that Shelley's friend Horace Smith was preparing for publication his *Amarynthus the Nympholept*. The Regency nymphaeum was becoming as crowded as Rotten Row or the circle at Covent Garden, and Peacock had had enough of the diversion. His pronouncement in "The Four Ages of Poetry" is at least as dispirited as the announcement reported by Plutarch in the first century that Great Pan is dead: "We know too that there are no Dryads in Hyde Park nor Naiads in Regent's canal."[27]

John Hamilton Reynolds, one of Keats's closest friends, contributed two documents to the natural history of the nymph. "The Pilgrimage of Living Poets to the Stream of Castaly" appeared in the *Champion* of April 1816, and is a dream vision relating an encounter with the guardian of the sacred spring which "so many poets rave of, though they know it not."[28] The dreamer is accosted by a creature with "a countenance full of life, and a form of living air," and fancies that he detects a dactylic motion in the dancing waters. There follows a less than serious enumeration of a queue of poets before the Castalian fount.

In the same year, shortly before meeting Keats, Reynolds published *The Naiad: A Tale with Other Poems*. It was dedicated to the high-minded painter Benjamin Robert Haydon, whom Reynolds reassured that "The Naiad is a truly respectable woman as far as personal appearance goes; I shall leave it to the world to decide on the beauty of her voice & the fascination of her Song."[29] Reynolds's protestations suggest that the reputation of the Regency nymph may have been languishing. The world beyond Haydon's breakfast circle at Lisson Grove, which included Reynolds, Hunt, and Horace Smith, and which would soon welcome Keats and occasional visits from Shelley, remained obdurate to her song. Wordsworth heard, but was unmoved. Reynolds had an inordinate admiration for the Lake Poet, whom he recognized as his master, and "The Eden of Imagination," published two years earlier, had already paid Wordsworth the compliment of an elaborate imitation of his "An Evening Walk." Perhaps the imitation of Wordsworth's juvenilia came too late to impress its begetter. Haydon was directed to send a copy of *The Naiad* to Wordsworth, and the poet's reply was laconic: "I will not scruple to say that your Poem would have told more upon me, if it had been shorter ... Your Fancy is too luxuriant and riots too much in its own creations."[30] Wordsworth's communication was a model of the brevity he enjoined upon Reynolds: he proposed that the author drop the first fifty-seven lines and the last one hundred and forty-six.

The phrase "luxuriant fancy" suggests that Wordsworth had already associated Reynolds and his poem with the versifiers gathered about Keats. His criticism, however peremptory, is a just pronouncement on most of these literary incursions into the pretty paganism of nymphology. The severity of Wordsworth's reaction can be better understood and sympathized with, however, when one recalls the poet's continuing preoccupation with reconstituting and rehabilitating this mythic figure in his own poetry with a subtlety which made obsolete the old practice of personification. It must have been particularly galling for Wordsworth to suffer a clamouring crowd of nymphs riding the tide of fashionable neo-Hellenism that conferred on them the same affectation which had marked their degeneration among the Augustans.

Horace Smith first met Shelley and Keats at Leigh Hunt's in 1816, and was already a member of the circle which frequented Haydon's and the Hunts'. He attracted Shelley at once, and engaged the poet in earnest discussion during an outing on Hampstead Heath. Shelley was astounded by the spectacle of a man who was Platonist, poet, writer of pastoral drama, and shrewd financier. Here indeed was poetry and the principle of self, God, and Mammon in one person. Shelley commended Smith to Maria Gisborne: "Wit and sense, / Virtue and human knowledge, all that might / Make this dull world a business of delight, / And all combined in Horace Smith."[31] Shelley placed his financial affairs in Smith's capable hands. The friendship produced "Ozymandias" as offspring of a competition between them. It continued throughout Shelley's removal to Italy, and the poet saw that Smith received copies of all of his works as they appeared.

Although the publication of Smith's *Amarynthus the Nympholept* was delayed until 1820, the poem was long in the works, and its inception probably belongs to the period of 1816–18 that saw the height of enthusiasm for the subject. It was most likely Shelley who halted Peacock's project by conveying to him news of Smith's poem's gestation.

Smith's pastoral drama, despite the absurdities of its plot, reveals none of the humour that established its author's literary reputation.

Smith introduces it, in the manner of Peacock, with a gravely learned preface calling upon the testimonies of Plutarch, Ovid, Festus, and Propertius about the "endemic complaint" which is his subject, and appends appropriate footnotes in the manner of Akenside. It is the most thorough account of the malady as it was understood by the circle.

The νυμφόληπτοι of the Greeks, and the Lymphati or Lymphatici of the Romans were men supposed to be possessed by the Nymphs, and driven to phrensy, either from having seen one of those mysterious beings, or from the maddening effect of the oracular caves in which they resided. Plutarch particularly mentions that the Nymphs Sphragitides haunted a cave on Mount Cithaeron, in Boeotia, in which there had formerly been an oracle, and where, from the inspiration they diffused, Nympholepsy became an endemic complaint. According to Festus, it was formerly thought that all those who had merely seen the figure of a nymph in a fountain were seized with madness during the remainder of their lives. Ovid himself dreaded this event, as appears by the lines in the fourth book of his Fasti.

Nec Dryadas, nec nos videamus labra Dianae,
Nec Faunum medio cum premit aura die:

and Propertius also alludes to the same belief, when in describing the happiness of the early ages, he exclaims,

Nec fuerat nudas poena videre deas.

It was the popular opinion throughout the whole of Greece, that the nymphs occasionally appeared to mortals, and that the consequences of beholding them were generally to be deprecated: the result among such a superstitious and imaginative people may easily be conjectured. Terror combined with religion in disposing the mind to adopt delusion for reality; and visions became frequent and indisputable in exact proportion to the prevalence of timidity and enthusiasm. Sometimes they were not altogether imaginary in their origin. Partial glimpses of some country girl, tripping, perhaps, through the twilight-grove to meet her lover, or stealing into the copse at day-break to bath in its embowered waters, were quite sufficient to inflame the combustible fancy of a Greek. Others, probably, without such excitement of the external sense would sit amid the solitude of the forest, brooding over the tales which peopled it with nymphs, fauns, and satyrs, until they realised them to their mind's eye, and became Nympholepts, the more incurable, because no tangible object had deranged their faculties, and they had consequently no means of proving the fallacy of their impressions.[32]

Smith's drama is set in "The Vale of Tempe and its Neighbourhood," but the chaste trystings of young love blossoming, bilked, and triumphant, abetted and plagued by meddlesome spirits in a cuckoo-infested wood, belong more to the heartland of "A Wood near Athens." A Shakespearean wood in Regency England is a somewhat self-conscious anachronism, an orangery rather than a wilderness, but it is true to the nature of pastoral worlds contrived by self-regarding urbanites to be self-conscious. Smith's indebtedness is extensive. He acknowledges Fletcher's *Faithful Shepherdess*, and on one occasion provides a startling echo of Wordsworth's account of his escape from London to the countryside, the gusty opening of *The Prelude* which serves to buoy the author through his fourteen books. Amarynthus, having quitted Athens and its material pursuits, contemplates the rustic world of his birthplace:

> ... so my soul
> Long in the city's peopled desert pent
> O holy Nature, to the freshness rushes,
> To bathe in leafy greeness, and inhale
> The rapture that to all my senses gushes.[33]

The pictorial elements in the poem are highly developed and suggest that Smith not only had an ear for literary echoes, but an eye to the Renaissance paintings which Hunt, Keats, and their friends "read" together in engraved copies. Urania's extended description of Amphitrite, her car, her attendant Tritons, and "sleepy Nereids of Peachy cheeks" may derive from the engraving of one of Hunt's and Shelley's favourites, Raphael's *Farnesina Galatea*. Smith's pictorial renderings are arrestingly detailed and not without an accomplished charm which establishes the work's superiority to Hunt's. But for all its merits, *Amarynthus* contributes nothing to the latter-day literature of Platonism, as Shelley might have hoped, and scant insight into the worlds of nymph and nympholept. Amarynthus's "nympholeptic pangs / And terror," it transpires, have been contracted from nothing more threatening than the sight of Amarillis, who in order to escape lifelong celibacy as priestess of Pan has hidden herself in a woodland cave. Although his condition is a spurious one, brought on by a case of mistaken identity, Amarynthus displays all the *bona fide* symptoms of madness and terror which plagued the nympholept, perhaps demonstrating that nympholeptic venery was a malaise, as Lawrence might have diagnosed it, of sex in the head. *Amarynthus the Nympholept* exists solely to charm, an entrancement which languishes, as Wordsworth pointed out to Reynolds, in the absence of brevity.

Byron had no need of Wordsworth's advice. The five brief stanzas of *Childe Harold's Pilgrimage* which sketch the career of the Egerean nymph and evoke the lonely Campagna spring which was popularly consecrated to her were the most celebrated and perhaps the most moving tribute of the age. Shelley wrote Peacock a note praying that Byron's accomplishment would not hinder his own poem on the subject: "You saw those beautiful stanzas in the 4th Canto about the nymph Egeria. Well, I did not whisper a word about nympholepsy, I hope you acquit me. – And I hope you will not carry delicacy so far as to let this suppress anything nympholeptic."[34]

Byron refuses to trouble the waters of mythogenesis, and is tolerant of all possible explanations concerning nymphs: she was the fictional creation of a despairing nympholept; she was an uncommonly beautiful woman, or indeed she may have been an ideal being; enough that "Thou wert a beautiful thought, and softly bodied forth." Whatever Byron might have written on the subject, he could rely on a knowledgeable public who had long venerated the Egerean spring and its legend. The spot was a mandatory secular station for the pilgrim to Rome throughout the eighteenth and nineteenth centuries. Wordsworth celebrated the site and its tenant on several occasions in his poetry before actually visiting it. On his Italian tour in 1837, literary allusion became an actuality, and he was moved to record his feelings once again.[35]

Although the origins of the nymph are obscure, nympholepsy appears to have entered English parlance in the revolutionary year of 1776, through the publication of Chandler's *Travels in Asia Minor and Greece*. "The Nymphs," Chandler writes, "it was the popular persuasion, occasionally appeared, and nympholepsy is characterized as a phrensy which arose from having beheld them."[36] Chandler's volumes are a plausible source for Keats, Shelley, Peacock, Hunt, and their friends. I will argue elsewhere Keats's own use of Chandler. The work was immensely popular since it afforded classical enthusiasts a detailed account of the holy land of their imaginings as fact, closed as it was by the Turk to all but the most intrepid of European travellers.

The use of the word "nymph" in Regency England was broadly applied, as it was by the ancient Greeks, to any young, beautiful, and unmarried woman. More particularly, it was applied, as in the case of Pope's Belinda, to women of the *ton*. In 1789 Mrs Piozzi confirmed that it had assumed a fashionable connotation by referring to "a pretty perking air which is infinitely nymphish and smart." The revival of classical costume and the relentless Attic attitudinizing of the Regency gave the term a new currency.

Like the creatures of myth, the Regency nymph sported in

treacherous waters, her title suggesting either the virgin charms she withheld or her more threatening aspect which drew her victims to account. It was not uncommonly applied to the "Cyprian" or "Fashionably Impure," the Regency whore. The nymph's subsequent history is one of decline. Her history of mantic powers and mythic charisma was diagnosed as mania, and suffered the indignity of preservation in treatises of sexual pathology. By 1859 the wet ones, as "nymphs of the pavement," essayed a new and seamier element. The later nineteenth century restored them to their proper element when the daughters of Ocean exchanged distaff for the scrub bucket, and "nymph" had become a euphemism for the London charlady.

CHAPTER SIX

Mistress of the Sounding Streams: "Endymion"

Praise ye, O maidens
her who delights in streams and the foliage of the groves.
Horace

There was never any so peevish to imagin the Moone
eyther capable of affectoun, or shape of a Mistris.   Lyly

After Apollo, who appears with greater frequency in Keats's poetry
than any of the Olympians, is his twin sister Diana, invoked in some
dozen poems.[1] Not since Michael Drayton and his contemporaries'
glorification of their virgin queen as Huntress had the goddess found so
ardent a follower. It seems unlikely, however, that Keats's ruling obses-
sions were divided between poetry and chastity, and certain that his
understanding of the complex nature of his goddess was more profound
than that single attribute implied. Artemis, Diana, Cynthia, Phoebe, or
Selene was, in fact, never worshipped, unless by Elizabethans, as an
exemplar of chastity; hers was a more profound and comprehensive
nature. Keats knew this, and his sonnet to Homer recognizes the goddess's triform nature as "Diana, Queen of Earth and Heaven and Hell,"
the same identification made by his Lemprière: "She was supposed to be
the same as the moon, and Proserpine or Hecate, and from that circumstance she was called Triformis, Terret, lustra, agit, Proserpina,
Luna, Diana, Inna, Supremas, and feras, sceptro, fulgone, saggita."[2]
Diana's many roles had long been celebrated in English poetry.
Drayton catalogued her titles in *Endymion and Phoebe*:

And now great Phoebe in her triumph comes
With all the tytles of her glorious name.
Diana, Delia, Lana, Cynthia,
Virago, Hecate, and Elythea

Protheria, Dictinna, Proserpine
Latona and Lucina.[3]

When Apollo was identified with Phoebus or Helios, it was inevitable that his twin sister would be cast in the role of the moon goddess Phoebe or Selene. Because of her changeable moon nature, and because she is assigned roles as protectress of earth, the night skies, and the underworld, Diana's character is highly paradoxical. She is associated with chastity and is a fierce upholder of its rule among her acolytes, but as effigies of the Ephesian Artemis Polymastos testify, she was also an Asian goddess of fertility.[4] As paramour of Endymion, she bore the narcoleptic shepherd some fifty daughters, testimony to her dexterity as much as her fecundity, a version of the myth which Keats left unexplored. Frazer pointed out that she was more preoccupied with the losing of virginity than its preservation, and with childbirth. She was venerated as the midwiving goddess Lucina or Ilithyia, since she had precociously assisted her mother's labour by delivering her twin brother. Unlike Apollo, Diana seems to have had no connection with music or poetry, other than a fondness for the dance, and she exhibited no oracular gifts. She is as benign as the moon, but a virago in her anger, never loath to inflict her brutal justice on erring mortals or nymphs. Her primitive cult in Sparta may have practised human sacrifice, which was in more humane times modified to mere flogging, and her grove at Aricia was bloodied with the ritual murders of priestly succession. These terrible aspects of the goddess's character correspond to part of her lunar nature: the unlucky days of the waning of the moon and the necromancy and mystery associated with its disappearance, when as Hecate or Proserpine she commands the powers of darkness.

Diana, standing a head taller than her retainers, is protectress and leader of the nymphs. Like them, she is associated with rivers and sacred wells, woodlands and hills, delighting in streams and leafy groves, as Horace described her.[5] She is Catullus's "lady of the mountains ... and / Of the rivers roaring."[6] She is Artemis Agrotera, the huntress, or Limnatis, the lady of the lake, or the Helean, lady of the bog. The goddess commands all those roles which naiads, dryads, and oreads exercised over their individual springs, streams, trees, and hills, and like the nymphs, she fosters human and natural kind, founding her shrines in spring-fed groves or grottoes where the water emerges from the rock, those places which powerfully express the mystery of the feminine creative nature and its power to bring forth life.

In less temperate climates, the fierce heat of the sun is hostile to human and natural life, and the sun's role as the giver of life is unknown. There it is the moon with its mysterious periodic rhythms and its association with seed-time and harvest which exercises the feminine power to command generation and fertility. "The moon," Plutarch wrote in *Isis and Osiris*, "having the light which makes moist and pregnant, is promotive of the generation of living things and the fructification of plants."[7] Moon goddesses like Diana and Ishtar were guardians of waters, as the tides, the rivers, brooks, and springs, or as the fertilizing dews. Artemis bore as did Ishtar before her the title "the all-dewy one," and her rites, the Hersephoria, were danced by Athenian maidens on nights of the full moon when dew-fall was heaviest.[8] The association of the feminine with moisture, darkness, fecundity, and the moon was as firmly secured in western mythology as it was in Chinese philosophy, where Yin, the feminine principle, is in direct opposition to the masculine principle of Yang. Yang is bright, hot, powerful creative energy, the power of the sun, while Yin is dark, moist, shadowy, and receptive, yet creative in that it gives birth and substance to the Yang energies. Keats knows his Diana's complex heritage, and *Endymion* unfolds the comprehensiveness of her rule through the language which poetry and myth command to dramatize the life of the psyche.

It is the god Pan, however, who presides over the opening scenes of Keats's poem, and whose rite occasions some of its finest poetry. Endymion, in spite of his dutiful attendance at woodland matins, is preoccupied and indifferent; the all-god fails to hold the young shepherd-king within his cult and his sway. Wordsworth was right, Keats's Hymn to Pan *is* a pretty piece of paganism, much too pretty for a religion of nature. It celebrates a conscientious pastoral deity who looks after the well-being and prosperity of his subjects. Pan is the bearer of all natural bounty, his responsibilities are homy and solicitous: he directs lost shepherds, cares for stray sheep, and preserves the grain from mildew, and even his fabled lusts are matters of dalliance rather than rape. His is a world of dawn and springtime, the conscious waking world of society, not unlike, as Keats admits, that of Chaucer and his pilgrims. Pan anticipates the Good Shepherd who would one day usurp his role. His sacred doings are interwoven with and a "leaven" to the lives and duties of men. On this occasion, his festival, the spiritual principle which is Pan informs the entire social nature of the observance. Dancing, pairing, rural games, and a sort of public confessional *cum catechism* in which each voices his inmost thoughts to his fellows and his priest speak of a world in which the sacred and the profane are neighbourly and compatible, where Pan's children live with unreflecting spontaneity. Their pastimes, their quoits and archery, are pursued with an awareness of the mythic analogues which gave them significance, tales of Hyacinthus and his foster mother the Huntress.[9] Here there is no inner life at odds with external circumstance, law, or destiny; all are reconciled within an order of nature which expresses and accommodates all human needs. It is a pastoral world in which Corinna might go a-maying, but of which Wordsworth's Michael knew nothing.

Only in the final stanza of the Hymn does Keats permit the god a dimension beyond the tame anthropomorphism afforded by "conception," but even the mystery of his transcendence serves and leavens human conduct. Even in Arcadia, tradition insists, lurk death and other incommodities, and the rural god, no matter how benign, also hides a dark and dreadful face. Where on these gentle slopes of Latmos is the riotous, frenetic Pan, the god of violent seizure, of rape and panic, the nameless terrors which Wordsworth knew were at one with the beauty of nature? The natural powers which paganism and its myths tried to grasp were not always obliging or pretty, and pastoral tradition, paganism's survivor and spokesman, preserves for us that sobering fact.

Endymion himself gives point to all this, since he alone stands aside: closed, inward, uncommunicative, bored to the point of extinction. He is on this morning as preoccupied with his night world and private dream as the unresponsive Madeline at the glittering ball of Saint Agnes's Eve. This inner night world speaks to him, not in the public language of rite and shepherd society, but in the compelling, private, and often disruptive language of dream. Endymion's confessor is Peona rather than Pan's priest, and his relationship to that shadowy unrealized figure who is at once sister, mother, guide, and nurse seems more psychic than consanguine. Peona, we are told repeatedly, is a guide, and she leads her somnolent charge, infantile in his passivity, to her own private and protected place, Peona's bowery isle. She has come to him while he sleeps or nods at his religious duties, and once they are enisled, she soothes him within her arms with a mother's lullaby, "as dove wings engender enduring love" in healing sleep. Peona is, as her name asserts, a healer, although her art is circumscribed, and she can offer no more than the temporary comfort of restorative sleep. Her influence on Endymion belongs to the early scenes, before his journey commences, but she is the first of many female figures who will guide him in his wanderings. The private paths they trace lead invariably toward the goddess, away from the god Pan and his patriarchal shepherd world. Their way lies within, within the womb of earth and within the unconscious world which is not subject to the *logos* of the god, but commanded by the feminine creatures who guard the dark recesses, the well-springs of instinct and action.

In his entry into Madeline's labyrinthine castle, Porphyro too encounters a guide, the wise old crone Angela who was once his nurse, with him, as it were, from the beginning. Angela is both psychopomp and palsy-twitch'd old woman; she is as real as Juliet's nurse and will share a natural death, but will lead her charges, the lovers, to a charmed escape from that ignominy. Like Angela, Peona exists at a conscious level of experience, but, through her association with sleep and its healing powers, she stands at the threshold of the unconscious world into which her brother must descend, to which sleep and dream give their fitful access. Her anxious inquiries as to the nature of Endymion's condition are framed in terms of the *logoi* of the conscious world (as are Angela's practical fears). She frets that he has "sinned," violated a law or taboo by viewing Diana at her bath or by hunting her sacred beasts, but she also arms her brother for his descent by the exercise of her healing powers, and like a dutiful psychoanalyst hears out his troubling dreams. Endymion's second glimpse of his goddess is mirrored within Latona's well, which he has known intimately since childhood, and which is associated with his sister, since it was here that he gathered, since childhood, flowers for Peona.

Endymion relates his successive epiphanies to his sister, and the imagery declares unambigously to all but its dreamer the presence and attributes of the goddess throughout these and all subsequent encounters. Endymion is not only somnolent, but slow-witted. Diana is present from the outset, and Peona, uncomprehending, but acting upon her instincts as woman, prepares her brother for his journey to her.

Rivers and streams wind an intricate and confounding course throughout the entire poem. The Panaeum of book one takes place beside a spring; Peona leads her brother between converging streams to her isle, and Endymion will pursue a skein of rivers into and throughout the underworld, to emerge where all streams end, in Ocean. The river on which he first embarks with his sister winds to the further end of the Latmian wood, where it sweeps into a semblance of the crescent moon. It is within the embrace of that crescent that Endymion finds the nuptial bed of poppy and dittany sacred to Diana of the horned moon.[10] This is the place, if not of hierogamy, of hierophany, the foreshadowing of their pleasures by means of a dizzying erotic flight, followed by the awakening to dawn and a dew-bedabbled poppy bed: "All the pleasant hues / Of heaven and earth had faded" (1.691–2). This post-visionary or post-coital desolation establishes a recurrent pattern throughout *Endymion*, but it is recognizable as a paradigmatic crisis in Romantic narrative in general. The scene's most obvious analogue, perhaps even its progenitor, is in Shelley's *Alastor*, when the hero wakes to cold dawn after the disturbing eroticism of his dream of the Indian Maid: "Wither have fled / The hues of heaven that canopied his bower / of yesternight?" (*Alastor*, 196–8). The situation need not be erotic in content. In *The Prelude* the desolation is occasioned by the disruptive assertion of unfathomable mystery in the midst of a boy's childish round of pleasures, effectively shattering that familiar world through a profound disorientation: "No familiar shapes / Remained, no pleasant images of trees / Of sea or sky, no colours of green fields ..." (1.395–7).

The goddess's second epiphany within or near the precincts of her mother Latona's temple establishes her as Artemis, the mother goddess of the Ephesians. The moss-fleeced well holding the element of life, the familiar sanctuary of the goddess and her nymphs, and the presence of the winged Eros speak of her procreative and generative nature. The moment and its passing are explicitly linked to the earlier encounter "when I wander'd from the poppy hill" (1.914). Again the epiphany is accompanied by the "all-dewy one" 's signature, a life-giving dew-fall at the improbable hour of midday, "Bathing my spirit in new delight." Noon is hardly dew-time, but it is the hour when gods and nymphs are afoot, when their temples are shut, and when it is hazardous to seek the shade by streams or springs. It is the dangerous hour when a glimpse of the guardians may craze the viewer.

A third meeting is occasioned by Endymion's following a brook that he has stumbled upon to its source within the mouth of a cave: "Overhead, / Hung a lush screen of drooping weeds, and spread / Thick, as to curtain up some wood-nymph's home" (1.939–41). Endymion guesses that it is the cave of the nymph Echo, or of the maid Proserpine when she mounts to the upper air in her yearly *anados*. Endymion has chosen figures associated or identified with Diana: Echo as nymph, and Proserpine, who, as Drayton and Lemprière maintained, represents the chthonic aspect of the goddess in her role as consort of the underworld. The voice from the cave seems to assert the claims of the nymph, and yet it compares the mysterious nature of the place with Delos, birthplace of Artemis and Apollo. With welcome discretion, Keats lowers his hymeneal screen of drooping weeds, and we are spared yet another account of their union. Welcome perhaps, but as a consequence the scene is dramatically inept. Keats carefully develops it and then perfunctorily dismisses the action with "Ah! where / Are those swift moments? Wither are they fled?", the familiar refrain which gives way to the inevitable questioning of the nature of what has passed and what remains (1.970–1). Endymion, with adolescent gravity, proposes a life of "demurest meditation" rather than of sensation, and we recognize a foretaste of the Keatsian paradigm in which, tolled back to his sole self, the dreamer or lover is capable of reflection only because of his distance from the all-absorbing moment, a distance at which he can weigh the contrasting claims of the dream and of reality.

The descent of the skyey Cynthia to the shepherd on his poppied rise, the goddess's image within Latona's well, and the encounter with the creature who tends or embodies the source establish through her manifestations the uranian, the chthonic, and the generative aspects of the goddess. Artemis rules earth and sky as Wordsworth's Lucy, violet and star beside her springs of Dove, ruled the world of her lover and elegist.

The remaining mythological configurations in Endymion's descent into the underworld and undersea are similarly expressive of Diana in her multiple aspects and roles. Our awareness of this fact, however, outstrips Endymion's. In spite of the nature of the last two encounters, it would seem that he persists in recognizing his lady only as moon, woodland queen, and leader of the nymphs, and is yet ignorant of her as queen of the underworld, just as he is unaware of Diana's nature as goal of the inner journey which he has reluctantly undertaken into the unessayed regions of his own subconscious. Consequently, in order to join his moon goddess, Endymion dim-wittedly proposes to scale her airy element; he would fly before he can walk with certainty. The way, as his new guide, the butterfly transformed into the nymph Echo, indicates, lies down; Endymion must seek out the well-springs, the sources of human and natural life.

On first entering this world, Endymion sees a shrine and effigy of the Huntress, and fails to recognize that these establish her sovereignty over the dim regions which are about to unfold. She is yet, to Endymion's reckoning, a creature solely of the upper air.

O Haunter chaste
Of river sides, and woods, and heathy waste,
...
O woodland Queen,
What smoothest air thy smoother forehead woos?
Where dost thou listen to the wide halloos
Of thy disparted nymphs? Through what dark tree
Glimmers thy crescent? (2.302-3, 305-8)

This journey down and within seems to Endymion perverse and misdirected: "Young goddess! Let me see my native bowers! / Deliver me from this rapacious deep" (2.331-2). Once the descent or journey is undertaken, even though by accident or misdirection, the deeps are indeed rapacious; so is his lady, its presiding goddess. Her demand, the demand of his own inner nature, once undertaken, is unrelenting. Endymion must descend, as all must descend, without bearings into the darkness; he must feel his way to the heart of the dark mystery to which only his instincts offer access. His progress through a maze of caverns and a snarl of rivers is scarcely chartable, and Keats deliberately confounds our spatial orientation as much as his hero's. We are left to read episode and indirections mythically, by surrendering to the peculiar logic of dream, the irresistible compulsion in which grottoed suite leads to suite, river to waterfall, source to stream to its demise within even more profound depths. The goddess is glimpsed through a swelling cast of avatars, and she is no less bewildering than the landscape to waking logic, as she insistently and repeatedly asserts her ineluctable nature. The Huntress is first among Keats's cruel mistresses: the Lamias and Belles Dames, deceiving elves whose absolute demand, along with our failure to meet it, is not their perversity but our inadequacy, the human failure to submit wholly to the logic of feeling or of imagination, and to gain entry to the heart of the mystery, the adyton where we, like Adam, might awake to find dream become truth.

As if in reply to Endymion's misguided plea for deliverance from the depths, the next scene unfolds at the goddess's behest, to the accompaniment of her "dew-dropping melody," and the wanderer finds himself within the Cave of Adonis. The riot of vegetation identifies Adonis as the living and dying fertility god, and Keats uses the myrtle sacred to Aphrodite in the same way he used dittany as emblematic of Diana. Aphrodite enters drawn by her doves. Her entrance is conventional enough in its iconography, but the doves sacred to Aphrodite have already been associated with the other principals, Peona and Diana, whose feminine influence has progressively undermined, or deepened, the limited patriarchal world of Pan. Doves were among the attributes of the mother goddess herself, as they were of Artemis the Ephesian, and of Aphrodite in her life-giving role as genetrix.

After admiring the subterranean *jeu d'eaux*, Endymion witnesses the majestic progress of Cybele. "To Him," as Gray wrote, "the mighty Mother did unveil / Her awful face."[11] The mural-crowned mother, who shared her Phrygian corona with the Ephesian and whose Cretan titles Britomartis and Diktynna were identified with Artemis, is the most unambiguous epiphany of the goddess in her chthonic guise, and introduces a further redaction of the motif of the love of a goddess for her lover-son who will aspire to and share her immortality. Like Aphrodite and Adonis, Cybele and her consort Attis adumbrate the inevitable union of Diana and Endymion.

Endymion is granted a third union with Diana. As in the cave of Echo, he first recognizes her as a nereid. The mating is suitably but distressingly lubricous, detailing the "slippery blisses" at "pleasure's nipple" which Keats's lowering curtain of drooping weeds tactfully elided in the Echo episode. An abandoned and downcast Endymion then follows the twin courses of springs which rise at his feet. Eavesdropping on the rushing streams' conversation, he hears Arethusa and

Alpheus recount their history. Keats's telling of the myth has Arethusa in a dither of indecision, willing to yield to Alpheus, but fearful of the judgment of "Great Dian, Oread Queen." She threatens the river god with a punishment at the hands of her mistress as debilitating as that which unmanned the Phrygian Attis:

> Cruel god,
> Desist! or my offended mistress' nod
> Will stagnate all thy fountains. (2.952–4)

Alpheus, who was once reckless enough to attempt an assault on the virgin goddess herself, holds out some hope that the unbending Huntress might weary of her buskins: "Dian's self must feel / Sometimes these very pangs" (2.984–5). But that moment has not yet arrived, and the fountain nymph cries: "What can I do, Alpheus? Dian stands / Severe before me: persecuting fate" (2.1005–6). The streams, divided, plunge into the abyss, and Endymion prays to his lady to extend her mercy. He, like Arethusa, now knows all too well her severity. He has known his goddess's waxings and wanings, the embracing fullness of her love and the stunning loss inflicted by her absence, the dark of his moon, and yet he seems to grasp that, contrary to the conflicting testimony of her caprice and cruelty, hers is a benevolent presence, the "gentle Goddess of my pilgrimage" (2.1014).

In book three, this dawning recognition is reaffirmed in the extended apostrophe to the moon in which Endymion speaks of those "thousand Powers [who] keep religious state, / In water, fiery realm, and airy bourne" (3.30–1), and from these powers he identifies one:

> I here swear,
> Eterne Apollo! that thy Sister fair
> Is of all these the gentlier-mightiest. (3.41–3)

Endymion has glimpsed the doubled visage of her power, Dian's mailed fist within its velvet glove, but his speech reveals that he understands more: that of all powers, Diana is paramount, because she comprehends all contradictions within herself. Endymion's speech extends her aegis from the realm of the sleeping earth of book two to the watery element of book three, where the welling tides are as responsive to her moon as the earth to her sway.

> The mighty deeps,
> The monstrous sea is thine – the myriad sea!
> O Moon! far-spooming Ocean bows to thee,
> And Tellus feels his forehead's cumbrous load. (3.68–71)

Endymion recalls the moony influences which fostered life and sensibility in his youth. The argument is equivalent to Wordsworth's apostrophes to nurse Nature and her lore, or Shelley's description of his childhood tutelage under Intellectual Beauty.

> When yet a child
> I oft have dried my tears when thou hast smil'd
> Thou seem'dst my sister: hand in hand we went
> From eve to morn across the firmament. (3.143–6)

The relation of moon to moon-child is indeed as sisterly as that of Peona, the first of Endymion's guides. Unlike Shelley, who shunned personifying the awesome abstraction of Intellectual Beauty, Keats humanizes this formulative power, scaling it to the natural and the childhood world. The moon nourished him: "No apples would I gather from the tree, / Till thou hadst cooled their cheeks deliciously." She was the messenger of all beauty: "No tumbling water ever spake romance / But when my eyes with thine thereon could dance." As well as beauty and pleasure, she fostered what Pan had neglected, pain and perhaps terror: "Yes, in my boyhood, every joy and pain / By thee were fashioned to the self-same end" (3.164–9). Here at last was a schooling Wordsworth might recognize. Keats's imagery is precipitated in a headlong Shelleyan rush to embrace the whole range of all possible experience:

> Thou wast the mountain-top – the sage's pen –
> The poet's harp – the voice of friends – the sun;
> Thou wast the river – thou wast glory won;
> Thou wast my clarion's blast – thou wast my steed –
> My goblet full of wine – my topmost deed: –
> Thou wast the charm of women, lovely Moon! (3.164–9)

The transformations, mutations, and adumbrations of the goddess which people the first three books of *Endymion* prepare us for her penultimate appearance in book four as the Indian Maid; yet this figure has offended many of Keats's readers, who see her as suggesting bad faith on Endymion's part, a stumble in his ascent toward the perfection of his goddess. These qualms have been a trouble to those who prefer to read the poem as an allegorical progress toward achieved perfection, each encounter serving to strengthen resolution or emending a moral weakness, as if Keats's shepherd prince were essaying admission to the Celestial city, Abraham's rather than Diana's bosom.

The elaborate masquings of a dramatis personae which, when

unmasked, reveals a cast of one suggest the highly complex psycho-machia of *Prometheus Unbound*, or, on a more modest scale, the complementary twinned natures of Coleridge's Geraldine and Christabel. The psychomachia, the projection and dramatization of the psychological attributes of a single individual, accommodated the psychological and metaphysical probings of Romantic narrative and framed its characteristic monodramatic form. Keats would return to it on a more manageable scale in *Lamia*, in which the antagonists within their triangular scenario enact the divided impulses of the central and perhaps the only character, Lycius. But *Lamia* is an exercise in the sort of formal discipline which *Endymion* eschewed, an attempt to achieve a dramatic form whose architecture is comparatively lean and unusually symmetrical.

The pace and narrative thrust of *Endymion* are less than compelling, and the finest of its excesses seem devised to allay breathlessness. Indeed the poem luxuriates in the leisure afforded by Keats's proposal that it unfold as expansively as the progress of three seasons. The miraculous inventiveness of episode and language which are the poem's glories undermine its architecture. There is no satisfying narrative thread to be traced in *Endymion*. Events, their causes and consequences, within a recognizable configuration of time and space, are as confounding as the poem's tangle of rivers, its underworld and undersea topography, and its deliberate blurring of dream with reality and dream within dream. The reader, casting about for his bearings, is hard put to determine whether and when his hero wakes or sleeps, or whether it matters. The narcoleptic Endymion is the Romantic dream quester *par excellence*, and his progress, such as it is, is no more physically active than that of Shelley's Prometheus, whose struggle and victory are enacted while the hero is splayed on the Caucasian talus. The questor, as it were, stands still. His name, "Endymion," means one who finds himself within. He is acted upon while events happen to him; landscapes unfold about him and are transformed in response to the inner transformation through which the hero moves toward a conscious recognition of the face of a truth which he and the reader have seen but darkly from the outset. The goddess acquires the dimensions of an all-embracing reality which transforms utterly all external circumstance, Endymion's waking world as well as that of his dreams.

Although the habit of reducing gods and goddesses to a single ur-figure, often of a solar character, or of discovering in each and every goddess of the pantheon the shadowy presence of the *magna mater* is generally associated with anthropological or psychological approaches to myth belonging to a period later than that of Keats, there was in his day, and earlier, no dearth of speculative attempts to submit the confusing genealogies of the gods to the government of reason or the over-riding efficacy of a single presiding deity or principle. In 1840, Müller, who rejected Apollo's status as a comprehensive solar deity, died of sunstroke at Delphi. Nonetheless, solar theories of godhead have fallen into disrepute, though Müller was neither the first nor the last to pursue them. The shadowy embrace of the Great Mother was recognized among her avatars in the classical pantheon long before the inquiries of Bachofen and Jung.

Among the most influential of the mythic syncretists of his day was Jacob Bryant, who argued in *A New System: or, the Analysis of Ancient Mythology* that all gods and goddesses were one personage, that their cults were degenerate forms of sun-worship, and that sun-worship itself was a degenerate form of the Israelite worship of one God. All mythologies were but a faint and warped recollection of antediluvian belief. Attempts to reconstruct the ur-myth were a con-tinuing preoccupation in the eighteenth century, since the congeries of gods and heroes and their tangled genealogies were a challenge to the rational image of a classical world. Bryant's stupefyingly massive researches, based on a fanciful investigation of word roots, fired Blake's imagination, and probably exerted considerably more than an indirect influence on Keats and his circle. Bryant's volumes explored subjects dear to the heart of a Romantic writer, particularly Keats. Volume one of *A System* considers the importance of rivers and fountains in all mythologies, and in the section "Worship paid at Caverns" Bryant explores the sanctity of the *temenos*, the innermost recess of temple or cavern, and in connection with this subject contributes a generous fund of information to contemporary lore concerning nymphs.

The question of the range and depth of Keats's acquaintance with classical mythology I reserve for consideration at the close of the next chapter, which follows the traces of Diana and her retinue through the landscape of Keats's Crete and Corinth and into mythologies other than classical.

CHAPTER SEVEN

Diana's Train:
Lamia, Belles Dames, and
Deceiving Elves

> Where is thy celebrated beauty, Doric Corinth? Where
> are the battlements of thy towers and thy ancient posses-
> sions? Where are the temples of the immortals, the horses
> and the matrons of the town of Sisyphus, and her myriads
> of people? Not even a trace is left of thee, most unhappy
> of towns, but war has seized on and devoured everything.
> We alone, the Nereids, Ocean's daughters, remain invio-
> late, and lament, like Halcyons, thy sorrows.
>
> The Greek Anthology

Keats's *Lamia* harbours one and possibly two nymphs. Of Herse, the
object of Hermes' attentions, there is no question; Keats identifies her as
a nymph, as did his sources. The poet is specific: Herse is a naiad or
river nymph identified with her charge, from her inland head or hidden
source in the Cretan highland to her feet, where she is received by the
foaming sea.

A nymph, to whom all hoofed Satyrs knelt:
At whose white feet the languid Tritons poured
Pearls, while on land they wither'd and adored.
Fast by the spring where she to bathe was wont,
And in those meads where sometimes she might haunt ... (1.14–17).

Herse testifies to Keats's especial mastery of personification. Here, as
with the presence of Autumn in her granary, he summons a creature
mediate between a natural landscape and a subtle evocation of human
form, as if an expressive feature of the landscape were endowed with an
elusive and pervasive female presence which refuses to coalesce into a
defined image. Herse is Keats's unique response to the challenge of her
mythic kind, the naiad who both dwells within and is identical with the
features of her river or stream.

The Homeric hymn to Aphrodite sings of these deep-breasted mountain nymphs of Cretan Ida: "with them the Silenoi and the quick-eyed slayer of Argos [Hermes] mate in love, deep in the pleasant caves."[1] But, the virgin Herse, through Lamia's necromancy, is hidden, a *fons ignote* as well as *signatus*, so that Hermes is unable to find his way to her chaste bed. Nymphs were loath to entertain the brusque attentions of Pan, satyrs, and silenoi, whose hirsute charms and attributes advertised their ruttish motives. Their reluctance to mate was attributed to their loyalty to the virgin Huntress Artemis, and was a gall to the ministrations of Eros, who urges them in the *Dionysiaca* into the service of his mother's cult.

Fountains also have known my shafts. I need not teach you of love in the waters; you have heard of the watery passion of Syracusan Aerthusa, that love-stricken fountain; you have heard of Alpheios, who in a watery bower embraces the indwelling nymph with watery hands. You – the offspring of a fountain – why are you pleased with the archeress? ... You ought rather to please Cypris.[2]

The plight of naiads and dryads before the arrows of Eros was familiar to Keats, who related the trials of Arethusa, Syrinx, and Daphne. There is every indication, moreover, that Lamia herself belongs with that watery breed rather than with the nursery bogies which her name customarily evokes; hence her sisterly concern for the vulnerable young Herse. Artemis, as Nonnus, Callimachus, and others maintained, preferred the company of like-minded maidens, recognizing that chastity's surest defence lay in numbers.[3] To that end she gathered her train of sixty nymphs, or sixty Oceanides and twenty Cretan naiads by some accounts, single-minded devotees of her hunt and celibacy. Arethusa was among these, and was delivered through the goddess's intercession from the impetuous rush of Alpheus. Daphne and Syrinx, both river daughters, were rescued from similar fates by hasty metamorphoses. Artemis was less sympathetically disposed, however, to those of her own company who, like Callisto, willingly transgressed their vows. Callisto was transformed into a bear, the victim of the hunt. Perhaps Keats's Lamia was among those who entertained Eros's shaft and suffered as punishment a disagreeable metamorphosis at the hands of the angry goddess. The "penanced lady elf" is not merely associated with, but clearly emblematic of, night and the rule of Diana as Selene or Phoebe. Her markings, "full of silver moons, that, as she breathed, / Dissolv'd or brighter shone," and crest of "wannish fire / Sprinkled with stars" (1.50–1, 57–8) are the heraldry of the moon goddess, and the shifting, fractured images are all suggestive of darting reflections within a moonlit stream.[4] The serpent prison is an appropriate metamorphosis for a creature of the stream, a naiad of Artemis's train. The serpent is the inevitable figuring of the winding flow and gathering which mark a stream's progress. The names of the Greek rivers Ophis and Ladon both signified a snake, and Hesiod described the Cephissus as flowing through Orchomenus "in winding serpent coils."[5] At her wedding feast Lamia is offered an appropriate garland, adder's tongue and the willow, the riverside tree sacred to the Artemis worshipped at Sparta, where her image was bound with withies and venerated within a willow grove.

Among those far-flung places which Lamia is able to visit in her dreams is the homeland of Ocean, father of all nymphs, where "Down through tress-lifting waves the Nereids fair / Wind into Thetis' bower by many a pearly stair" (1.207–8). Lamia's father, according to Plutarch, was Poseidon.[6] If Keats did not know Plutarch's tract "The Oracles at Delphi," the information was available to him in Bryant's *A New System*.[7]

Lycius, on first seeing Lamia, greets her as one of the race of nymphs, perhaps because the encounter takes place near the Pierean rills where the nymph Pierene wept herself into a fountain in sorrow for her son Cenchreae, who was slain by the Huntress. The renovated Lamia disposes herself like mother Eve, preening her newly created charms before a mirroring pool.

> Stay! though a Naiad of the rivers, stay!
> To thy far wishes will thy streams obey:
> Stay! though the greenest woods be thy domain,
> Alone they can drink up the morning rain. (1.261–4)

Her woodland course, Lycius implies, must make do with nurturing rain in her absence. Meanwhile she will serve as inexhaustible nourishment to the stricken novice, who proposes to live on love, whose eyes had "drunk her beauty up, / Leaving no drop in the bewildering cup, / And still the cup was full" (1.251–3). Lycius tries again to identify his lady. He still insists upon her identity as nymph, and reveals himself as much a student of Corinthian lore as of nymphology.

> Though a descended Pleiade, will not one
> Of thine harmonious sisters keep in tune
> Thy spheres, and as thy silver proxy shine? (1.265–7)

The flattering proposition is perfectly appropriate to the occasion and the place, and to the young Corinthian. The miracle is that it occurred to Keats. Of the Atlantides, who were translated at death into the Pleiades, only one deigned to descend and mate with a mortal, and she, the nymph Merope, chose Sisyphus, king and founder of the city of Corinth.

The allegiance to Diana that Lamia's form and markings betoken vanishes as her stars are licked up and crescents eclipsed in the searing blight of her metamorphosis, "as the lava ravishes the meads," the water meadows congenial to Lamia, her kind, and their mistress.[8] Lamia's impromptu Corinthian palace preserves a dim memory of her watery world arrested in its sea of cold marble, but the silver lamp which presides over her threshold is emblematic, not of the eclipsed crescent of Diana, but of the lone star of the sea which is Aphrodite's.

> Where hung a silver lamp, whose phosphor glow
> Reflected in the slabbed steps below,
> Mild as a star in water; for so new,
> And so unsullied was the marble's hue,
> So through the crystal polish, liquid fine,
> Ran the dark veins, that none but feet divine
> Could e'er have touched there. (1.380-6)

Lamia has responded, as she may have done in the past, to the prompt-ings of Eros and transferred her allegiance to the goddess of love. Her efforts to recreate a green recessed wood, an ersatz counterpart of the Cretan setting which accommodated the consummation of Hermes and Herse, include a stream of lamps flowing through a mock glade, but for all her ingenuity, the appointments are lavishly claptrap with groves of sham palm and plantain and groaning tables more reminiscent of a Prince Regent's banquet at Brighton Pavilion than the tender trap of an Acrasia's bower.

Lamia appears to have suffered a drastic sea change in her flight from pastoral Crete to urban Corinth, where she is clearly out of her element in spite of her unconvincing claims that the city is her home. The fascination and menacing undertones which accompanied her in Crete and followed her even on the road from Cenchreas have been forgot-ten. We are reminded of her deceptive nature only through her lies to Lycius, but these are harmless lover's lies framed to veil her past, and the Cretan serpent has become a memory no more threatening than the conventional skeletons in every lover's cupboard. Lamia's account of her first sight of Lycius is cunningly devised to align their love with all those fabled, irresistible loves undertaken at Venus's temple porch: Troilus and his Criseyde, Hero and her Leander, or, when the temple became Santa Clara and the feast Paschal rather than Adonian,

Petrarch and his Madonna Laura. These spectres of lovers past and yet to come serve to veil the true nature of the jaded dealings at the porch of Aphrodite's Corinthian temple. Corinth was the city of love and the home of Lais, most celebrated of history's courtesans. According to Strabo, Aphrodite's temple boasted a thousand sacred prostitutes who practised unimaginable refinements in the arts of love.[9] In Alciphron the Rhetor's imaginary *Letters of Courtesans*, a communication from the Courtesans in Corinth to their Athenian sisters details Lais's triumphs. "There is one woman now who has all Greece agog – just one: Lais in the barber shops, Lais in the theatres, in the assemblies, in the courts, in the council chamber, everywhere. All men have her on their tongues, by Aphrodite, and the deaf and dumb nod her beauty to one another; so does Lais give speech even to those who cannot talk."[10] Plato, in *The Republic*, used the phrase "Corinthian girl" as synonymous with prostitute, and not for nothing did Saint Paul discharge two canonical epistles addressed to Corinth's Christians: "It is actually reported that there is fornication among you, and such fornication as is not found even among the Gentiles. ... Do you not know that he who cleaves to a harlot becomes one body with her?"[11] Small wonder that Lycius furtively conceals his lady from the eyes of his moral tutor, Apollonius, in the twilight streets of Corinth. Did Keats know that among the letters of Alciphron's *grandes horizontales* Phryne and Thais were those of one Lamia, Athenian courtesan and lavish hostess?

The opening lines of part two of Keats's poem with their jarring note of Byronic cynicism effectively deflate the mythic context of the Cretan setting and transport the action to crowded, commercial Corinth. Lamia has left Crete to become a compliant courtesan in what looks suspiciously like a luxurious bagnio under the sign of Aphrodite in the city dedicated to the refinement of her arts. What Lamia preserves of Diana's cult of chastity merely serves to compound her appeal; chastity has become a desirable commodity pressed into the service of the erotic: "A virgin purest lipp'd, yet in the lore / Of love deep learn'd to the red heart's core." Lamia is all things to all men: innocence and experience, age and youth, nun and whore, and "of sciential brain / To unperplex bliss from its neighbour pain" (1.189–92). She offers a love of greater finesse than the most cunning of her city's courtesans. Matters have gone seriously awry since the meddling trumpet clarion "from the slope side of a suburb hill" first dispelled the lovers' cloistered idyll, a threat averted in "The Eve of St. Agnes" by the simple expedient of closing the door. The buzz which remains in Lycius's head, as unnerving as the buzz of the *putto* like a jealous hornet at their lintel, precipitates a scene which suggests that Keats's comic instincts lie not far beneath the surface:

she began to moan and sigh
Because he mused beyond her, knowing well
That but a moment's thought is passion's passing bell.
"Why do you sigh, fair creature?" whispered he ... (2.37–40)

Lamia urgently counters with her variation on the perennial lovers' question: "Why do you think?"

All might have succeeded with the lovers, Lycius claims, had he shared Lamia's expertise:

How to entangle, trammel up and snare
Your soul in mine, and labyrinth you there
Like the hid scent in an unbudded rose? (2.52–4)

Love, literary tradition insists, is more at home in the rose-bed than the conjugal. The unbudded rose is plucked from the bed of images with which Keats consistently portrays the dalliance of immortals or those special human beings whose perishable loves have been "saved by miracle." Herse, "self-enfolding like a flower," and Madeline abed "as though a rose should shut and be a bud again," enact their eager passage from modest innocence to the embrace of experience. Madeline and her lover engage "as the rose / Blendeth its odour with the violet," while the nymph "Bloomed and gave up her honey to the lees," their awakening carnality promising the perfected love of unfulfilled fulfilment, the eternity of passion of which mere mortals can only dream.

Lycius's proposal, however, is framed by the forked tongue of mortality, and we are aware that the role of the predator is displaced. His words describing his dream of fulfilment, "entangle, trammel up and snare," are an eerie echo of those of the narrator describing Lamia when she still exercised something of her predatory nature, waylaying "the life she had so tangled in her mesh." No longer the serpent, she is the victim of the youth who proposes to flaunt their private and perishable mysteries in a gaudy fling through the streets of Corinth.

Theirs is a dulled affair. The eternal honeymoon promised Hermes and Herse, Porphyro and Madeline, has yielded to the prosaic mortal dilemma, *post coitum tristitia*. Whether pursued in palace or hut, the narrator confides, the course of mortal love is undeviating, even comic in its predictable banality. Lamia has lost all trace of the *frisson* of threat and horror which gave their affair its risky fascination. She is scarcely the beguiling predator Philostratus described as engaged in "fattening up Menippus the Lycian with dainties so that she might devour his body."[12] Her preparations for the banqueting chamber are suggestive of the caterer's rather than the sorcerer's arts, and she is reduced to a fretting, disillusioned suburban matron who, having passed the first flush of romance, finds distraction by redecorating the house and pettishly arranging a party for her husband's associates. Without struggle or any attempt to redirect events, she seems to succumb to what she knows is inevitable, and her weary compliance hints that she, like Keats's La Belle Dame Sans Merci, may indeed have seen and enacted all this before. La Belle Dame weeps with helpless foreknowledge of where this latest episode in her perennial career will lead. Coleridge's Geraldine, soul-sister to Keats's ladies, exhibits the same weary *déjà vu*.

Their literary type, or archetype, is familiar enough, and Keats assumes its familiarity among his readers. Both Lamia and his Belle Dame bring to their poems a bad press, the fabulously destructive reputation of the *femme fatale*. Keats ensures this by quoting Burton's *Philostratus* and by preserving the title of the Alain Chartier poem. In spite of the borrowed *frisson* which they bring from their literary forebears, Keats's ladies are disclosed as disarmingly benign, as if, having advertised their traditional role, the poet must deliberately dispel or undermine that reputation. There is nothing in Keats's ballad that accuses La Belle Dame of being wilfully and perversely *sans merci*. The knight's disruptive warning dream is his own, and as such scarcely permits us to accept it as an objective account of the proceedings. It is a dramatization of the dreamer's own fears and inadequacies, and we are unable to judge whether they are reliable or not. The description of the lady's contentious sidelong glance intimates no more of stealth or calculation than did Keats's application of the phrase to his Kentuckian sister-in-law Georgiana, attributing to her the disarming modesty which his generation prized in the celebrated turn of head of the Venus di Medici. Moreover, a more direct glance might have tumbled the elfin lady from her knight's charger.

It is unnecessary to identify the fairy child of "La Belle Dame Sans Merci" with the naiad of classical mythology, although the family resemblance is strong and her haunts are the familiar settings of meads or water-meadows.[13] She is, Keats maintains, of the naiad's progeny, the usurpers which the opening lines of *Lamia* identify as the fairy brood who "drove Nymph and Satyrs from the prosperous woods." She traffics with knights errant rather than fledgling Platonists, but enacts the same role. The Cretan has become a Celt; her context is the Celtic folklore which enriched the middle ages and preserved her family resemblance to her elder sisters. The lovely lady of Keats's poem is scarcely the loathly lady of balladry or the false Duessa of Spenserian romance, but one of the race the Irish knew as the Sidhe, the immortal children of Dana whose dwellings "were in the depths of the earth, in hills, or under ridges more or less elevated." Keats's Endymion proposed to live with his Indian maid "Under the brow / Of some steep mossy hill" (4.670–1), like the knight-at-arms, within the *mons veneris*, but instead wins the heights with his goddess on a loftier Latmian mount.

Such creatures commonly take mortals as their lemans and offer them love and immortality, an immortal love. There is nothing deceptive or arbitrarily cruel in their offers or their motives unless it is to extend a call to a love of such perfection that it can be entertained only in dream. The nature of such love, to Keats's doubting knight, is as incomprehensible as the language of his immortal lady.

The *femme fatale*, as Keats dramatizes her, reveals an insight into the nature of that role which could scarcely be served by the traditional bogy, the lamia who indulged her appetites on plump children rather than Platonists. The true *femme fatale*, as Keats knew her, merely goes about the business of being herself. Whether she is Keats's Lady, Coleridge's Geraldine, Wedekind's Lulu, or Heinrich Mann's Lola Lola, she is culpable by all conceivable moral standards, but these scarcely apply to one who is wholly unaware of their existence. She is neither ravening nor destructive, merely self-sufficient and surpassingly, fatally, desirable.

To pass an eternity awakening on one's fair love's ripening breast, or even within her elfin grot, risks considerably more than a stiff neck; indeed it is to embrace more than mortality affords, although this scarcely inhibits our readiness to dream of the possibility. To lie with eternity is by all mortal calculations to lie with death, and our unsettling awareness of this mistranslation of eternity into our world of time renders such moments both dangerous and threatening. Such reckonings permit the simple alternative: "and so live for ever – or swoon to death." The numinous moment of dream having passed, the visionary can only conclude from his temporal perspective that he has "been half in love with easeful Death," and be plagued by his awareness of "aching Pleasure nigh, / Turning to Poison while the bee-mouth sips."

The element of danger which is compellingly dramatized by the knight's nightmare or the veiled threat which haunts Lamia's past provides the *frisson* which must accompany the demand to love. In "The Eve of St. Agnes" the threat is externalized, so that it lies not within the relationship itself but within the larger precincts of the castle, with Hildebrand and his bloodthirsty crew, with the sleeping dragons which guard the labyrinth of thresholds, corridors, and mounting stairs. Finally, it is in the outer world of winter storm, wintry age, and ignoble death. These are the hazards, the perilous seas which must be crossed to reach the ripening promise of a mythic rather than geographic south.

✒ OUT OF THE RIVER AND
UNDER THE HILL

Nymphes and faunes apoun every side
Qwilk Farefolkens or than Elfis clepenwe. Gavin Douglas

The location of the initial encounter in Keats's poems is a familiar one and notably dampish: the meads bordering the sedgy lake, the river nymph's hidden bed unveiled by Lamia's powers for Hermes' eyes, the poolside where Lamia meets Lycius, the place where the narrator first encounters Cupid and Psyche "In deepest grass ... where there ran / A brooklet scarce espied: / Mid hushed, cool-rooted flowers" (10–13). Such places were known to the ancients and to the medieval world, and were remembered by folklore and by Renaissance writers such as Michael Drayton.

In Meadowes, and in Marshes found
Of them so call'd the Fayrie ground,
Of which they have the keeping.[14]

The labyrinthine wood of verdurous glooms and winding mossy ways in which the poet of the Nightingale ode is exiled, after his brief experience of paradise with its "melodious plot of beechen green," offers him the "coming musk rose full of dewy wing." It is within the embrace of a winding, partly hidden river, on a bed of flowers sacred to Diana, that Endymion first dreams of his perfected love, to awake with the poppies hanging "Dewdabbled on their stalks." Small wonder an unsympathetic and mythologically obtuse Byron excoriated the "self-pollutings of John Piss-a-bed Keats."[15] We first encounter Madeline "hoodwink'd with faery fancy," and we are permitted a fleeting glimpse of her disrobing, when she appears to Porphyro in that most improbable of settings as the most unlikely of creatures, "a mermaid in sea-weed."

There is a weighty body of esoteric speculation on the subject of humidity and the soul, from Thales through Heraclitus to the Neoplatonists, preserved in Thomas Taylor's commentary on Porphyry's *De antro nympharum*. "A dry soul," as Heraclitus maintained, "was wisest"; as exegetes and scholiasts understood it, the dry soul was worthiest because it shunned the humid and flowing condition characteristic of generative nature, and aspired to the arid heights of the unchanging and permanent.[16] Homer's nymphs in book thirteen of the *Odyssey*, Taylor contended, were *pegae* and naiads, guardians of fountain and stream who presided over this watery world of flux where, following their weavers' trade, they robed souls with the generative body.[17]

I have no intention of arguing that Keats plied the more esoteric channels of Neoplatonism, thus delivering him into the hands of those of his readers who prefer to bathe in the fiery fountain rather than drink the waters of Hippocrene. It can be argued, however, that Neoplatonic imagery is more widely disseminated than in the learned and subtle arguments of a Taylor. The images are perennial, their argument or their rationale perishable, or at least open to revision. Shelley made use of a dialectic of images tracing the moist soul's progress toward the dehydrated spirituality which is the condition of fire in *Adonais*, and even Leigh Hunt seems to have dimly groped toward the principle in his vapid cloud nymphs, the nepheliads.

The language of image has always spoken compellingly and less esoterically of moisture and water as the female procreative element, the first of all elements, Thales claimed, from which all others, indeed the entire world of becoming, flows. Michael Psellus writes:

As many demons as live in damp places, and enjoy a softer way of living, give themselves the forms of birds or women. That is why the Greeks gave them a feminine designation, Naiads, Nereids, or Dryads.[18]

The watery breed maintained their liking for these congenial haunts long after Artemis Limnatos, the marshland Diana, yielded her sway to Titania and her miniaturized court. Agrippa announces the appearance of the fairy band in the familiar classical setting:

But the waterie and such as dwell upon the moist surfaces of the earth, are by reason of the moistness of the elements, for the most part like to women; of such kind are fayries of the Rivers & Nymphs of the wood. ...[19]

Keats would have known from Lemprière that Titania was another name for Artemis. The *Daemonologie* of James I demonstrates the uninhibited manner in which the Renaissance mixed its mythologies and tolerated their fruitful coexistence.

That fourth kinde of spirites, which by the Gentiles was called *Diana*, and her wandering court and amongst us was called the *Phairie* (as I tould you) or our good neighboures, was one of the sortes of illusiones that was rifest in the time of *Papistrie*: for although it was holden odious to Prophesie by the devill, yet whome these kinde of Spirites carryed awaie, and informed, they were thought to be sonsiest and of best life.[20]

Just as food or drink invariably accompanies the communion or coupling of Keatsian lovers, so the place of consummation or of consummate vision, Keats's holy of holies, is recognizable throughout the poems. As contrasted with the plashy lowlands which witness the initial encounter, it invariably occupies or is associated with heights, physical as well as emotional. The characteristic Keatsian narrative describes a passage from beside or out of the river and onto the heights, or at least under the hill. Lamia's palace is "high built," and it is from an inferior "slope side of a suburb hill" (possibly the worst line Keats ever penned) that profane trumpets dispel her idyll with Lycius, even as the sound of clarinet and boistrous kettledrum mounts from the great hall to Madeline's lofty bedchamber. The Nightingale's melodious plot of beechen green, although it lies at the heart of a dark wood, is the empery of the Queen Moon and all her starry fays, and can be reached only by flight. Hermes and Herse fly to their green-recessed wood, Herse's source and hidden bed in the highlands of Crete. Moneta's temple is lofty, and the tryst with La Belle Dame may take place under the hill, but it also commands the heights associated with the Venus Mount.

It is "La Belle Dame Sans Merci" which limns with its masterly economy this paradigmatic situation and its imaginative topography: the encounter and its setting, consummation and vision, disorientation and the human failure to sustain visionary or erotic fulfilment. Keats's knight-at-arms has forfeited the knightly role, the purposeful life of questing, saving beleaguered maidens, and impaling offending dragons. The substitution of "woeful wight" at Hunt's behest has no virtue other than alliterative, describing only what is obvious, the hero's condition after the episode, and preserving no sense of the heightened contrast between before and after. Lycius, too, was a quester, a journeying philosopher and a pilgrim to the house of Jove at Aegina before he was waylaid on the road to Corinth. His questing nature is emphasized by his passage from the Saronic island:

> ... his galley now
> Grated the quaystones with her brazen prow
> In port Cenchreas, from Egina isle ... (1.223–5)

Cenchreas was the port which saw the end of the greatest of mythic quests, the Argonauts' voyage and the beaching of Argo.

 *LAMIA: DEI EX MACHINA*

Like Eliot's Tiresias, the *femme fatale* has known and "foresuffered all / Enacted on this same divan or bed," and Lamia abets the workings of a foreordinated mechanism all too familiar to her. Since Keats divulges the outcome of his narrative at the beginning of part two, and his title alone would indicate to his reader the conclusion, we share her fore-knowledge. In this respect Keats's plot is a mummery, a variation on a familiar theme. I do not denigrate Keats's narrative invention: the same might be said of Greek tragedy. *Lamia's* mechanism is set in motion by the Olympians, Hermes and Jove, and is ultimately resolved by the intercession of the trickster god.[21]

The wily Hermes had "escaped the sight / Of his great summoner," and has stolen away under the cloud cover of the mortal world in order to pursue his "amorous theft" (1.11, 12). He has, in fact, duped or caught napping all-seeing Jove. Hermes, who even as an infant man-aged to bilk Apollo of his prized cattle, is adroit at such matters: he is the trickster god of thieves described in the Homeric hymn to Hermes. As "star of Lethe" he is also *psychopompos*, the conductor of souls to the underworld, while his "lythe caducean charm" establishes him as the Hellenic god of changes, Trismegistus, latter-day patron of alchemical transformations. The god of commerce's attributes of elo-quence, duplicity, and theft bewildered Pausanias, but seemed emin-ently compatible with the Homeric age, as they do with our own.

The Hermes-Herse episode has been treated by many of *Lamia's* readers somewhat sentimentally as a foil to the more squalid under-taking of Keats's Corinthian lovers. It deserves, however, to be seen for what it is. Keats attributes nothing but loveliness to Hermes' quarry: she is as faceless as she is, in Keats's rendering, nameless. She is merely the latest and not the last episode in the amorous career of "ever-smitten Hermes," proverbial for his "celestial heat" and barnstorming couplings. Lamia, who facilitates the conquest, is a woodlot madam exacting her price as procuress. As a result of the transaction she is translated to womanhood and her fateful station on the Cenchreas road.

Jove, apparently placated by Lycius's pious sacrifice at his Aegina temple, responds to the young Platonist's petition for love ("Jove heard his vows and bettered his desire"), delivering him into the arms of Lamia by engineering an opportune estrangement from his comrades on the road (1.229). Since it is unlikely that Jove would reward a faithful pilgrim and suppliant with a monster contriving his destruction, these puzzling events must be directed by a collision rather than collusion of divine motives. For all their abilities to enjoy what is denied to mortals ("Real are the dreams of God, and smoothly pass / Their pleasures in a long immortal dream"), the course of divine affairs seldom ran smoothly (1.127–8). Keats's Jove is less than omniscient; Hermes is deceitful and as prone to jealousy as any lesser creature. Thwarted in his search for Herse, and fretful that the silenoi might have already deflowered his budding nymph, Hermes is found by Lamia in a jealous snit as ill-tempered as that of his son Eros, who buzzes angrily about the door of the lovers' bedchamber. Jealousy, deception, and discord are as much a part of the divine pantheon as they are of the mortal arena to which these gods are less than passive spectators. Discord, Ares' sister Eris, it will be recalled, was honoured among the Olympians, and rolled the apple precipitating the squalid family quarrel among immortals and mortals known as the Trojan War.

It is necessary to labour this point, so much in evidence in the workings of Keats's plot, in order to counter readings of the poem, such as Wasserman's, arguing that the homeland of ethereal essences beyond heaven's bourne is the perfected, timeless consummation of imperfect mortal aspiration. Being is as discordant and disharmonious as Becoming in Keats's vale of soul-making. Such misreadings result from inadvertently employing the same elements of platonic dualism which Wasserman disclaimed as incompatible with Keats's world of hierarchical intensity.

The mythology Keats espouses has nothing to do with a scale of progressively disembodied essences: it belongs to a living mythology antecedent to allegorizations by Neoplatonists, Pythagoreans, or those positing an unmoved mover at the apex of his scale of emanations. Jove's mythic dignity was not compromised by his behaviour as a just, arbitrary, forgiving, vengeful, zealous, and jealous philandering father and husband; nor was that of his siblings and offspring who bore the family likeness and character. Even within the realm of godhead, the brightest virtues cast the longest and darkest shadows. Matters above, as Trismegistus maintained, indeed correspond with those below, and the Olympians are paradigms neither of abstract virtues nor of unalloyed essence, but of the roistering contrariness of human nature in all its muddled splendour. These are the gods Keats acknowledges and serves in *Lamia* as well as *Endymion*.

The dour gate-crasher Apollonius is usually credited with disrupting the festivities and precipitating Lamia's last, fatal transformation. But Apollonius's agon with Lamia is a pyrrhic victory resulting in the destruction of his own pupil. It is the juggling trickster's "caducean charm" as much as Apollonius's "juggling eyes" that effects the second of Lamia's metamorphoses. Hermes, who, apart from the brief appearance of his nettled son Eros, would seem to have been discarded with part one, resolves the poem as he inaugurated its action, by his continuing influence and a last-minute intercession.

The "fluent Greek" of the wedding party, the stately music ("sole perhaps and lone / Supportress of the fairy-roof") of Lamia's hollow festive illusion

Grew hush ...
By faint degrees, voice, lute, and pleasures ceased;
A deadly silence step by step increased,
Until it seemed a horrid presence there,
And not a man but felt the terror in his hair. (1.263–8)

Lamia's pulse is stilled and all is blight.[22] The ominous silence gripping the assembly is the signature of the trickster's god's transforming presence. Erasmus, who probably had it from Plutarch's *De garrulitate*, records in his *Adagia* that, in past times, whenever a sudden silence fell in the midst of a feast, it was understood that Mercury passed over, and that even in his own day such moments were feared as portentous. More enlightened generations have attributed them to a passing angel.[23]

Lycius, at the close of *Lamia*, is dead; the nightingale's ecstatic poet is become a sod. Keats's knight-at-arms, left to wander aimlessly about the cold hillside, is as good as dead. The assertion of point and meaning in his life, compelling beyond all his vows of chivalry, has been withdrawn, or he has apprehensively withdrawn from it. Knights-at-arms have no business loitering; theirs is a life of going forth, of commissions. Nothing remains but to hopelessly circle the height that he has known and lost. The spring world of the lakeside meeting slips into winter, and the sun-filled water-meadows no longer promise paradise but a land of the dead. The lakeside setting is become *avernus* or *aornos*, the underworld portal of the dead, where, the ancients maintained, there are no birds to sing.

✑❧ KEATS'S CLASSICS

Keats's familiarity with classical literature and mythology has usually been slighted as a matter of handbook gleanings from Lemprière and Potter, along with a smattering of Sandys' translations of Ovid and other Elizabethan translations. Douglas Bush, who proposed to uncover Romantic roots in classical mythology, in fact planted them firmly in the Renaissance. Bush, the Renaissance scholar, surveyed his Romantics and discovered an image of himself. His Keats turned to the Elizabethans for his mythology and a congenial luxuriance of language. Bush detected the influence of "William Browne, Chapman, Spenser, John Fletcher, Sandys, Ben Jonson, Marston and others" on Keats's list of the god's attributes from the "Hymn to Pan," and adds to them, as an afterthought, Wordsworth.[24] With magisterial brilliance Bush once dismissed generations of pious rhetoric attributing Marlowe's *Hero and Leander* to a purest draught from the classical Pierean spring by unmasking it as a Cellini salt cellar. It might be objected, however, that the Venus and Adonis of Keats's *Endymion* are no more Cellini's than they are Bion's.

Certainly Keats's education and medical training fitted him less admirably for the role of classicist than did the backgrounds of Words-worth, Coleridge, Shelley, and Byron, and the reputation of the un-tutored wunderkind still plagues a Keats who chose to follow his pulses rather than his head. The caricature is a disservice to a not ill educated, not unlettered young man who was sensitively and passionately re-sponsive to the intellectual, literary, and artistic currents of his day. Of all the Romantics, it is Keats who turns most frequently to classical myth. Are we to believe that the writer of *Endymion*, of *Lamia*, of odes to Maia, Psyche, and the Grecian Urn, of the two Hyperions and the "Hymn to Apollo," of sonnets to Homer, and of poems such as the "Epistle to Matthews" and "I Stood Tiptoe," rich in classical subject matter, had acquired the authority and command of his materials by recourse to Lemprière, handbooks, and a knack for allusion?

Keats's friend Reynolds recognized this aspect of his genius, and in 1818 tellingly compared Keats's classical impulse with that of one for-mally schooled in a classical education, and whose professed models were Neoclassical: Byron.

The genius of Mr. Keats is peculiarly classical; and, with the exception of a few faults, which are the natural followers of youth, his imagination and his lan-guage have a spirit and an intensity which we should in vain look for in half the popular poets of the day. Lord Byron is a splendid and noble egotist. – He visits Classical shores; roams over romantic lands, and wanders through magnificent forests; courses the dark and restless waves of the sea, and rocks his spirit on the midnight lakes; but no spot is conveyed to our minds, that is not peopled by the gloomy and ghastly feelings of one proud and solitary man. ...[25]

Reynolds, it will be remembered, was privy to Keats's speculations in 1818 concerning negative capability and the egotistical sublime, and these frame his comparison of the two poets, but the estimate is a fair and a telling one. Byron fixes a celebrated place in a phrase of stunning resonance and sonority, so that the reader nods a cowed assent while the face of a dowager and memory-raddled Europe is invoked in trium-phant if somewhat ejaculatory variations on the *ubi sunt* topos.

Clarens! sweet Clarens, birthplace of deep love!

Lo, Nemi! navell'd in the woody hills

Italia! oh Italia! thou who hast
The fatal gift of beauty.

She looks a sea Cybele, fresh from ocean
Rising with her tiara of proud towers

The castled crag of Drachenfels
Frowns o'er the wide and winding Rhine.

Byron's are rhetorical triumphs; Keats's imaginative incursions into the realms of gold are of a different order. *Lamia* has been called the most classical of Keats's poems, and I have indicated the poet's impressive familiarity with the mythic landscape of his Cretan and Corinthian setting. His surefootedness among the physical details of the classical landscape is no less uncanny, and this is strikingly demonstrated in the scene from *Lamia* on the road to Corinth.

Apollonius's pupil, in spite of his studious nature, was, according to Philostratus, susceptible to Venus. Keats establishes his character and the nature of his piety by portraying Lycius as a pilgrim returning from religious duties at the temple of Jove on the Island of Aegina. The Aegina pilgrimage is Keats's invention; Philostratus merely placed Lycius on the road from Cenchreas. Lycius, like Porphyro, is a famish'd pilgrim pining for the sweetmeats of love's antechamber. It is unfulfilled desire which motivated his pilgrimage: "Jove heard his vows, and bettered his desire," and Lamia materializes by the roadside.

To sail from Aegina, Lycius would indeed ride the eastern wind, as Keats tells us, across the Saronic gulf to debark at Cenchreas rather than Corinth's western port on the Corinthian gulf. Even more striking is the accuracy of Keats's account of the topography from the port to the city.

She fled into that valley they pass o'er
Who go to Corinth from Cenchreas' shore;
And rested at the foot of those wild hills,
The rugged founts of the Peraean rills,
And of that other ridge whose barren back
Stretches, with all its mist and cloudy rack,
South-westward to Cleone. (1.173–9)

Some thirty-five years later Smith's *Geography of Greece* described the scene: "The road from Cenchreae to Corinth ran in a southwest direction through a narrow valley, shut in by two ranges of mountains, which almost served the purpose of long walls. On the left hand were the high ranges of the Oneian mountains."[26] Keats's ridge with its "barren back" is the "asses' back," the Oneian ridge extending from Homer's "wealthy Corinth" to "well-built Cleone."

Such details were not available to Keats in Lemprière or the handbooks, or even by a meticulous reconstruction from details of the Corinthia by Pausanias or Strabo. Keats's account, in fact, is entirely accurate, while the Greek geographer Strabo, who confuses his mountain ranges, is muddled. Keats's most plausible source is contemporary travel literature, through which his classical Greece acquires an assured concreteness and authority. Chandler's *Travels in Asia Minor and Greece*, sponsored by the Dilettanti Society, was the most celebrated account at a time when Greece was all but closed by the Turk to the western traveller and authoritative accounts were scarce. Chandler supplies a map and all the essential details behind the *Lamia* passages. Chandler also attributes the Aegina temple to Jupiter Panhellenius. The "temple of Jove" at Aegina is Keats's only false step. There is no temple of Zeus on the island, but the temple of Aphaiea was commonly misidentified as such in Keats's day. Turner's painting *The Temple of Jupiter on Island of Aegina* of 1814, now in the Northumberland Collection, was well known, and the temple was attributed to Zeus as late as 1860 when Cockerell published his study of its remains. It is tempting to conjecture that Keats stationed his Lamia beside the warm salt spring described by Chandler and known to Pausanias as the bath of Helen near Cenchreas on the Corinth road.[27]

Perhaps a second Turner canvas played a role in the genesis of Keats's poem. Keats identified the source of his principal episode, the love of Lycius for Lamia, by quoting Burton's version of Philostratus. Neither Burton nor Philostratus, however, mentions the Cretan episode. The story of Hermes and Herse is told by Ovid, but Herse's role is secondary to that of her sister Aglaurus, and Ovid, Apollodorus, and Hyginus offer little more than Herse's genealogy and that of her son by Hermes.[28] Keats's details, along with the introduction of Lamia in Crete, are his own invention, and he identifies Herse only as a nymph and not by name. The source for the episode probably belongs with the visual arts which so often served Keats as inspiration.

In 1811 Turner exhibited his Claudean idyll *Mercury and Herse*, and, although Keats was still serving his apprenticeship at Hammond, he may have known it, since the painting acquired unusual celebrity because of its rumoured sale to the Prince Regent. The sale fell through, and it was seen by the public long after that date. Hazlitt, while reviewing the British Institution show of 1814, recalled Turner's "never-enough-to-be-admired picture of "Mercury and Herse" of three years earlier.[29] Turner's work was based on the brief account from the *Metamorphoses* and shows Hermes gazing at Herse with a train of Cretan nymphs.

Keats's landscapes and his mythologies are never bookish, even when sources can be traced to such dryasdust compilations as those of Lemprière, Tooke, Potter, and Bryant. Ian Jack has shown the dimension that the visual arts, the works of Poussin, Titian, and others, contributed to the fleshing out of Keats's world of Flora and old Pan.[30] The influence of Renaissance painting was at least as potent on the young poet as that of its literature. So was the heady conversation, the punning, the interminably playful classicizing beloved of Hunt, Peacock, and their circle. From plaster casts to engravings of Renaissance masters – Keats's influences ranged from the sublime to the trivial – from the Elgin marbles to Tassies' gems and their cheap reproduction of classical motifs, to contemporary dress and Regency architecture with their modish neo-Hellenism. Keats's classicism was not a matter of literary archaeology but the heady and potent London ferment of which he was a part.

CHAPTER EIGHT

Shelley's Anabasis: Heroic Landscape and the River Journey in "Alastor"

> ... and midway between the sea and the sky, they saw white snow peaks hanging, glittering sharp and bright above the clouds. And they knew that they were come to Caucasus, at the end of all the earth: Caucasus the highest of all mountains, the father of the rivers of the east.
> Kingsley

> Here we, in our impatience of the steps,
> Get back to the beginning of beginnings,
> The stream of everything that runs away.
> ...
> It is this backward motion toward the source,
> Against the stream, that most we see ourselves in,
> The tribute of the current to the source.
> Frost, "West-running Brook"

Contemporary criticism has alerted us to the perils of confusing the singer with his song, and Ariadne's thread, the simple narrative skein that served to direct us to and from our encounters with mystery, crisis, and recognition, has become treacherously snarled. And so the critical prospect of Shelley's *Alastor* is giddier than ever, fractured by a maze of mirrors, personae, and ironic perspectives.[1] The poem appears to have generated a critical impasse. Failure to disengage *Alastor's* teller from his tale and to dissociate each from the author's preface invites charges of critical naïveté, while to do so involves treading a slippery trail of red herrings. Perhaps the discomfort occasioned by Shelley's often frenetic impulsiveness, his intensity and candour, continues to haunt the squeamish modern reader, who would render him more tolerable through the removes afforded by ironic structures. But it is Shelley's habit to mince his readers rather than words.

The distinction between the narrator and his hero has been drawn with such ingenuity that it has become necessary to reaffirm what was once obvious, that the narrator spins a tale about someone remarkably like himself in character, temper, and background. Both narrator and hero are innocent, celibate, solitary, youthfully idealistic, and obsessively devoted to the worship or pursuit of a common ideal. They are on intimate and harmonious terms with the natural world; they are fellow poets, vegetarians, and, just possibly, necrophiles.

The narrator describes the intimations which have moulded his life through "incommunicable dreams," "twilight phantoms," and "deep noonday thought." His hero has been nurtured since infancy by "bright silver dreams"; his crucial encounter with the Kashmiri is an erotic dream and his second major epiphany, the bright-eyed phantom by the wellside, appears in an umbrageous "Silence and Twilight" beneath "a noonday sun." Narrator and hero devotedly dog the footsteps of their ineluctable mystery: "I have watched / Thy shadow, and the darkness of thy steps" the narrator confesses, while his hero "Nature's most secret steps / He like her shadow has pursued" (20–1, 81–2). But there is a single major and crucial distinction: one watches, the other pursues; one waits, the other acts. This salient distinction derives from the comparative passivity of the narrator, the meditative pose appropriate to the teller or teacher as opposed to the more strenuous exertions of his hero. The narrator's communion with the maternal mysteries is conducted by gazing, by bedding down with the dead, through "asking looks" and fruitless bouts with necromancy. He is the stay-at-home who watches, dreams, thinks, and tells tales. He awaits the unveiling of the "inmost sanctuary" while his hero seeks it out and undertakes the penetration of its mysteries. The dense texture of Wordsworthian tags in *Alastor* argues that the narrator is exemplary of the wise passivity that for Shelley produced only visionary impotence.[2] But the narrator's "solemn song" is, like all deeply felt songs, a song of himself, a freeing or projection of the moribund farer within him, whose chronicle is cast with appropriate complementarity in the recognizable mould of heroic action.

The tale to which the narrator is privy alters conspicuously his view of things in the course of its telling. At the close of the poem there is no further talk of the mothering universe or the beloved confraternity of man and elemental nature of the invocations, only "pale despair and cold tranquillity," the sober recognition of the indifference of universal process to human aspiration. It is as if Coleridge's ancient mariner and wedding guest were one and the same person, stunned by the impact of a self-revelation effected by the telling of the tale. The story-teller's creative act is a cognitive act, and the final vision which has claimed the *Alastor* narrator is recognition, a bleak confirmation of the desperation and unsuccess that beset him from the outset.

Alastor owes its title to Peacock and much of its reputation to circumstances which provide scant service to the issue of its integrity as a poem. Romantics and later readers appear to have received it as a portrait of arrested adolescence (a circumstance even more poetical than childhood) drawn against an imaginary landscape whose features were disposed to sate contemporary tastes for the sublime, the exotic, and the unworldly. Devout Shelleyans and those who insist upon real toads in real gardens praised or damned a hero who was nameless and rootless, a poem which was possibly mindless, and a poet who might well have been a literary panderer.

"The picture is not barren of instruction to actual men," Shelley warns in his preface to *Alastor*, and one experiences the sinking sensation which augurs the onset of an exemplary tale. Shelley, however, protests while *Alastor* does not, and his preface introduces a homiletic tone which the narrative mercifully evades. *Alastor* probably touched upon a personal nerve which compelled Shelley, as in *Epipsychidion*, to hide behind a covering preface, but to unveil Shelley himself is perhaps no more seemly or profitable than unveiling *Alastor*'s maid. My primary concern is with the poem as a quest embracing three continents and an inner geography of no less consequence. The psychological dimension of *Alastor* unfolds in terms of the hero's night sea voyage and his river journey tending, in Frost's words, "against the stream," toward the source. Unlike *Endymion*'s anonymous rivers, or Alph, sounding with analogues from a mythic and literary past, the landscape that Alastor's hero traverses is an actual one; the mythic resonance of the journey is already secured through its connection with the most heroic of historical expeditions, beginning as it does with the geographical and moving toward its source in the mythic highlands and inner geography associated with the "beginnings of beginnings." This reading will argue that Shelley is firmly in control of those historic and geographic elements which cast his narrative in the form of heroic myth. To identify the narrative as such, however, is to defend the central figure of *Alastor* from the implied criticism of Shelley's preface. His exertions are crowned with a failure confirming the barren passivity of the narrator of the invocations. Each route terminates in a common impasse, but the narrator wakes to the implacable truth which he has been reluctant to face at the outset.

The preface's account of the youthful poet's education and career introduces the *pothos* of the young man, his desire for the "infinite and unmeasured," and his subsequent discovery of a "prototype of his conception," or in Yeats's words an "image of desire," which serves to marshal his energies and direct his course, but which is no more attainable than the infinite. The remainder of Shelley's preface, insisting upon the admonitory nature of his "allegory," is troublesome. There are, Shelley insists, two classes of humanity: those who seek, whether through an abundance of love or "generous error," and those who do not, who lack vision as well as the sacred thirst. These last are the morally dead because they conceive neither of a heaven nor of a hell and languish in an indiscriminate moral indifference. They are blind and unmotivated, and decay as in *Adonais* "Like corpses in a charnel." Blake would have consigned them to his London, and Shelley, who twinned that city with hell, would have concurred.

By singling out their moral apathy, Shelley scourges them for their uncompanionable character, and appears to tar his young quester with the same brush: "Those who love not their fellow beings live unfruitful lives, and prepare for their old age a miserable grave." There is some ambivalence in Shelley's position, but it is incautious to conclude that Shelley was so out of love with his own errant hero that, as Donald Reiman suggests, he cast a wholly admonitory fable: "Although the poem has its autobiographical aspects, it should be read primarily as Shelley's warning to men not to abandon their social concerns."[3] The quester's death, however, is hardly ignoble; it boasts its own splendour, and whatever the nature of his pursuit, as hero he has no alternative. He can form no lasting attachment to the human community, at least until his quest is complete. His *pothos* is love, but not the kind which might have gratified the slighted maidens he passes on his journey, nor is it that serviceable Shelleyan altruism which might regenerate society. Nor is it love of self as an exclusive narcissism, an assumption which has led some readers to interpret the poem as a version of the Narcissus myth and its pining hero who seeks nothing beyond his own mirrored image.[4] If Shelley indeed condemns his hero and consigns him to the moral indigents, then the poet is out of love with mankind at large.

Such readings as these force the moral ambivalence which is at the heart of the myth of the romantic quester into a straitened ethical formula which the myth's very nature strives to transcend; viewed from the limited perspective they afford, questing can only appear wrongheaded and self-indulgent, and the quester pathetically frustrated rather than heroic. Heroes have always founded their own court of appeal on their own terms, and their heroics cannot be weighed by those who, in Yeats's words, "were born to pray and save." Shelley, like the Romantic reader in general, was more than half in love with his hero's quest and his less-than-easeful death. Perhaps some of Shelley's ambivalence clings to the lines from *The Excursion* with which he closes his preface, lines which might well serve as an epitaph for Romanticism itself:

> The good die first,
> And those whose hearts are dry as summer dust,
> Burn to the socket.

There is certainly a moral judgment here, but to whom is it directed? We have been provided with two orders of humanity: the seekers and the sluggards. The *Alastor* hero's heart is full, too full to secure an object for its affections, and he, with the "good" or the hero, must die in the elegiac glow of an autumnal splendour.

⤳ THE WANDERER

Before his encounter with the veiled maid, at least two earlier stages of the wanderer's spiritual progress are established: infancy and early youth. Infancy is, appropriately enough, the time for nurturing, and because an explicit mother and father are notably absent from this childhood hearth, the presence of the universal Mother of the invocation is realized in her fostering role. "By solemn vision and bright silver dream, / His infancy was nurtured." Fables instil his love for the past, and "The fountains of divinest philosophy / Fled not his thirsting lips." This nurturing world invoked in the opening lines of the poem presides over the "beloved brotherhood" of the elements and universal process, the passage of days and seasons unfolding under the aegis of the great Mother. She is not to be understood exclusively in her customary tellurgic role, since Shelley assigns earth to the brotherhood of elements, but as emblem of the mystery of primary wholeness. As such she belongs to the world of the unconscious, and her sanctuaries lie in shadow, within the depths, in dream and death.

Youth commences with the inevitable departure from the maternal Eden: home and fireside have grown cold and alien and exile begins. The lessons of history and "divine philosophy" are no longer accommodatingly served up to the thirsting lips of the child, but must be actively sought in undiscovered lands, the *terrae incognitae* of the external world. It is a sharply divided world; to experience it to the full one must live in the extremes of heat and cold, height and depth, past and present. The youth's earliest wanderings are not entirely aimless, and are directed by his need to embrace these extremes of the physical world in order to recover the lost coherence of infancy. The volcano and its molten core promise warmth, the hearth of infancy rekindled, but its crater lies above the high ranges of ice and snow; bitumen lakes and secret caves offer access to the depths "of thy deep mysteries" on which the childish heart habitually fed. The journey after the relics of the past is the wanderer's attempt to turn back time, to rediscover the fabled ages which infancy embraced and held in communion. But this youthful quest delivers no rewards: contraries beget contraries and fail to reconstitute what was so lightly lost.

The youth's early travels suggest the *Wanderjahr*, a journey for knowledge pursued with the genteel dilettantism of the traveller of the Grand Tour sampling the pleasure of ruins. He visits Athens, Tyre, Balbec, Jerusalem, Babylon, Memphis, Thebes, and the wilds of Ethiopia, gazing on "memorials of the world's youth,"

> but ever gazed
> And gazed, till meaning on his vacant mind
> Flashed like strong inspiration, and he saw
> The thrilling secrets of the birth of time. (125–8)

His illumination is a victory as handily won as that of Wordsworth over a host of golden daffodils, as momentous as, if less arduous than, that of Victor Frankenstein, who "after days and nights of incredible labour and fatigue ... succeeded in discovering the cause and generation of life" – and it is about as convincing.[5] Whatever the nature of this illumination in the search for beginnings is, it provides him with scant pause and little satisfaction.

Undirected though he may be, this traveller does accumulate impressive mileage. His journey has usually been admired as a random gathering of splendours defying physical geography. We know nothing of his origins, and the site of his death has occasioned considerable conjecture, but we are furnished with ample directions on the journey, so that his progress is carefully annotated. G. Wilson Knight pronounced the mythic orientation of the journey "significant," and identified it as eastward.[6] The journey to the east, however, is only half of the hero's passage, which in its career reverses its eastward thrust into the Caucasus Indicus, as they were known to ancient geographers, toward the west.

Having penetrated the "thrilling secrets of the birth of time," time and time's works no longer hold any fascination for the wanderer, and landmarks bearing the imprint of man are left behind. An apparent aimlessness takes over his wanderings; no longer does the detritus of the human past draw his steps, but places which are vast, trackless, and uncharted, lying toward what Yeats called the "fabulous, formless east." He crosses Arabia through Kerman to the east of Persia and the wastes of Asia, to the embrace of a "natural bower" in the Vale of Kashmir, where he dreams of a maiden who will transform wandering into quest and lend it a new urgency.

⤳ THE QUESTER AND THE LADY
OF THE HOUSE OF SLEEP

Donald Cameron has described unequivocally the explicitly sexual nature of the dream and its culmination.[7] It is curious to note how many readers have accorded this episode their decorous inattention and described it as a wholly spiritual epiphany. The encounter with the veiled maid begins tamely enough, even absurdly so, with the young poet conducting a stilted drawing-room *conversazione* on knowledge, truth, virtue, liberty, and poetry, an episode as improbable as Donna Julia's high-minded tutelage of the young Don Juan. As the pair scale the ladder of discourse, mere talk yields to song and harping, shuddering limbs, and parting of lips and of her veil, and a solitary early morning awakening on the cold hillside of spent passion.

There is in the description of the dream no more confusion between the spiritual and the frankly sensual than in *Epipsychidion*. Such confusion lies in part with those of the poem's readers who insist on the eviscerated nature of Shelley's ecstasies, or accuse him of a sublimated sexuality in his aerial incursions, or of wanting it both ways.[8] The generalized sentiment of *pothos* has found its coveted image and is powerfully transformed into *himeros*, the fleeting pleasures of the winged Eros.[9] The image of the maiden has welled up from the world of the hero's dream, and is of the quintessential and undifferentiated feminine: priestess (for she too, is portrayed as poet), virgin, witch, and whore. She is, as Joseph Campbell has described her in her mythic role, "The Lady of the House of Sleep," the mother-sister-bride who haunted Shelley's personal and imaginative life.

She is the paragon of all paragons of beauty, the reply to all desire, the bliss-bestowing goal of every hero's earthly and unearthly quest. She is mother, sister, mistress, bride. Whatever in the world has lured, whatever has seemed to promise joy, has been premonitory of her existence – in the deep of sleep, if not in the cities and forests of the world. For she is the incarnation of the promise of perfection; the soul's assurance that, at the conclusion of its exile in a world of organized inadequacies, the bliss that once was known will be known again; the comforting, the nourishing, the "good" mother – young and beautiful – who was known to us, and even tasted, in our remotest past.[10]

The quintessential feminine has, as well, her threatening aspect, as Pater understood when attempting to interpret her as the Gioconda. Campbell has identified her with the remembered image of the real mother in her nourishing and protective role in the paradise of infancy from which we are exiled, but she continues to exert an autonomous life in the adult unconscious, and finds her mythic expression in the great Goddess or universal Mother who embodies the whole complex of female attributes both benign and threatening. "Heroes," Carl Jung writes, citing Gilgamesh, Dionysius, Heracles, and Mithras, "are usually wanderers and wandering is the symbol of longing of the restless urge which never finds its object, of nostalgia for the lost mother."[11]

Shelley's wanderer has but one mother as far as the narrative is concerned, and she is the Mother goddess, who first appears in her benign aspect. As in *Endymion*, the quester's dream of union with his maid promises the *hieros gamos* or sacred wedding of the questing hero of tradition with the goddess herself. For Shelley's hero it will remain a promise unfulfilled, and, in her indifference to his efforts, the Mother reveals her obverse face, that of the "fair fiend."

"Whither have fled / The hues of heaven that canopied his bower / Of yesternight?" (196–8). The quester has won his vision of heaven, and its loss in the cold morning light will be his hell. After the vision is spent, he is as radically divided within as was the physical world he explored at the outset of his journey. "He eagerly pursues / Beyond the realms of dream that fleeting shade; / He overleaps the bounds" (205–7), and he is for a time sundered: the old wanderer by day, and the quester born in the womb of night.

> While daylight held
> The sky, the Poet kept mute conference
> With his still soul. At night the passion came,
> Like the fierce fiend of a distempered dream,
> And shook him from his rest, and led him forth
> Into the darkness. (222–7)

The overmastering ascendancy of the night creature over the mild poet by day is established in the emblems of the serpent, associated with night and the moon, and the sun-assailing eagle.[12]

> – As an eagle grasped
> In folds of the green serpent, feels her breast
> Burn with the poison, and precipitates
> Through night and day, tempest, and calm, and cloud,
> Frantic with dizzying anguish, her blind flight
> O'er the wide aery wilderness; thus driven
> By the bright shadow of that lovely dream,
> Beneath the cold glare of the desolate night
> Through tangled swamps and deep precipitous dells,
> Startling with careless step the moonlight snake,
> He fled. (227–37)

Shelley's hero has enlisted in the haunted company of Romantic out-casts with his body consumed and a smouldering if not a glittering eye, moon-dogged, a wanderer by night.

The overwhelming power of the image possessing the dreamer lies in its undifferentiated character, for which there can be no equivalent in the waking world. Only the cold moon sinking in the west before his waking eyes remains, the pallid emblem of her presence. He puzzles over the nature of her dominions, and hence the subsequent direction of his quest. Sleep and dream have provided their fitful access, but he now asks "Does the dark gate of death / Conduct to thy mysterious para-dise?" In reply, he turns his steps toward that western gate and the westering moon.

ALASTOR AND ALEXANDER

The new direction takes Shelley's hero beyond Mount Aornos, where no birds fly, where a towering fortress withstood the assaults of Krishna and Hercules only to fall to Alexander the Great. The wanderer surveys Aornos from Petra, not the Arabian city of the Nabataeans but the rock stronghold seized by Alexander near the River Oxus. He con-tinues the journey afoot beyond Balk, or Bactria as it was known in Alexander's day, to the Chorasmian shore or eastern banks, as Hero-dotus located them, of the Caspian Sea.[13]

The landscape of the westward odyssey is not a province of Shelley's imagination: its landmarks derive from and are perhaps intended to evoke the expedition of Alexander of Macedonia. All the sites named in the poem figure in the Alexandrian chronicles, including the shores of the Hyrcanean or Caspian Sea, which Alexander proposed to explore in order to determine its presumed connection with Ocean. No record of Shelley's reading survives from Bishopsgate, where he wrote *Alastor* in the autumn of 1815, but in August of the following year, and in November at Geneva and Bath, he read with Mary the *Vita Alexandria* of Curtius, and went directly from it to Plutarch's life of Alexander.[14] Alexander's expedition and its geography held a continuing fascination for him, so that he read in 1817 Arrian's *Historia Indica*, and in the following year Mount-Stuart Elphinstone's *An Account of the King-dom of Kabul*.[15] Shelley would have been familiar with the lie of the Alexandrian landscape and its features from school-days at Eton, and the details of the early wanderings of his *Alastor* hero correspond to those of Alexander. Athens, Tyre, Jerusalem (for which Josephus claimed the distinction of the conqueror's visit), Babylon, Memphis, Arabia, Persia, and Carmania were all stations of Alexander's progress. Of the places mentioned by Shelley, only Balbec, which was famed in his own day but still in its infancy in Alexander's, the Egyptian Thebes, and Ethiopia escaped the conqueror's attentions. Perhaps Shelley's hero was intended to overreach the Macedonian, who, as Curtius reports, longed to journey to Upper Egypt and Ethiopia but had not the time. Eliade has described the abiding fascination with the Alexandrian chronicles in terms which illuminate Shelley's own preference for the ancient mythographers and historians over the more prosaic accounts of his contemporaries: "If the memory of Alexander's journey to India never faded it was because, being classed with the great myths, it satisfied the longing for mythical geography – the only sort of geography man could never do without."[16]

Alexander's own instincts were no less mythopoeic than those of his chroniclers. His urge to master what Hercules could not, to outstrip the eastern wanderings of Dionysius, and his readiness to claim his own semi-divine parentage suggest a talent for heroics in the mythic mould. If Shelley's hero is less canny or self-conscious in this respect, we may be certain that Shelley was not. It was not simply that the Alexandrian itinerary corresponds closely with that of Shelley's hero; the motives that goad the two heroes on are identical. *Pothos*, as the etymology of the *Cratylus* would have it, is a yearning desire for a distant object, a longing for the unattainable for which German Romantics supplied the less euphonious term *Sehnsucht*. The word *pothos* was not only frequently applied to Alexander, but almost exclusively appropriated for him by his chroniclers. The regularity with which Arrian invokes it and describes his hero as "seized by *pothos*" gave rise to the conjecture that the word might well have been coined by Alexander himself.[17] The analogy with Alexander furnishes Shelley's hero with heroic dimensions, a precedent for his heroic unrest, the poem's psychological rationale, and a resonance fusing the mythic and historical.

Although the *Alastor* hero's odyssey has suggested to many of Shelley's readers a transcontinental amble toward transcendence, and its narrative a shambles, the poem is in fact tightly, almost schematically, deployed. Its twin invocations and closing threnody establish a striking symmetry, and are within a single line of equal length. The poem unfolds in four principal acts: the double invocation, a retrospective summary, the narrative, and the threnody. The lengthiest section, the narrative, has three distinct thrusts: the poet-hero's history until his encounter in Kashmir, the epiphany of the lady by the well, and the hero's subsequent history and death. Each of these segments provides a climactic confrontation which alters or resolves the course of action. Moreover, all of these epiphanic confrontations take place in similar if not identical settings: a bowery enclosed place with its well or running river, a natural chamber, cavern, dell, or hollow with its rivulet.

... in the vale of Cashmire, far within
Its loneliest dell, where odorous plants entwine
Beneath the hollow rocks a natural bower,
Beside a sparkline rivulet he stretched
His languid limbs. A vision on his sleep
There came ... (145–50)

Within another narrow vale, the bowery world which is "Nature's dearest haunt," in its "one darkest glen" beneath a "foliaged lattice" runs the "sweet brook that from the secret springs / Of that dark fountain rose" (429, 451, 464, 478–9). It is here that the hero encounters the spectral eyes that redirect him on his journey. The third of these precincts is the place where death is met, the "green recess" of "that obscurest chasm," inviolate, embowered "with leaves forever green," clasped in the foliage's entwining arms, "one silent nook" (625, 637, 580, 579, 572). Here the stream, now become a river, gathers for its final leap into oblivion.

These are the sacred places won by the hero which direct the course of the narrative action. They are explicitly contrasted with the frame and its narrator, who can only dream of such places and fail to penetrate their mysteries: "though ne'er yet / Thou hast unveil'd thy inmost sanctuary" (37–8).

ANABASIS AND THE RIVER

Shelley probably knew of or even read at Bishopsgate Arrian's account of the campaigns of Alexander, the *Anabasis*. The title itself, translated as "The Journey Up Country," bears a striking relevance to *Alastor*'s geography. Shelley's hero passes through the venerable cities of the plain, through the trackless desert itself, and essays the heights at three crucial points: in Kashmir where he dreams, on the massif of the Caucasus where he encounters his vision, and on the lofty escarpment where he dies. But it is to the highland eyrie that the entire journey tends. The Caucasus assumes as central a role in *Alastor* as in the mythic geography of *Prometheus Unbound*. Where, then, lie the mountains and the river of *Alastor*? Where is their location both geographically and mythically? And what did the river mean to Shelley?

Alastor was written following a ten-day excursion in late August 1815 to the source of the Thames. Peacock claimed it was this outing which fired Shelley's abiding appetite for boating. It certainly whetted his appetite for rivers. A year later Shelley would negotiate the Rhine, seek out the sources of the Rhone and Arveiron; he would sail the navigable reaches of the Serchio and launch an extravagant poem following the course of the Nile from its fabled sources on Mount Atlas. Describing his Rhine journey in the Preface to *Laon and Cythna*, Shelley displayed the same sort of self-dramatization that may have produced *Alastor*.

I have been a wanderer among distant fields. I have sailed down mighty rivers, and seen the sun rise and set, and the stars come forth, whilst I have sailed night and day down a rapid stream among mountains.[18]

In the same year Shelley's horizons spread as wide as his own poet-hero's wanderings, and in a letter to Peacock from Geneva he reveals that not only was he still thinking about rivers but they had become, for him, representative of the human mind. Shelley proposed to traverse the entire continent by negotiating an intricate passage of rivers, the Black Sea, and the Mediterranean, embracing Europe, as it were, in the living metaphors of river, sea, and the great circular journey. His letter to Peacock is an inimitable gathering of the varying strands of the poet's complex character: the brilliant speculations of the grandiose schemer combined with the practical irony of the impecunious traveller.

If possible we think of descending the Danube in a boat, of visiting Constantinople and Athens, then Rome and the Tuscan cities, and returning by the south of France, always following great rivers. The Danube, the Po, the Rhone and the Garonne; rivers are not like roads, the works of the hands of man; they imitate the mind, which wanders at will over pathless deserts, and flows through natures which are inaccessible to anything besides. They have the vile advantage also of affording a cheaper mode of conveyance.[19]

"Mont Blanc" is Shelley's most calculated exploration of the affinities between mind and river, but his essay "Difficulty of Analyzing the Human Mind," which may have been contemporaneous with *Alastor*'s composition, addresses itself to both the Alpine and his Caucasian river by supplying a resonant vocabulary for the mental processes he chose to explore.

But thought can with difficulty visit the intricate and winding chambers which it inhabits. It is like a river whose rapid and perpetual stream flows outwards. The caverns of the mind are obscure, and shadowy; or pervaded with a lustre, beautifully bright indeed, but shining not beyond their portals.[20]

Led by "strong impulse," the logic of feeling rather than that of the compass or of reason, to the shores of the inland sea, the quester finds a swan, startles it, and envies its homing flight westward across the Caspian:

> Thou hast a home,
> Beautiful bird; thou voyagest to thine home
>
> ...
>
> And what am I that I should linger here? (280–1, 285)

As if in reply, in the swan's stead is a small boat floating offshore, which will spirit him effortlessly across the sea. A storm drives him, amid "the mutual war of ocean's mountainous wastes," toward the western shore and to the foot of the great Caucasus shining under the moon. He is preserved from destruction on the rockbound coast by being swept into the mouth and windings of a great cavern and along its hidden river. The river bears him upwards against its natural flow toward the crest of the Caucasian massif by what has been described with some desperation as the impulse of mysterious Shelleyan hydrau- lics, or even more implausibly as a variation of the great Deluge.[21]

The subterranean river yields to a chasm winding through the riven mountain, a descent or penetration into darkness, the skirting of a threatening maelstrom, and an ascent into light and the easy calm of the now placid stream. The underworld descent and return to the light of day provide the physical counterpart to the dream of the Kashmiri. Their symbolic import is clearly established, although they beggar explanation in terms of the strictest realism. The question arises at this point whether Shelley has abandoned all pretence at geography in order to depict an unfolding landscape of the mind. Not entirely, or, more precisely, the two coexist within a deepening mythic dimension. The river is probably Shelley's version of the river Aras or Araxes, as it was known to the ancient geographers, whose name, as Strabo explains, was derived from the Greek *a paraxae*, a cleft. Strabo describes its pre- cipitous descent from the Caucasus to the western shore of the Caspian, stressing its turbulence, which, according to Virgil, even Alexander was powerless to bridge.[22] Lemprière asserts that it "arises in the Antitaurus, only a few miles from the source of the Euphrates," and flows a length of six hundred miles into the Caspian.[23]

The Araxes, as the ancients understood it, plunged through a myste- rious but highly charged mytho-geographic landscape. Even its course was disputed. Herodutus and Aristotle seem to have confused it with the Oxus on the eastern shore of the Caspian. The usual passage from the Black to the Caspian Sea was by way of the Cyrus and the Phasis, which flows west into the southeast of the Black Sea north of the Araxes, and was considered by Strabo and Herodotus, as was the entire massif, to mark the boundary of Asia and Europe.[24] Arrian and others thought the highlands from the Hindu Kush to the Caucasus (the Indicus and the Scythian Caucasus) and southward to the Taurus to be a single massif, and that it was from these highlands that all the great rivers of the east took their beginnings. The source of the Araxes is not far distant from Mount Ararat, the sacred mount of Noah on the Armenian plateau from which the river takes its modern name, Aras. It was perhaps for this reason that Genesis 2 was understood as sanctioning the location of the Garden of Eden near the Araxes Valley in the highlands which gave rise to the Tigris, Euphrates, Araxes, and Phasis, contenders for the four rivers of paradise. It is possible, moreover, that Shelley may have been aware of the several versions of the medieval *Iter Alexandri Magni ad Paradisum* which preserve accounts of Alexander's expedition to the gates of paradise at the head of a raging river navigable only with the greatest difficulty. The legend locating paradise in the region is at least anterior to 500 AD, and is told in the Babylonian Talmud. In the *Iter* and its French versions, the *Faits des Romains* and *Voyage d'Alexandre*, the river is identified variously as the Ganges, the Physon, the Gyon, and the Tigris.[25]

Alastor's geography is indebted to the Greek historians' accounts of the east, but within its lineaments there unfolds a landscape of the mind disclosed by the familiar landmarks of the mythic inner journey. It is this twofold nature of the quest, geographical and psychological, which accounts for *Alastor's* curious double invocation, a feature which is hardly excused by the assumption that two attendant muses are more propitious than one. The narrator first implores the "wonted favour" of the elements of earth, ocean, and air, and proceeds to enlist the "Mother of this unfathomable world" to "Favour my solemn song." Earth, ocean, and air are the elements with which the hero traffics in his preliminary journey east and west, but the unfathomable world which the inner journey essays, that which lies under the aegis of the great Mother, has left its traces not in the historic accounts of the Alexandrian chroniclers but among the mythic renderings of the heroic quest.

The passage toward the east is traditionally one toward light and consciousness, but its reversal, the westering journey, tends toward the darkness of the unconscious or of death. The nature of the poet-hero's wanderings has altered dramatically since his encounter within the Vale of Kashmir. "A strong impulse urged / His steps to the sea-shore" (274–5); he is now "driven" or fleeing. Rather than motivated by idle curiosity or conscious design, his steps are directed by unconscious impulse. The quester's surrender to instinct or the logic of feeling is his surrender to the personal daimon or drive which Heraclitus and Freud identified with destiny. The swan that serves to reveal his direction and his conveyance is one of those simple instinctive creatures, birds, beasts, children, or fools, who direct heroes on their quests, and it seals the young poet's surrender to the inner promptings first revealed to him in his transforming dream. The voyage to the western shores of the Caspian in the frail boat is the night sea journey of the perennial quest in which the hero is threatened by adverse elements and the devouring sea monster from whose belly he will be reborn. From the point at which Shelley's hero spreads his traveller's cloak to the winds as sail, the direction and thrust of the voyage give it an impetus entirely its own. The aimless wanderings toward the east are behind him, and the crossing of the dark sea among a chaos of warring elements demands the surrender of the conscious will to the tides and currents of the unconscious.

Shelley's hero is swept into or, more aptly, devoured by the yawning cavern revealed by moonlight at the foot of the Caucasus. If the movement is indeed an anabasis or journey to the high country, this is the necessary descent preliminary to that rise in the dark, the *katabasis eis antro* or penetration into the secret chthonic world which is the womb of nature and the self.

The river flows through a labyrinth at once familiar and baffling, and a threatening whirlpool bars the way. Fabulous forces and antagonists must be met and overcome by the hero. These barriers, however, when confronted directly are no longer barriers, their threats less than threatening, and our deepest fears and bafflements lose their potency and become our allies. So it is with the symplegades or the whirlpool. Within the maelstrom's turbulent embrace lies its most potent threat, the calm pool, deceptive counterpart to the mirroring pool which awaits the hero at the summit. It is a beguilingly false image of the self, "Reflecting yet distorting every cloud / A pool of treacherous and tremendous calm," and it offers a dubious haven from questing. The threat is overcome by the sail, the quester's cloak, and the whirlpool is transformed into a threshold rather than a barrier, driving him upwards on its mounting ridges even as the whirlwinds of the Caspian furthered his progress across the sea. All personal effort has yielded to irresistible force, and the subsequent climb of the boat to the highlands against the current of the rushing river may be *contra naturam*, but it enacts the inner logic of the mythic quest. The high road of the quest is never simply a fixed route to be pursued at will: it takes on the character of something alive in its own right, drawing the quester along irresistibly. Something of this property belongs to the quest in Browning's "Childe Roland," where, once the hero's steps are committed for good or ill by the wretched cripple who points the way, the threshold has been crossed and the remainder of the journey unfolds about him almost as if he were standing still. He is wholly subject to it, and it unfolds with the compelling logic and fluid forms of nightmare, as surely as do the terrible consequences of the ancient mariner's killing of the albatross.

The river, now a placid stream between mossy banks, bears the boat through the heart of a forest, a beguiling pastoral world contrasting with the natural violence of the sea and river journey. It is pastoral in the fullest sense of the word: a retreat of natural harmony and peace, a world where nature is arrested in a vast embrace. Leaves weave patterns of twilight, the vale embosoms the forest, the oak embraces the beech, overarching cedars form solemn domes, blossoming vines flow around grey trunks:

> and, as gamesome infants' eyes,
> With gentle meanings, and most innocent wiles,
> Fold their beams round the hearts of those that love,
> These twine their tendrils with the wedded boughs
> Uniting their close union ...
> ...
> ... Soft mossy lawns
> Beneath these canopies extend their swells,
> Fragrant with perfumed herbs, and eyed with blooms
> Minute yet beautiful. (441–5, 448–51)

The wood is redolent of matrimony, innocence, maternal harmony, and infancy; it is Shelley's version of the moony married world of Blake's Beulah, charged with a Keatsian richness and ripeness.

> One darkest glen
> Sends from its woods of musk-rose, twined with jasmine,
> A soul-destroying odour, to invite
> To some more lovely mystery. (451–4)

This Shelleyan "plot of beechen green and shadows numberless" lacks only the song of Keat's nightingale within its deepening twilight, but breathes what Keats's grove did not, a lingering femininity no less sexual in tone than "Nutting's" "green and mossy bower" with its "fairy water-breaks" or the birthplace of Xanadu's sacred river.

Touching upon the heart of mystery, now more than ever seems it rich for Shelley's hero to die, and he seeks "in Nature's dearest haunt, some bank, / Her cradle, and his sepulchre." Its cynosure is the dark well, the source of a second young river, perhaps the secret source of the first, indeed of all rivers. This, the *Urquelle* and its setting, is the goal denied the sedentary narrator, who complained, "ne'er yet / Thou has unveiled thy inmost sanctuary." It is a *temenos*, the place of beginnings and, as Shelley's deployment of his mythic Caucasian geography implies, the Eden of childhood as well as the Eden of the childhood of man. But Eden, the happy maternal valley of childhood vision or the pastoral world of wedded bliss, is for all its idyllic promise a retreat, Milton's "narrow room," Shelley's "narrow vale." Blake understood that to linger there was to forfeit the possibility of vision, and to waste in a regressively childish nursery world. Beulah is properly a way-station, not a terminus, and the valley, like all sheltering valleys, must be traversed.

Reflected within the sacred well, the quester sees only his own image, his reflected eyes, and a mysterious presence standing beside him. Her identity has troubled *Alastor's* readers. She has been identified as the Caucasian maid, as Nature, as the Great Mother herself. It is not merely conciliatory to insist that none of these possibilities need be excluded: they are all aspects of the Mother goddess or her Greek avatar Demeter, whose inconography depicts her standing by her sacred well. Shelley is deliberately ambiguous here, refusing to accord the presence a reality independent of his hero. The palimpsest image glimpsed within the sacred well is as much a psychological *ens* as a metaphysical one. The dark fountain and its burden, however, will not slake the sacred thirst, and the starry eyes which beckon are identical with the dream image "hung in the gloom of thought," in the inner world of the quester.

From here the way lies down from the watershed with its leaping rivulet, away from the perpetual twilight of embowered noon in the direction of the westering moon to an autumnal eyrie and its night world. The young stream, too, is a mirror of sorts, and the hero reads in it the course of his own life.[26]

> Whither do thy mysterious waters tend?
> Thou imagest my life. Thy darksome stillness,
> Thy dazzling waves, thy loud and hollow gulfs,
> Thy searchless fountain, and invisible course
> Have each their type in me. (504–8)

He follows it beyond the first giddy leaps of infancy through maturity into an increasingly spare landscape.

Yet ghastly. For, as fast years flow away,
The smooth brow gathers, and the hair grows thin
And white, and where irradiate dewy eyes
Had shone, gleam stony orbs: – so from his steps
Bright flowers departed, and the beautiful shade
Of the green groves, with all their odorous winds
And musical motions. (533–9)

The stream gathers "with its wintry speed" through desolation, to
plunge over the talus in a torrent. The quester dies on his lonely
eminence in circumstances befitting heroic death: among autumnal
elegies of fallen leaves, overlooking a vast panorama, the battleground
of life on which he has fallen, where for the hero victory and defeat are
one.

                    his last sight
Was the great moon, which o'er the western line
Of the wide world her mighty horn suspended,
With whose dun beams inwoven darkness seemed
To mingle. (645–9)

He dies with its setting, "when two lessening points of light alone /
Gleamed through the darkness"

                    – till the minutest ray
Was quenched, the pulse yet lingered in his heart.
It paused – it fluttered. But when heaven remained
Utterly black, the murky shades involved
An image, silent, cold, and motionless,
As their own voiceless earth and vacant air. (657–62)

If the poet-quester is vouchsafed his dying moment on the Mount of
Vision, the prospect is indeed bleak and comfortless. While the sinking
horns of the crescent moon resolve themselves into the ubiquitous eyes
which drew him through his austere life of pursuit, they hold no promise of union with the dream through death. That goal, Shelley insists, is
baseless as dream, at one with Medea's lost alchemy, the dream of
Christian immortality, the labours of the alchemists and necromancers.
The closing threnody anticipates the imagery of *Adonais*, but it is an
Adonais arrested in the first stage of the elegy's progress: inconsolable
and powerless grief before the finality of death.

   It will be recalled that the invocation to *Alastor*, calling upon earth,
air, and ocean, neglected fire, the element completing the traditional

tetrad. Shelley's omission is not without point. Harold Bloom has attempted to supply the missing fourth element by positing a Blakean narrator who speaks out of the fires of the imagination, but there is no fire and little warmth to be found in *Alastor*.[27] In spite of deserts crossed and heights scaled, *Alastor* is a world of shadowy dells and bowers, dark chasms, cold firesides, cold white light, pale or blue moons, and prosaic daylight. Only on one occasion is the sun described, as a harsh noonday light excluded from the pastoral world embowered in twilight at the summit of the Caucasus. It is only in the steamy embrace with his dream maiden that the hero finds warmth. But this is dream, promising more than life can deliver, and dissolving in the cold white light of morning. The final epiphany, the spirit presiding over her sacred well, is "clothed in no bright robes / Of shadowy silver or enshrining light," and the dying hero's last glimpse of his world is of "An image, silent, cold, and motionless" (480–1, 661).

The exclusion of the element of fire from *Alastor* is as rigorous as its absence from the icebound world of act one of *Prometheus*, or from the wintry arrest which blinds natural process in the opening passages of *Adonais*. These are worlds locked in generation, the cradling arms of the Great Mother, beyond whom there is nothing but the vast, the impersonal, and the impenetrable. Hers is the world of Shelley's Urania, mother and mistress, whose embrace is both comfort and confinement, a blunting of pain and a quenching of the visionary fire. She launches her child-lover on his worldly or his inner quest; she is there at the setting out, she is guide, and she awaits his return at the close. The heroic life pursues a passage like the rising and setting of her moon: it runs its brief course in the circuiting sublunary world of beginnings and endings which is her empery. Muse, mother, and mistress, Shelley's Urania and her realm must be overcome if one is to reach the transforming fires of the fountainhead, or herself be transformed by the millennial renewal offered by a new Promethean age.

Shelley knew that tradition also posited a primary triad of elements, recognizing in fire the unique transforming principle which altered their states. *Prometheus Unbound* and *Adonais* essay that fiery transformation which was denied *Alastor*'s hero and his thwarted chronicler in the autumn of 1815 when, having weighed his world, Shelley found a voiceless earth and vacant air.

CHAPTER NINE

"The Witch of Atlas" and the Mythic Geography of the Nile

> But so far is he from having any desire for a more accurate knowledge of the earth's surface, that he said he should prefer not to know the sources of the Nile, and that there should be some unknown regions preserved as hunting-grounds for the poetic imagination. *Middlemarch*

> But alas! alas! that Nature is a wary wily long-breathed old Witch, tough-lived as a Turtle and divisible as the Polyp, repullulative in a thousand Snips and Cuttings, integra et in toto! Coleridge, Letter to Gillman

Mary Shelley's notes and her husband's introduction to his "three-day wonder" stress the purely imaginative nature of Shelley's poem as a playful flight of fancy: his spinning, to Mary's evident chagrin, of an ideal world, shunning plot, character, and any element of human interest. T.S. Eliot hardly needed to read beyond Mary's hesitant praise and Shelley's introductory stanzas to dismiss *The Witch of Atlas* as a trifle.[1] Eliot's judgment and Harold Bloom's evaluation of *The Witch* as Shelley's finest longer poem establish the poles of critical opinion.[2] Bloom's admiration for the poem as a mythopoeic creation risks equating the practice of myth-making with superlative poetry, when at best it is only a condition for poetry's creation. All myths, lamentably, are not necessarily equal, no more than are poems themselves, and a facility with the one need not guarantee the excellence of the other. Bloom's praise, however, does have the virtue of countering a cavalier dismissal of the poem, although his discussion of Shelley's myth largely ignores the roots of a personal Shelleyan mythology among the shards of traditional historical and mythological accounts. Shelley is no less deeply indebted to tradition than Yeats or Blake.

In spite of Shelley's own caveat, that his verses "tell no story, false or true," there is narrative continuity to *The Witch*, fragmentary or incomplete though it may appear. Its coherence is the subject of this reading, which is not simply an identification of the classical sources for Shelley's Nile, but an inquiry into source and course, into the witch and her river. Shelley's last-minute promise to provide a further instalment of the witch's pranks among the Olympians, throwing in for good measure the subsequent bedding of his chaste heroine, scarcely argues that his work is incomplete, and is even less convincing than Coleridge's yarn about his inopportune visit from the visitor of Porlock.

Like Tristram Shandy's, the witch's biography commences with her conception and an inquiry into her provenance. Her credentials and her journey are more coherent and closely oriented to traditional sources than Shelley's rapid speed of composition and the poem's barrelling narrative pace might suggest. The passage of time is at least as confounding as in *Prometheus Unbound*, but like that poem's mythic geography, it can be determined in the broadest terms of mythic and historic time.

While *Prometheus Unbound* spans geographic Europe and Asia, and culminates in an apotheosis in the cave lying "beyond the Bacchic Nyssa," in what W.B. Yeats called the formless, fecundating east, the setting of *The Witch of Atlas* is Africa. Shelley's principal source for the witch's mountain stronghold, her river journey, and many of its episodes is Herodotus's account of Africa in books two to four of his *History*, augmented occasionally with the elaborations of Pausanias and Strabo.

That Shelley should prefer the accounts of the classical historians and geographers to the less fanciful ones of his contemporaries should be no more surprising than Yeats's dismissal of anything smacking of modern science for the allure of more arcane accounts, or Blake's spurning of the myth of rationalist objectivity for his own eclectic mythical constructs. Moreover, in the first quarter of the nineteenth century, the perennial question of the sources of the Nile was as open as it was in the days of Herodotus, Hecataeus, and Ptolemy. Major James Rennell, who published in 1800 *The Geographical System of Herodotus Examined and Explained*, could yet state that "to us it appears more probable than the remote sources of the Nile are rather to the south than to the west," thereby calling into question one aspect of the Herodotean account, and advancing the course of contemporary European speculation to the position held in the second century BC by Ptolemy.[3] The Nile question was in Shelley's day still fraught with the mystery it had commanded for over two and a quarter millennia.

Readings of *The Witch of Atlas* have neglected to take into account the poem's bearings, its mythic orientation in terms of space and time. Curiously, no one has charted adequately the course of the river which is central to the poem, either ignoring it entirely, assuming the existence of several rivers as in *Alastor*, or peremptorily consigning it to a mental landscape peculiarly and inexplicably Shelleyan. I shall discuss the various Herodotean elements as they arise in the course of Shelley's narrative, since it is clear that the witch's voyage and the exotic riverscape through which she passes are less kaleidoscopic or random than readers have assumed, that the controlling narrative thread is the course of the Nile from its mysterious fountain source within the witch's Atlas cave to the final descent toward the Nile delta when, in the final stanzas, she turns her attentions from the natural and preternatural world to the affairs of men.

It was Herodotus who, in his visit to Egypt in 450 BC, concluded that, beyond his own vantage point at the city of Elephantine on the first Nile cataract, "this river flows from the west and the setting of the sun; but beyond this no one is able to speak of with certainty, for the rest of the country is desert by reason of excessive heat."[4] Probably Herodotus had mistaken the great east-west bend in the river beyond the Ethiopian capital of Meroe for a permanent westerly direction, and he bases his conclusion on an account of credulous Nasamonean travellers who identified as the Nile a river which they saw in western Libya, apparently because it bore crocodiles.[5] As a Greek, Herodotus respected the laws of symmetry, geographic as well as dialectical, and opined that the Nile in its eastward course could be compared with the Danube, traversing the greater part of Africa as the European river traversed central and eastern Europe in its course to the Black Sea. Although Herodotus failed to identify its source in the Atlas range of West Africa, he at least indicated that direction, and firmly established the heresy of the western source of the Nile. It was only a matter of time before cohesive but uninformed minds would seek to connect two knowns, the Atlas range to the west and the Nile to the east, thus spanning the great *terra incognita* of the Sahara. The task fell to Juba II, heir to the first king of Numidea, who wrote from a comfortable captivity in Rome an armchair geography of his native continent. Juba, who was given as wife Cleopatra Selene, the daughter of Antony and Cleopatra, had every reason to be concerned with reconciling the geographical dialectics of east and west. His account survives in fragments cited by Pliny.[6] Juba claimed that the Nile rose in a mountain of lower Mauritania, and that the river in its descent to the desert formed a lake, plunged under the sands to reappear in a second lake, became subterranean once again, and reemerged in the Ethiopian highlands. Juba is clearly responsible for Pliny's speculations, and it appears that Pausanias, too, had it from Juba. "Not a few," Pausanias wrote, "have supposed that this water, reappearing out of the sand, forms the Egyptian Nile."[7]

Pausanias stresses, as did Herodotus before him, the inaccessibility and loftiness of the great Atlas mountain, which had already achieved mythic status by the time of Hesiod, "reaching to the skies with rushing torrents and impenetrable forests blanketing its slopes."[8] Lest Shelley appear perverse in his redrafting of such fanciful accounts, it should be pointed out that it was not until long after his death that the Niger, flowing eastward near the city of Timbuctoo, was charted and dismissed as a possible upper arm of the Nile.

A WATER WITCH: GENEALOGY AND BIRTH

The opening stanza of Shelley's poem refers affectionately to the Saturnian age antecedent to the primal rupture effected by the appearance of Error and Truth, the knowledge of good and evil that banished the age of gold and troubled its amiable creatures. But it was our less than ideal world, riven by the true and the false, which Mary Shelley and the "viperish critics" doggedly maintained was the proper arena for the poet's art. Mary seemed grimly determined that her husband live out his days closeted in the Palazzo Cenci, and her two critical objections, the poem's apparent lack of narrative line and its absence of a moral poise, are disarmingly answered by Shelley's visionary rhyme.

Carlos Baker has indicated the indebtedness of the opening lines to "L'Allegro," and he and D.L. Clark jointly combated J.L. Lowes's claims for indebtedness to *Endymion* by amassing a collection of Spenserian analogues.[9] The opening lines constitute, in fact, a Shelleyan theogony, and begin with a gravity not entirely free of premonitions of mock gravity. In tone as well as in subject matter, the closest analogue to these lines is Keats's *Lamia*. Keats opens his poem with a similar evocation of a golden age long past, and later points his accusing finger at villainous philosophy, or what Shelley called "reasoned wrong, glozed on by ignorance." The startling shifts in Keats's tone, from the solemnly serious to a cavalier Byronic mockery, evident in the opening lines of the second part of *Lamia*, find a striking counterpart in Shelley's poem. Yet, analogous though the two poems may be as instances of common romantic preoccupations or techniques, Shelley is not in Keats's debt. Keats posted his poem with his advice to Shelley "to load every rift of your subject with ore" from Hampstead on the same day on which Shelley was completing *The Witch of Atlas* in San Giuliano. One must either accept the similarity as an example of synchronicity, or more plausibly, see the two poems as instances of what Harold Bloom calls "barbed vision" or visionary cynicism, "a peculiar and effective attitude shared only by Blake and the later Yeats."[10]

The witch, we are told, is a daughter of an Atlantide and Phoebus Apollo. She was immaculately conceived in an *aura seminalis*; her mother faded away in her transport (less incendiary a fate than that of Danae), and was translated into an asteroid. The witch gestates in a womblike cave within the mountain, scene of her mother's hierogamy, and materializes at full term. Do we, or did Shelley, know any more concerning her provenance than this? We can be certain that Shelley did.

The Atlantides, according to Lemprière, were an African race living near Mount Atlas; their first emperor was Uranus, and their country was that in which all the ancient gods were born.[11] These gods and their Atlantidean children belonged to the Saturnian age. Elsewhere the Atlantides are identified as the seven daughters of Atlas and Pleione, species of the genus *nymphae*, who after fortunes and misadventures were translated into the constellation known as the Pleiades. Nymphs, as we have seen, were numerous. Artemis had sixty sea nymphs or Oceanides in her retinue, and Oceanus is said to have sired at least three thousand. Among their offices were weaving purple garments in their grottoes and watching benevolently over the fates of mortals.[12] Shelley's witch resides in her proper maternal home, a cave, and as spinner and weaver follows her mother's trade. She is Shelley's rather than Apollo's conception: Phoebus's couplings with nymphs were maculate and they bore him sons rather than daughters.

Nymphs, unless apotheosized to more durable circumstances, were not immortal, nor were they conventionally mortal. Although Aristotle protested that neither nymphs nor satyrs were immortal, Plutarch established that they enjoyed unfading youth for a life-span of 9720 years, "less than most mathematicians think." His estimates were based on the calculations of Hesiod:

The crow lives 9 generations
4 crows = 1 stag
3 stags = 1 raven
9 ravens = 1 phoenix
10 phoenix = 1 nymph[13]

This in itself serves to distinguish the witch, daughter of Apollo, from her aunts, the nymphs, although she preserves certain of their characteristics. She, along with Plutarch, Hesiod, and Milton, knows what the nymphs do not know, that although they may be "Of her sweet presence – each a satellite," their tenure is limited.

From haunted spring and dale
Edged with poplar pale
The parting genius is with sighing sent.

> ("On the Morning of Christ's Nativity")

Their golden age must pass as the seasons of the year, and like Urania or Earth, Shelley's witch complains:

I cannot die as ye must – over me
Your leaves shall glance – the streams in which ye dwell
Shall be my paths henceforth, and so – farewell! (238–40)

The primal epoch has passed, the natural world is emptied of its ministering presences, and there survives only the solitary witch, who now identifies herself with the flowing streams, their springs, and the river which issues from its mountain source. These now know but one presiding genius, and it is to their secret sources within the mountains that she will repair at the outset of her journey, climbing the plunging torrents with her consort Hermaphroditus. ("The pinnace, oared by those enchanted wings, / Clove the fierce streams towards their upper springs," 407–8). The witch now takes over the offices of her former satellites, the Crenae or Pegae, the vanished nymphs who were ministrants and guardians of springs and fountains.

Of the witch's appearance, we know only her eyes and her voice, and that she has dark hair. Her eyes, like "unfathomable night / Seen through a Temple's cloven roof" (83–4), suggest Shelley's description of Pompeiian temples in a letter to Peacock.[14] Her voice, low "like love," attracts, and the beasts it summons appear, as early as stanza four, to belong to an already fallen or declining world. These passages may be, as D.L. Clark suggests, indebted to *Comus*, although it is doubtful whether Shelley would have shared Milton's confidence in the impregnable armour of chastity and its efficacy in taming the savage beast, or indeed whether the witch's curious brand of chastity is even of that order.[15] Her looks "made tame sanguine beasts"; "The magic circle of her voice and eyes / All savage natures did imparadise" (103–4). The days of the natural fellowship of the lion and lamb have passed, but the witch wields a power like that of the hidden scrolls and phials of her grotto, which can rekindle a fallen paradise. She enacts, rather than that of the lady of *Comus*, the role of her own half-brother, son of the muse Calliope and Apollo. Orpheus's paternity has been disputed, but it is clear that he acquired his musical talents from Phoebus. The savage beasts must learn love at her feet; it is no longer theirs by natural right. She, as the sole surviving creature and creation of the age of gold, revives the ruling harmonies of love as Orpheus recaptured and sang the lost music of universal concord.

Although the entranced and mollified beasts belong to the fallen world, the witch's charmed circle widens to embrace or evoke the superannuated denizens of the pastoral age: Dryope, Faunus, the silenoi, nymphs, Oceanides and their sire Oceanus, the rulers of pastoral Garamant (whom Herodotus placed at a twenty-day journey from the foot of Atlas),[16] as well as all manner of beings ranging from the invisible All-god, Pan, to hybrids and grotesques: Priapus, Pigmies, Polyphemes, centaurs, satyrs, and the lowest forms of life: "lumps neither alive nor dead, / Dog-headed, bosom-eyed and birdfooted" (135–6). Rather than representing a delegation from the theriomorphic gods of ancient Egypt, these last creatures, according to Herodotus, inhabited the land west of the Libyan river Triton: "Monsters with dog's heads and without heads, who have eyes in their breasts, at least as the Libyans say," primordial kin to the bosom-eyed horror Shelley once glimpsed in his wife Mary on a story-spinning Swiss night with Byron and Polidori.[17] But even this motley assembly, from the Great God himself to lesser classical Calibans, pales before the witch's numinous presence, as does the natural world which serves to mask her presence, even as the subtle veil she herself wove and wore. "Her beauty made / The bright world dim, and everything beside / Seemed like the fleeting image of a shade" (137–9). And in terms of her lease on life, her listeners are precisely that, fleeting as shades.

✎❦ THE CAVE AND ITS TROVE

Sealed in crystal cells is the witch's hoard: essences of sounds, visions, colours, and tastes, themselves as fleeting as the stuff of the world of sense, captured here in undying perfection: sound within silence, the evanescent snared within the permanent, a larder of oxymora to be administered by their chatelaine at her will to those deserving of her attentions. In the fourth of her reliquaries is the panacea that will "change eternal death into a night of glorious dreams," which she will bring to the living and the dead in her descent of the Nile, to those who "lived thenceforward as if some control / Mightier than life, were in them" (596–7). The crystal cells, their contents and their power of transforming life and death, and Shelley's subsequent references to the inferior embalmers' arts of Egypt probably owe something to Herodotus's account of the treatment accorded the Ethiopian dead. Unlike the Egyptians, the Ethiopians displayed their dead, not in the pomp of windings and mummy-cases, but in ingenious crystal monstrances. Herodotus explains:

When they have dried the body, whether as the Egyptians do or in some other way, they plaster it all over with gypsum, and paint it, making it as much as possible resemble real life; they then put round it a hollow column made of crystal, which they dig up in abundance, and is easily wrought. The body being in the middle of the column is plainly seen, nor does it emit an unpleasant smell, nor is it in any way offensive and it is all visible as the body itself.[18]

The witch is, moreover, a bibliophile, collector and custodian of the accumulated lore of the Saturnian age. Within her scrolls are wisdom's secrets: the lost knowledge of living in universal harmony, the inmost lore of love, wisdom's transforming power over recalcitrant fact. Here are those powerful spells that might awaken the golden age – not the millennium itself, but the golden age as it is known to the lover, the magus, or the artist: "Men from the Gods might win that happy age / Too lightly lost, redeeming native vice" (188–9). The Atlas cave and its mistress are identifiable with the "still cave of the witch poesy" in the fastness of Shelley's Mont Blanc, and it is these witches' common lot to sow the narrow plot which the poet cultivates – to attain the hard-won perfection which is the fruit of the artist's pursuit of his or her art or science. As Auden described it, "With the farming of a verse / Make a vineyard of the curse."

The witch harbours further treasure:

And wondrous works of substances unknown,
To which the enchantment of her father's power
Had changed those ragged blocks of savage stone,
Were heaped in the recesses of her bower;
Carved lamps and chalices, and vials which shone
In their own golden beams – each like a flower ... (201–6)

These, too, are the fruits of a secret knowledge, which like the Arch-image's scrolls are directed toward transformation or, more precisely, transmutation. The heaped treasure is the handiwork of the father who conceived her in a golden mist: Apollo, Helios, or Sol, as he was known to the alchemists who laboured under his aegis and honoured him with the goal of their science – gold, the coveted element of the sun.

 MOUNTAIN AND FOUNTAIN

The witch is guardian of two wells: the secret, sacred fount which lies within her cave where she lies entranced in hieratic posture while its emerald waters reflect the constellations in their dance, and the second, her winter couch, the burning fountain. Like her father, Apollo, who withdraws from his mountain eyrie at Delphi to winter in the more temperate climes of the Hyperboreans, she seeks out her congenial seasonal elements. It is not certain whether the burning fountain can be considered as a second source of the river spawned on Atlas, but Shelley knew that tradition persisted in citing twin fountains as sources of the Nile, and because the fountain is hers, it is related to the river of Egypt. Her element is as much fire as water, and her habitat is as paradoxical as her own nature, as her mercurial temperament, as her hoard. She is identifiable with, and perhaps more than, the *mysterium conjunctionis* effected by her crystal cells, her alchemical knowledge and transformer's arts. Hers is a transcendent nature of which all constituent elements seem no more than quixotic faceting. As with the witch, so it is with her avatar or embodiment, the vivifying river which first summoned Egypt – the Nile's gift, as Hecataeus of Miletus called it – from the eastern Sahara wastes.

Although the fiery fountain occupies no role in traditional speculation concerning the source of the great river, the Nile was known to have sprung from two fountains variously located: near the city of Elephantine, or in the highlands of Ethiopia, or beyond the river's unknown upper reaches, persistently retreating into the uncharted as exploration pushed the boundaries of the known further upstream. The fiery fountain is, of course, a purely and characteristically Shelleyan invention, as is the hermaphrodite who, fostered by the warring elements, comprehends the apparent contradictions of physical existence.

Within the heart of the heaven-shouldering mountain, the witch receives homage seated upon an emerald throne, the seat of power referred to in both stanzas nine and ten. Her couch, the sacred fount, is bathed in green splendour and edged with emerald crags, while her seasonal retreat on the Austral Lake in the southern hemisphere "Was as a gem to copy Heaven engraven" (448). There, on the reflecting surface of the lake, her floor, the southern constellations, the obverse side of the heavens, move as the northern stars danced before her eyes within the sacred fount on Atlas. Here, too, she receives her news of the universe "on a throne in-laden with starlight," weeping and rejoicing over the dispatches of the day. The emerald thrones, whether several or portable, and the haven which "was as a gem to copy Heaven engraven" suggest the emerald tablet of Hermes Trismegistus, which affirmed the correspondence of earthly things with the heavens, the hermetic assumption underlying both the exoteric and esoteric pursuits of the alchemists, implications of which have already been established in the juncture of the heavens with her eyes and in the reflecting mirror of the Austral palace.

Atlas, Herodotus reported in his *History*, "is narrow and circular on all sides, and is said to be so lofty, that its top can never be seen; for it is never free from clouds, either in summer or winter. The inhabitants say that it is the Pillar of Heaven."[19] Pliny wrote that this "most fabulous of African mountains" soared into the very orbit of the moon.[20] Atlas is a central point of Africa, if not of earth itself, interpenetrating the planes of earth and heaven, and as such is sacred ground as well as source of the sacred river traversing the continent. It is an *omphalos*, a point of mythic orientation corresponding to that of Apollo at Delphi, the navel of the Greek world. As each culture identified or occasionally reared its own holy mountain from which all meaningful orientation proceeded, so do we find in Shelley's "Mont Blanc," *Epipsychidion*, *Prometheus Unbound*, and *The Witch of the Atlas* a carefully delineated sacred space at the heart of the matter, or occasionally of a continent. The cave "beyond the Peak / Of Bacchic Nysa, Maenad-haunted moun- tain / And beyond Indus and its tribute rivers" in which Prometheus seals his reunion with the estranged Asia in the central highlands of the continent and from which unfolds the transforming presence of uni- versal love, the seat of power at the awesome summit of Mont Blanc, and the Ionian isle of *Epipsychidion*, "Beautiful as a wreck of Paradise" suspended "twixt Heaven, Air, Earth and Sea," harbouring the cave in which the lovers essay their apotheosis, are further examples. Less obvious, but no less crucial, is the pyramid of Caius Cestius which heralds the climactic movement and resolution of Shelley's elegy *Adonais*, mounting from the mouldering sepulchre of Rome to the blue Italian sky, from the cycles of birth, death, and decay to the burning fountain and the eternal star.

There may be those who object to an inattentive delicacy in my terms, preferring to recognize in this congeries of caves something more vulval than umbilical. They indeed function as places of conception: they serve as wombs incubating a new order, personal or universal. The delights of the senses stored in their nascent purity in the witch's cave and her association with love all support this identification. Such readings are no more Freudian than Shelleyan, and Shelley would not object. Traditionally, the mountain is the *omphalos*, the cave is the uterus of the earth, and the two are frequently conjoined or associated as the source of power and of creation. The manifestation of that power is the mountain's issue, the Nile, coursing from the frontiers of myth through the heart of historical Egypt. The river source must lie on high ground, but, as Hippocrates maintains, the best of springs flow from the highest places, such as the upper Pierene and Aganippe, which rise on the peaks of the Acrocorinth and Helicon.

The juxtaposition of cave, fountain, and an issuing river, Shelley's favourite symbolic locations, is common to *Alastor* and "Mont Blanc" as well as to *The Witch of Atlas*. Mary Shelley described her husband's fascination with rivers, his descent of the Rhine from its source in Switzerland in 1814, and the ascent of the Thames to its source in the following year, and associated these with the composition of *Alastor*.[21] Mountains play a role not only within the poems but in their inception and execution. Shelley's visit to Mont Blanc is the obvious example, but he conceived *Prometheus Unbound* in the high Echelles in Savoy in March 1818. He wrote act one at Byron's villa, and also "Lines Written among the Euganean Hills," surveying the northern Italian plain from these hills' abrupt eminence. Act II of *Prometheus* owes much to the Shelleys' ascent of Vesuvius. Nietzsche, it is said, conceived his wise man of the Caucasus in the Alps of the upper Engadine, and wrote of Zarathustra's descent from the mount of meditation while residing in the mountain village of Eze in southern France. Even the claustrophobic Roman world of the Cenci unfolded from Shelley's roof-top eyrie at the Villa Valsavano with Mount Montanaro filling his horizon. *The Witch of Atlas* was begun the day after Shelley's two-day ascent of Monte San Pellegrino in August 1820.

⁂ THE BOAT AND ITS PILOT: THE HERMAPHRODITE

The witch's barque probably owes its existence to Wordsworth's Introduction to *Peter Bell* and Shelley's resolve to launch his own craft in the treacherous ether of poetic fantasy rather than on Wordsworth's homy green earth with its creature comforts. "There's something in a flying horse," Wordsworth noted in his opening lines, "there's something in a huge balloon," but for Shelley, the giddy prospect from Pegasus more than compensated for an afflatus of hot air. "The over-busy gardener's blundering toil" was no way to hoe in the vineyard of poetry, and Wordsworth's truculent Peter Bell was its ungainly fruit.

Like the witch herself, the boat is furnished with credentials: a genealogy of the sort which the epic commonly affixed to weapons or heroic conveyances. Shelley's account is invested with a mock heroic gravity duly deflated when a chariot forged by Venus's cuckolded husband, the smith Vulcan, is sold by her to Apollo. The goddess seems to have been alarmed by its fragility, a hazard in the pursuit of her amours. Apollo, who had one of his own, divested his purchase of its wheels, refitted it as a boat, and gave it to his daughter, the witch. That, Shelley implies, reducing the history to a used-car transaction, is the more prosaic account, but he provides an alternative version of the boat's genesis, a pretty redress of the Orphic theogony.

The primordial Eros who sowed chaos with the seed of love and brought forth the cosmos sows another seed, harbouring it in the home of his mother, the evening star, coddling it to maturity. The burgeoning gourd-like fruit, responsive to the ministrations of love, transmutes light and dew into its own substance. Cored and hulled, it is jockeyed by Eros about the world-encircling streams of Ocean.

Eros's craft is found moored upon the witch's fount. No longer piloted by the winged Love, however, it lacks a means of locomotion, and this the witch amends by her oddest creation, the hermaphrodite.

The witch's wiles and arts – the pacifying power of her voice and eye, her crystal hoard, her archimagean and alchemical lore, the creation of the hermaphrodite and the rearing of the Austral palace, as well as her pranks among the mortals of the lower Nile – reenact the fundamental reconciliation of Eros with Eris, the primordial act of creation itself. With her knowledge of alchemy and her universal solvent, the liquid love which she dispenses, she weds the warring elements of fire and snow and draws forth a perfected purity, a miraculous synthesis of the sexes as well as the elements. Her reasons for playing Pygmalion have led to much serious conjecture. Carlos Baker saw the witch motivated by a need for companionship, while Bloom dismissed her consort as a robot.[22] For all its beauty, its smiles and tears, the "Image" is distinctly uncompanionable; moreover it is probably mute, mute as perfection itself. F.A.C. Wilson maintained that it was created as the witch's lover, a perfect match for her sexless nature.[23] Some match, some lover. G. Wilson Knight chose to see Hermaphroditus as a supra-sexual being transcending the limitations of the divided sexes, an ultimate synthesis like Goethe's homunculus or perhaps Knight's own Lord Byron.[24] Questions of sexuality hardly seem germane if supra-sexuality implies, as in Aristophanes' account of the androgynes in the *Symposium*, no sexuality. Perfect, the hermaphrodite knows nothing of the imperfections of the divided sexes and their lack of completeness, and is no more than a somnolent, highly ornamental Narcissus, self-contained and without the urge or power to procreate. But it does know how to act the oarsman to the witch's piloting. Shelley probably drew his "Image" from his recollections of the sleeping hermaphrodites belonging to the Uffizi and Villa Borghese collections – both wingless – but Hermaphroditus's wings may serve to identify him as the winged hermaphrodite known to the alchemists, "the symbol of the spiritual body wherein spirit has mastery over the elements."[25]

The witch herself, who remains a maid throughout the poem, is another sexual conundrum. She is a curiously sexless being for an incarnation or executrix of love: consummate loveliness, but unloving and unloved. The witch harbours all knowledge, all love, but does she herself know love? "The Heliad doth not know its value yet," Shelley hints, and drops the matter. Presumably the telling of this story belongs to her further adventures among the sprites and Olympians promised by the final stanza. Perhaps the only clue to the nature of Shelley's improbable sequel lies within the passage describing the reflected stars on the stilled surface of the Austral Lake. Of the Antarctic constellations, only the star Canopus is singled out, appropriately enough, since it lies in the constellation Argo, demarking the rudder of the ship purported to have been the first built to sail the seas. Its pilot was Tiphys, but the guiding hand behind the tiller was that of the sorceress Medea, who rescued the adventurers and rewarded their expedition with the golden fleece. Like the witch, Ovid's Medea commanded preternatural powers over the course of rivers and their springs: "the crooked banks much wondering at the thing / I have compelled streams to run clean backward to their spring" (*Metamorphoses* 7.199–200).

Medea was the niece of Circe; she transformed Aeson from old age to youth, and practised those same skills in which the pilot witch of Atlas was adept. Shelley describes her arts in *Alastor*:

O, for Medea's wondrous alchemy,
Which whereso'er it fell made the earth gleam
With bright flowers, and the wintry boughs exhale
From vernal blooms fresh fragrance. (672–5)

Medea, in Shelley's mythology, might well be an avatar of the witch, her shadow in the mortal world, and perhaps Medea's fate, her intemperate love for Jason and its dark consequences, bears some relation to that of Shelley's witch, as he promises to chronicle it – "A Tale more fit for the weird winter nights / Than for these garish summer days" (670–1).

⟆✹⟅ THE NILE JOURNEY

The first leg of the Nile journey begins, and if the witch grasps the tiller, Herodotus guides her hand. They plunge downstream, hurled by the impetus of the young river, and pass "panther-peopled forests," "a country abounding with wild beasts" which Herodotus associates with the Garamantes, the tract to the south of Mount Atlas, and beyond "many a star-surrounded pyramid / Of icy crag cleaving the purple sky" (350–1), the strangely conical mountains which litter the Herodotean landscape, of which Mount Atlas itself is the cynosure.[26] Beyond islands and caverns, through winding dells and mountain gorges, rapids, cataracts, and chasms, they sweep through a subterranean portal where the Nile plunges in its *katavothra* beneath the Sahara. It is within this subterranean world that Hermaphroditus is roused into service, propelling the craft upstream with beating wings to attend to the neglected sources of the river's tributaries within the mountains.

The witch pilots her craft toward the Austral waters, and her course takes her "beyond the fabulous Thamondocana," Timbuctoo as it was known to Shelley's contemporaries, although it was unknown to Herodotus, who predated the city's zenith by some two thousand years.[27] Nor did the city, synonymous with the unattainably remote, the exotic, and untold wealth, flourish in Shelley's own day, except in the dreams and collective fantasies of all Europe. Leo Africanus was known to have visited Timbuctoo in 1526 and spread word of the crossroads of the Sahara caravans as a city of mighty mosques and houses roofed with gold, an African El Dorado. No one in the nineteenth century failed to hear of the city, but no European had travelled there and returned. Its renown reached a feverish height in Shelley's lifetime. One Benjamin Rose, alias Robert Adams, an illiterate American seaman, claimed to have been taken there in captivity and to have escaped in 1811. His account was hotly disputed and dismissed as fraudulent because it was too prosaic.[28] In 1816 an ill-fated British expedition under Peddie vanished in the Sahara. Four years after Shelley's death, Captain Gordon Laing reached Timbuctoo, to be murdered while returning, and the following year a Frenchman, René Caillié, did return, without silk or gold, with reports of a drearily monotonous waste of mud huts, a squalid, exhausted desert outpost beneath a punishing sun. The dream, however, proved more durable than Caillié's reality, which fell on deaf ears, and in 1829 a sceptical young Tennyson at Oxford was awarded the chancellor's medal for English verse for his "Timbuctoo."

Shelley did not know, nor did Europe, that the westward flowing river near his Thamondocana was the Niger and not the Nile, not one of the reputed arms of the upper Nile. In fact, they knew little more than Herodotus.

✐ THE AUSTRAL LAKE

Beyond Thamondocana lies the Austral Lake. The lake, as its name implies and the constellations mirrored on its surface reveal, lies beyond the equatorial zone. Though subject to incessant hail and the buffeting of fierce winds, it is not the Antarctic, as Harold Bloom identifies it.[29] The Antarctic constellations are visible to the entire southern hemisphere and the crags hemming the lake only look "like a shore of wintry mountains." Moreover, it is identified as a lake and not the streams of Ocean which encircled the world known to antiquity, and which Shelley refers to in his account of Eros's antics in his boat. The lake has no counterpart in the *History* of Herodotus. Its surface and skies suggest a fierce maelstrom of bursting natural energy. The surface "foamed like a wounded thing," lacerated by tempests (442). The atmosphere is a turmoil of hail, lightning flashes, and the fire-balls' roar. It is here that the witch rears her flamboyant bivouac in her southern dominions, its walls sheltering proud pavilions as if becalmed in the eye of a hurricane.

Shelley would have heard reports of a vast lake far to the south through which the Nile or one of its arms was reputed to pass, a lake which had yet to take its name from an Englishwoman born in the previous year to be queen.[30] Herodotus had no intelligence of this, but he did review at length the theories purporting to explain the summer flooding of the Nile, adding his own outlandish speculations. One of the theories which Herodotus discards explains how the strong Etesian winds cause the swelling of the river by blowing against its natural flow, thus damming the river until it is released by their subsidence. Herodotus's own explanation also hinges upon winds, violent winter storms to the south which drive the sun from its appointed course into retirement in the upper parts of Libya.[31]

The witch's power to reconcile and control the dissident elements is evident in her stronghold, its imperial tent, and its appointments. Within the charmed circle of her walls the angry lake is tamed to a calm mere; the tent is pavilioned with a cunning fabric "Of woven exhalations, underlaid / With lambent lightning-fire," while underfoot is spread a carpet of "fleece-like mist ... / Dyed in the beams of the ascending moon" (466–7, 471–2). This preternatural magnificence is drawn from the same loom which, in the Atlas cave, worked mist, strands of dawn light, and starbeams into the fabric of poesy, the high tales woven upon the witch's growing woof.

Nor does she hesitate to extend her empery to the heavens themselves and the listening earth below:

> And like Arion on the dolphin's back
> Ride singing through the shoreless air; – oft-time
> Following the serpent lightning's winding track,
> She ran upon the platforms of the wind,
> And laughed to hear the fire-balls roar behind. (484–8)

The heavens echo her laughter in a spirit of cosmic hilarity, and when she blends her own voice with those of the spirits of the moving spheres, the mortal's day is transfigured, filled with the harmonies which lie in her power to command as she rekindles the Orphic strains which tamed the wild and recall the age of gold.

But has the witch left unattended her seat on Atlas? Her quarters on the Austral Lake, her crafts, and her antics are all strikingly familiar to those who first knew her in her mountain grotto. Indeed, when she pursues her pleasures toward the mouth of the great river, has she in fact left her grotto or the Austral Lake emptied of her animating presence? No more than the river in its coursing toward the sea ever leaves behind the source from which it rises. The Nile remains one, presence and process, and so intimately is the witch identified with the river and its gift of life that the extended metaphor of her journey never entirely teases us out of recognizing this.

⁓✦⁓ THE JOURNEY INTO TIME

The highlands behind her, the witch glides through the Egyptian plain. The sequence of her itinerary becomes less crucial. Lake Moeris, above the city of Memphis, is bracketed with the Mareotid Lake in the lower Delta for no perceptible reason other than alliteration. Details are still informed by Herodotus: the two lakes are as he described them, connected with the Nile by channels choked with lotus, and so is the Great Labyrinth built by the Twelve Kings near the city of Crocodilopolis, with its twelve courts. "The labyrinth surpasses even the pyramids," wrote the historian, ever susceptible to wonders, who described a vast number of rooms above, with a corresponding number below ground – those which he was forbidden to enter – the sepulchres of kings and the sacred crocodiles.[32] Herodotus provides no information concerning boys riding the crocodiles Arion-fashion, but he does explain how the sacred beasts were honoured, braceleted with gold, with rings of crystal and gold hanging in their ears, fed with sacred food, and trained to come at the call of the priests.

The Baedeker account of the Nile journey is over, and the witch turns from natural and man-made marvels to observe human kind in the hours of sleep. She not only observes but sees into the nature of their dreams, as if she glides through the tides of sleep. The first group of dreamers (stanza sixty-one) have no need of her. Infants and lovers lie within each others' arms, old age embraces the calm of life fulfilled, and the lone youth who weeps in his sleep sighs for that fulfilment which he already possesses in his dreams. All possess or dream of concord achieved, the gift of Eros. She passes on.

The second group, troubled sleepers, sleep as they live, in a world radically out of whack. Supernatural awe is unspeakably distorted

(Eros perverted): "imaginings of visioned wrong," spectral and pallid like Blake's Urizen, haunt the dreamer and those who render themselves "subject to custom's lawless law." These are the restless dreams of Eris: " 'This,' said the wizard maiden, 'is the strife / Which stirs the liquid surface of man's life' " (543–4). She passes on, unmoved. This same liquid surface, however, is the witch's own watery element, and although she moves within its untroubled depths, she is no stranger to wild and windswept lakes, metaphorical or otherwise, or to the strife which troubles their surface. Here she exercises the powers which she employed on the Austral Lake, drawing from fury a haven of concord.

> We, the weak mariners of that wide lake
> Where'er its shores extend or billows roll,
> Our course unpiloted and starless make
> O'er its wild surface to an unknown goal: –
> But she in the calm depths her way could take,
> Where in bright bowers immortal forms abide
> Beneath the weltering of the restless tide. (546–52)

Shelley has extended and wedded his central metaphors, the witch's watery element and the shifting tides of human life. But the witch moves under the restless shiftings as she moves under the surface of the Nile by night, within those unconscious depths of the mind to which our sole access lies in dream. There she may, or may not, work her alchemy. We move rudderless, unpiloted across the conscious surface of our lives, while she steers purposefully, silently in the deeps.[33]

The witch passes men of all degrees – princes, priests, peasants, and mariners – and those beyond degree – the dead in their dreamless graves, each neatly disposed within his appointed niche and content with his lot. These can neither dream nor imagine other than their own limited roles. Without vision or desire they slumber on, ignorant of their limitations within their own smug cells.

Because the witch moves from within and traffics in their subaqueous depths with souls, she is moved by and attracted solely to inner beauty rather than the accident of surface appearances. With her favoured souls, she mingles the liquid element of which she is guardian, the panacea stored in her crystal cell.

> Strange panacea in a crystal bowl: –
> They drank in their deep sleep of that sweet wave,
> And lived thenceforward as if some control,
> Mightier than life, were in them ... (594–7)

"That sweet wave" and its power transform even the wearied soul's forebodings of death; Eros confronts Thanatos, and for these fortunates the grave offers no dreamless sleep but a green and overarching bower, a paradisiac grove beyond time and decay peopled with a wealth of dream. Again the witch has transmuted the dissident elements (now of life and death) into a state of perfected completion, not unlike that embodied in her former creation, the *mysterium conjunctionis* of fire and ice and of the sexes, the hermaphrodite. The nurtured corpse slumbers, now at one with its own dreams of perfection, and it is indistinguishable from her own sleeping hermaphrodite.

With gentle smiles about its eyelids playing,
And living in its dream beyond the rage
Of death or life; while they were still arraying
In liveries ever new, the rapid, blind
And fleeting generations of mankind. (612–16)

FROM MYTH TO SATIRE

Until the Nile plunges from its Ethiopian highland, the witch's career has unfolded in a world which is characteristically mythic in its ordering of space and time. The identification of the witch with the Nile is established as a *pars pro toto* relationship, and the witch herself, her habitat, and her activities partake in a micro-macrocosmic relationship expressive of the workings of universal order. Her acts are a repetition in small of the primary theogonic act which first drew cosmic order from chaos or discord through the agency of Eros. Because of this, her repertory of stunts at various stages in her career reveals (albeit with variations) a certain repetitiousness, since her nature and role are unchanging, and it is various and changing circumstances that make her appear arbitrary and capricious. She preserves a continuity founded in the golden age, enduring in a fallen world, and informing the historic present of the final passages of the poem, in the manner in which myth and ritual customarily affirm or enact a changeless presence coexistent with the passing of clock time – human history. She endures through the vicissitudes of time, change, and the various – the fleeting landscapes of her passage – in a nascent present. In this respect, she may be understood simply as a persona, surrogate for the same Power Shelley addresses in his "Hymn to Intellectual Beauty," handmaid to the mighty seat of power which is the glacier of Mont Blanc, or sister to the west wind. Whether she serves the power or is that power itself in its effective role is beside the point, and the question risks the threat of heresy which Shelley raised in his introduction: "If you unveil my Witch, no Priest or Primate can shrive you of that sin." A maid unveiled, whether handmaid or witch, is a maid diminished. If Shelley's witch must suffer the indifferent scrutiny of analysis, causality, and what Keats called the "irritable reaching after fact and reason," she will be pronounced agent to the Power, serving, like the shadowy figure of Demogorgon, a larger and deeper mystery. But in the world framed by myth or religious ritual, she is that power or its hypostasis, and to analyse the nature of that mystery in logical terms is to reduce her to a scamp, or godhead to a crust of bread.

I have already raised the question of whether or not she leaves her mountain cave on her journey – whether the river as a river ever leaves behind its source – and it has been necessary throughout this inquiry to refer to her progress as a journey. In a curious way, it is as if there were no journey at all, as if the natural world in its flickering brilliance and the mortal in its petty squalor were slipping by her, illuminated, transfigured, or mocked by her presence, as the beasts and the genii, gods, and kings of the golden age brought their homage to her feet. It is this property and not the witch's nature which lends the kaleidoscopic and arbitrary character frequently attributed to the poem's imagery. There is, of course, nothing arbitrary about the poem and its deployment; its informing centre, whether we consider it as moving or at rest, is the witch and her river, from which all else derives relevance and beauty.

In a further sense the term "journey" is inadequate, particularly if it should suggest the archetypal literary quest. The traditional quest, a journey in time and space or within the mind, dictates that the quester is himself altered in his passage. The Witch of Atlas does not, nor can she, change. She is a constant like the river, herself unchanged by all she passes. But unaltered, she alters all.

After the descent from its mythic heights, it is as if the Nile widens in its passage into the shallows of a historic and recognizably human world. In spite of its setting in an exotic Egyptian past, it is also our world, not unlike the world of Swift's Houyhnhnms or Johnson's Rasselas – remote, bizarre, yet uncomfortably near. The river glides from its mythic antecedents into the world of satire, past proud temples, pyramids, princedoms, dioceses, and the cities of the plain. Consequently, the dimensions of the witch herself seem diminished, although her presence is everywhere critical. She has left behind her boat and oarsman and moves within the water, and it is likely that Shelley identifies her with the annual Nile flood and its gift. Her presence, like the river, constitutes a watery glass in which human foibles and institutions are reflected with mocking clarity.

Her pranks are still rehearsed in the dreams of the living, but now transform their waking hours as well. It is a breathlessly topsy-turvy world "where the beggars raffle the bank notes / And Jill goes down on her back." Bewitched dreams flesh out the exclusiveness and crabbed one-sidedness of human experience by revealing its obverse face, and the crooked is made straight from within. The remorseless one-sidedness of human motive is translated into multifaceted comedy. The transition to the shallows of satire is strikingly signalled by an altered tone and language, terse and flippant, and unceremoniously heralded by the crude cinching couplet of stanza seventy.

And she unwound the woven imagery
Of second childhood's swaddling bands, and took
The coffin, its last cradle, from its niche,
And threw it with contempt into a ditch. (605–8)

In his dreams the miser throws away his hoard, the lying scribe admits his lies, priests confess their pious frauds, even to playing at the ultimate apostasy, profaning the sacred menagerie of Egypt by nailing, like Luther, their denunciations to the temple door.[34] The king enthrones an ape in his stead and appoints a parrot as prime minister, while fawning courtiers kiss his arse. Soldiers play the smith, beating swords into ploughshares, jailers free the jailed, hesitant lovers dreamily act out what they dared only dream and are in due term confronted with the burden of the proof. Broken friendships are mended.

These wonders are no less wondrous than those the Greek historian observed among the Egyptians. Herodotus's Egypt, however, pursued its customs without the intercession of a witch of Atlas. Shelley may have found in the following passage the model for his portrayal of the inverted behaviour of his Cloud Cuckoo-Land on the Nile:

I now proceed to give a more particular account of Egypt; it possesses more wonders than any other country, and exhibits works greater than can be described, in comparison with all other regions; therefore more must be said about it. The Egyptians, besides having a climate peculiar to themselves, and a river differing in its nature from all other rivers, have adopted customs and usages in almost every respect different from the rest of mankind. Amongst them the women attend markets and traffic, but the men stay home and weave. Other nations, in weaving throw the wool upwards; the Egyptians, downwards. The men carry burdens on their heads; the women, on their shoulders. The women stand up when they make water, but the men sit down. They ease themselves in their houses, but eat out of doors; alleging that, whatever is indecent, though necessary, ought to be done in private; ... In other countries the priests of the gods wear long hair, in Egypt they have it

shaved ... They knead the dough with their feet; but mix clay and take up
dung in their hands.[35]

Shelley read Herodotus in July and August of 1818 at Bagni di Lucca,
two years before writing *The Witch of Atlas* under Edenic if not Saturnian circumstances beside a transparent woodland pool surrounded by
precipitous rocks and fed by a waterfall. "My custom is to undress and
sit on the rocks, reading Herodotus, until the perspiration has subsided,
and then to slip from the edge of the rock into the fountain."[36] This was
not necessarily his first acquaintance with the mythical landscape of the
Nile or its geographers.[37] Mary Shelley's accounting of her husband's
reading must be treated with caution; her records cannot establish that
Shelley had no previous knowledge of the works cited. His early readings of the classical geographers probably belonged to the days of classicizing with Peacock and his circle at Marlow that left their mark on
Alastor. It was at the time of his departure from Marlow in February
1818 that Shelley wrote his sonnet "To the Nile." The poem reveals that
not only had Shelley already charted the fabled course of his river from
its "aereal urn" on Atlas, but that the fundamental oppositions which
inform the later poem were already drawn, awaiting further exploration:

> Month after month the gathered rains descend
> Drenching yon secret Aethiopian dells,
> And from the desert's ice-girt pinnacles
> Where Frost and Heat in strange embraces blend
> On Atlas, fields of moist snow half depend.
> Girt there with blasts and meteors Tempest dwells
> By Nile's aereal urn, with rapid spells
> Urging those waters to their mighty end.
> O'er Egypt's land of Memory floods are level
> And they are thine, O Nile – and well thou knowest
> That soul-sustaining airs and blasts of evil
> And fruits and poisons spring where'er thou flowest.
> Beware, O Man – for knowledge must to thee,
> Like the great flood to Egypt, ever be.

The blasts, meteors, and tempests that gird Atlas, vexing the Nile's
creation, are translated to the Austral Lake; the elemental conflict of
"frost and heat in strange embraces" recurs in the creation of Hermaphroditus and is implicit in the witch's twin founts and her own paradoxical nature. The renovating river's "fruits" and "soul-sustaining
airs" retreat, leaving in their wake the mixed bounty of "poisons" and

"blasts of evil" which is the lot of the temporal world, Egypt's plain, "the land of memory."

The density of Herodotean materials throughout *The Witch of Atlas* either indicates a miracle of recollection or, more plausibly, argues the likelihood that Shelley reread the *History* at least in part in the summer of 1820. All of his Herodotean sources lie within three of the nine books of the *History*: books two, three, and four, the sections which posterity dedicated to the muses Euterpe, Thalia, and Terpsichore. Almost all of Shelley's historical and geographical details find at least an equivalent if not a positive source in Herodotus.[38] Unveiling Shelley's witch, however, bares more than a versified Herodotus, and hers is more than a borrowed splendour. She is invested with and at one with the perennial mystery which veiled the Nile, its source, its path, and its bounty.

Wordsworth, the "over-busy gardener," Shelley informs us in the prologue to *The Witch of Atlas*, passed nineteen years cultivating his *Peter Bell*:

Watering his laurels with the killing tears
    Of slow, dull care, so that their roots to Hell
Might pierce, and their wide branches blot the spheres
    Of Heaven, with dewy leaves and flowers ... (27–30)

"I send you the 'Witch of Atlas,' a fanciful poem, which, if its merit be measured by the labour which it cost, is worth nothing ..."[39] The three-day delivery of *The Witch of Atlas* does not disguise the fact that its germ lay fallow for at least two and a half years in Shelley's imagination, where, like Eros's boat,

The plant grew strong and green, the snowy flower
Fell, and the long and gourd-like fruit began
To turn the light and dew by inward power
To its own substance ... (305–8)

– a briefer term than *Peter Bell*, but a finer bravery.

Epilogue

These readings of Romantic poems have been directed toward the confluence of myth and psychology figured by the symbolic riverscape and its features. Some further explanation of their psychological underpinnings is in order.

The psychology I have found most serviceable in these matters is the psychology of the unconscious, depth psychology, engaged as it is with the business of translating the archaic language of myth into its own modern mythologems. I have not proposed Jungian readings of the poems, but I have found at least two features of the psychology of Carl Jung helpful in illuminating what appear here as recurrent themes or preoccupations. These are *anima* and the theory of projections, and the mechanism of psychic complementarity.

Anima is identified as the guardian of the unconscious and the executor of its imaginal expression. She is Jung's version of classical mythology's naiad at the river source, or the muse at the well-spring of poetic inspiration. Such figures furnish examples of projection, the means by which we personify or externalize subjective experience, so that what is "in here" is translated "out there" where we can protect ourselves from it or negotiate with it, where understanding is possible. This projective mechanism should be familiar to the reader of Romantic poetry: it is one of the most characteristic features of the Romantic preoccupation with natural and interior landscape. The role of *anima* and her avatars is ubiquitous throughout Romantic poetry, preoccupied as it is with the nature and dynamic of the creative process.

The principle of psychic complementarity has been introduced at a number of points in these essays; it too calls for further elaboration here. Jung fashioned his theory from the complementary or supplementary systems proposed by Adler's psychology of neuroses, although he characteristically looked for further corroboration as far afield as the Heraclitean *enantiodromia*, the arcana of alchemistry, and the physics of Niels Bohr. The mechanism of complementarity and its workings are discernible not only in Romantic poetry and biographical material but in the philosophical and aesthetic rationalizations of Romantic prose.

Because consciousness is characterized by its directed, discriminatory, and selective operations, it excludes or represses that which seems irrelevant to the thrust of its inquiry. As a consequence, its orientation often becomes increasingly precarious through an exclusive one-sidedness. Catastrophe or pathology threaten when we fail to respond to the realities of our survival or to imperatives of feeling which have been systematically overlooked. Mounting pressure is reduced and a normative redress is effected when these repressed contents are thrust upon consciousness through dream, spontaneous imagery, or, as already suggested, projection onto external elements where they can command our attention. Complementarity, whether a natural regulating mechanism or something fostered by clinical intervention, assumes the allopathic method of traditional medicine in which health, or organic equilibrium, is restored through treating a condition or pathology with its opposite.

Coleridge furnishes the most comprehensive instance of a Romantic essaying ontological, metaphysical, and aesthetic integrity predicated upon a dialectic of opposites. Jung, like Coleridge, saw opposites as constitutive of things: of synthesis, symbol, generation and growth, and art. Opposites are not merely modes of analytic discourse fashioned for the sake of argument. I have suggested that a play of opposites, a conscious idealization and its compensatory demonization, informs Coleridge's highly problematic personal relationships as well as the fantasy life recorded in the notebooks and reconstituted in the poetry. The Coleridgean symbolic landscape with its characteristic dramatis personae is drawn and peopled by the same countering impulses. Art, the "miracle of rare device," is itself a *tertium aliquid* achieved by the precarious equilibration of conscious intellect with unconscious impulse, the province of feeling.

Keats's negative capability is a matter of psychological projection, and the critical behaviour of Endymion, Lycius, and the knight-at-arms is defined by their response to inner imperatives at odds with the roles of their waking lives. The Latmian shepherd's odyssey toward his goddess is launched by his restless discontent with the paternally directed world of Pan with its insipid pastoralism, while the fledgling Corinthian Platonist is introduced at the point of abandoning the rigors of cold philosophy for the arms of his changeling mistress whose pursuits are directed by Eros and the thieving god of changes. Knights-at-arms are purposive, directed souls. As such, they are susceptible to the siren song of a faery's child and the lure of her elfin grot.

The turning point in Shelley's *Alastor* occurs when its genteel tourism is transformed into the urgent heroic quest, when that which was excluded from life (as rigorously as that repressed by Coleridge's ascetic in "The Picture") asserts itself in a dream confrontation that cannot be denied.

These readings end with Shelley's mythopoeic account of the Nile, not simply because *The Witch of Atlas* recalls their point of embarkation – *The Prelude*, *The River Duddon*, and the *Ecclesiastical Sonnets*, poems structured in terms of the river and its passage – but because Shelley's poem masters all the diverse elements which have been the subject of this inquiry. Among these are the paradoxes of being and becoming and of identify and change enacted by the river passage, its coming into being at the source, and the guardian who is both at home and at one with its waters, and who presides over the mysteries of creation, recreation, generation, and nurture. The Nile guardian's peculiar witchery preserved by her archimagean lore contrives the reconciliation of Eros with Eris, the theogonic act which gave birth to cosmos and our first age. In her piloting beneath the "liquid surface of man's life," Shelley's physician mends souls and redirects their one-sided pursuits by challenging them with healing counter-images. Through her miraculous devising they are made anew and made whole. In her physic can be recognized the allopathy, psychological and metaphysical, with which the Romantic sought to reconstitute his art and his world.

Notes

Unless otherwise noted, translations from Greek and Latin sources are from the Loeb Classics editions.

ABBREVIATIONS

CN   *The Notebooks of Samuel Taylor Coleridge*, ed. Kathleen Coburn, 3 vols. (New York: Pantheon 1957–72)

EHC   *The Complete Poetical Works of Samuel Taylor Coleridge*, ed. E.H. Coleridge, 2 vols. (Oxford: Clarendon Press 1912)

STC Letters *Collected Letters of Samuel Taylor Coleridge*, ed. E.L. Griggs, 6 vols. (Oxford: Clarendon Press 1956–9)

Prelude *The Prelude, 1799, 1805, 1850*, ed. Jonathan Wordsworth, M.H. Abrams, and Stephen Gill (New York: W.W. Norton 1970). All quotations, unless otherwise indicated, are from the 1805 *Prelude*.

WPW   *The Poetical Works of William Wordsworth*, ed. E. de Selincourt and Helen Darbishire, 5 vols. (Oxford: Clarendon Press 1963)

All quotations are from these editions unless otherwise noted. Quotations from the poetry of Keats and Shelley are from the following:

- *The Poetical Works of John Keats*, ed. H.W. Garrod (London: Oxford University Press 1956)
- *The Complete Poetical Works of Percy Bysshe Shelley*, ed. Thomas Hutchinson (London: Oxford University Press 1956)

RIVERSCAPES: A PROLOGUE

1 Quoted from the *Bhavisyottarapurana*, in Mircea Eliade, *Patterns in Comparative Religion*, trans. Rosemary Sheed (New York: Meridian 1965), 188.
2 "The Canticle of Brother Sun," in L.S. Cunningham, *Saint Francis of Assisi* (Boston: G.K. Hall 1976), 58.
3 Eliade, *Patterns*, 200.

CHAPTER ONE

1 Kenneth MacLean, "The Water Symbol in *The Prelude* (1805–6)," *UTQ*, 17 (July 1948): 372–89 provides an indiscriminate gathering of water references culled from *The Prelude* (lakes, rivers, oceans, waterfalls), and observes that they are frequent. James Applewhite, *Seas and Inland Journeys: Landscape and Consciousness from Wordsworth to Roethke* (Athens: University of Georgia Press 1985) deals largely with seas and overlooks the fact that the inland journey is frequently a river journey from or to the sea. John Beer's essay "Coleridge and Wordsworth: Influence and Confluence," in Donald Sultana, ed., *New Approaches to Coleridge: Biographical and Critical Essays* (London and Totowa, NJ: Vision and Barnes and Noble 1981), 192–211 anticipates the thrust of this inquiry. Beer notes the currency of springs and rivers and Wordsworth's and Coleridge's interest in them. He likens the form of *The Prelude* to a river and relates it to the Duddon sonnets (205). See also Jonathan Wordsworth, *William Wordsworth: The Borders of Vision* (Oxford: Clarendon Press 1982) and his chapter "The Image of a Mighty Mind," in which he discusses rivers in connection with the Snowdon episode.
2 Geoffrey Hartman in "Blessing the Torrent: On Wordsworth's Later Style," *PMLA*, 93 (March 1978): 196–203 makes the untenable assertion that Derwent is the infant's nurse or foster mother. Derwent and all other Wordsworthian rivers are masculine: the nurse fulfils the feminine role.
3 R.A. Foakes, *The Romantic Assertion* (London: Methuen 1958) has considered *The Prelude* as a voyage or pilgrimage poem; A.F. Potts, *Wordsworth's Prelude* (New York: Octagon 1972) suggests as much. Those who read it as epic narrative have identified other heroic patterns. None, I think, have considered the circumstances of the hero's birth.
4 Wordsworth, unlike that other poet of memory, Proust, preserved few recollections of his mother, although he was eight years old at the time of her death. In "Autobiographical Memoranda" he cites two of these, which are surprisingly slight and impersonal. Nor did his father fare better. There is a single oblique reference to him in *The Prelude* ("my father's house"), so that John Wordsworth seems more of a place than a person.

5 Marcel Proust, *Swann's Way*, in *Remembrance of Things Past*, trans. C.K. Scott-Moncrieff, 2 vols. (New York: Random House 1934), 1:35.

6 Wordsworth's account of his Cambridge days is not wholly an annual of unrelieved gloom, and the poet attempts to convey something of its fascination and gaieties ("and yet this was a gladsome time"). That "yet" is characteristic. The clouds swag heavily on the fens, and the Cambridge imagery speaks tellingly of the poet's ambivalence. In his revisions Wordsworth heightened considerably the impact of his return to Windermere, casting Cambridge by contrast in deeper glooms.

7 Quoted in Mary Moorman, *William Wordsworth: A Biography. The Early Years, 1770-1803* (Oxford: Clarendon Press 1957), 105.

8 The allusion to Charon and his river has vexed Wordsworth's editors. De Selincourt found it inept, and W.J.B. Owen concurs, noting that Charon is always surly and unsavoury, and that he plies a river and not a lake. "Literary Echoes in *The Prelude*," *Wordsworth Circle*, 3 (Summer 1972): 3-16. Wordsworth's apparently churlish gesture toward the ferryman George Robinson seems undeserved, particularly since he extends a cordial welcome. The returning scholar may be stuffed with ill-digested classical allusion but, aside from the issue of Charon's character, the allusion is perfectly apt if we consider the oarsman as ferrying his charge from immurement in the cloistered land of shades to this spacious world of glancing light. Moreover, Wordsworth's Charon does cross a "Windermere / Like a vast river." In *Select Views* Wordsworth quoted with approval Gray's description of the lake in a letter to Joseph Wharton: "It is ten miles in length and at most a mile over, resembling the course of some vast and magnificent river." W.J.B. Owen and J.M. Smyser, eds., *The Prose Works of William Wordsworth*, 3 vols. (Oxford: Clarendon Press 1974), 2:261n.

9 I have adopted the names of the streams in the Simplon-Viamala region as identified by Max Wildi in "Wordsworth and the Simplon Pass," *ES*, 41 (1959): 224-32.

10 *WPW*, 3:503.

11 Stewart Wilcox, "Wordsworth's River Duddon Sonnets," *PMLA*, 69 (1954): 131-41. Wilcox gives a thorough and persuasive reading of the sonnets, except for his rigid Platonic rendering of the final poem, which is less than convincing.

12 Ibid., 135.

13 M.W. to S.H. (1 December 1818), *WPW*, 3:506.

14 *WPW*, 3:523-4.

15 "Goredale," *WPW*, 3:37-8.

16 A.F. Potts, *The Ecclesiastical Sonnets of William Wordsworth* (New Haven: Yale University Press 1922). Potts's is the exhaustive account of sources, analogues, and echoes.

17 *WPW*, 3:569.

CHAPTER TWO

1 L.R. Farnell, *The Cults of the Greek States*, 5 vols. (Oxford: Clarendon Press 1907), 5:420.
2 H.D. Kitto, *In the Mountains of Greece* (London: Methuen 1933).
3 Symmachus to Ausonius 10.
4 Ausonius, *Mosella* 10.169–85.
5 R.A. Aubin, *Topographical Poetry in Eighteenth-Century England* (New York: Modern Language Association of America 1936). Aubin's "*hortus siccus* of withered pedantries" is a garden of informative delights.
6 *The Lay of the Last Minstrel*, in J.L. Robertson, ed., *The Poetical Works of Sir Walter Scott* (London: Frowde 1910), 159.
7 *CN*, 3:3463.
8 Homer, *Iliad* 2.303–8.
9 Pausanius 14.3.9. Plutarch, *De defectu oraculorum* 432.
10 Barbara E. Rooke, ed., *The Friend*, 2 vols. in *The Collected Works of Samuel Taylor Coleridge* (London: Routledge 1969), 1:18.
11 Pausanius 1.34.9. Thomas Taylor, trans., *Iamblichus on the Mysteries* (London: Dobell 1895), 141.
12 Varro, *De lingua Latina* 5.61.
13 *The Greek Anthology* 9.607.
14 Ibid. 9.329.
15 Ibid. 9.663.
16 Ibid. 9.327.
17 Mircea Eliade, *Patterns in Comparative Religion* (New York: Meridian 1965), 204.
18 Robert Kirk, *The Secret Commonwealth* (Stirling: the Observer Press 1933), 81.
19 Ulrich von Wilamowitz-Moellendorff, *Der Glaube der Hellenen*, 2 vols. (Berlin: Weidmannsche 1931), 1:17. Walter F. Otto, *Dionysus: Myth and Cult*, trans. R.B. Palmer (Bloomington: Indiana University Press 1965), 32.
20 For instances of the persistence of nymphs in modern Greece see J.C. Lawson, *Modern Greek Folklore and Ancient Greek Religion: A Study in Survivals* (New York: University Books 1966), 130–73. Also Richard and Eva Blum, *The Dangerous Hour: The Lore of Crisis and Mystery in Rural Greece* (London: Chatto and Windus 1970), 112–18.
21 Horace, *Odes* 3.1.13. Martial 6.47.5.
22 Aubrey's "Remaines of Gentilisme and Judaisme" also refers to contemporary instances of well-dressing. John Buchanan-Brown, ed., *John Aubrey: Three Prose Works* (Fontwell: Centaur Press 1972), 188–9.
23 Eliade, *Patterns*, 200. Robert Charles Hope, *The Legendary Lore of the Holy Wells of England: Including Rivers, Lakes, Fountains, and Springs* (London 1893), xx.

24 Hope, *Legendary Lore*, 211.

25 Ausonius, *Ordo urbium nobilium* 20.30–4.

26 Sir James Frazer, ed., *The Fasti of Ovid*, 6 vols. (London: Macmillan 1929), 3:289.

27 Hope, *Legendary Lore*, 81.

28 Eleanor Hull, *Folklore of the British Isles* (London: Methuen 1928), 110.

29 Hope, *Legendary Lore*, 164.

30 Ibid., 43.

31 Ibid., 40.

32 Ibid., 39.

CHAPTER THREE

1 *WPW*, 1:260. "Essay upon Epitaphs," in W.J.B. Owen and J.W. Smyser, eds., *The Prose Works of William Wordsworth*, 3 vols. (Oxford: Clarendon Press 1974), 2:51.

2 "Did Sabine grace adorn my living line, / Bandusia's praise, wild stream, should yield to thine" (*WPW*, 1:11, 72–3). "Or Sabine vales explored inspire a wish / To meet the shade of Horace by the side / Of his Bandusian fount … "(*WPW*, 3:209, 255–7).

3 Wordsworth, *Prose*, 3:34. Coleridge attributed such "godkins and goddesslings" to the workings of Greek fancy, reserving imaginative vision for the Hebrews.

4 J. Lemprière, *A Classical Dictionary* (London 1815), no pag. Entry under "nymphae."

5 The poem is printed by de Selincourt, *WPW*, 4:381–7 (appendix B).

6 Mary Moorman, *William Wordsworth: A Biography*, 2 vols. (Oxford: Clarendon Press 1965), 2:422.

7 *WPW*, 4:382n.

8 Plutarch, *De defectu oraculorum* 432.

9 Ibid., 435.

10 *WPW*, 4:423.

11 Virgil, *Georgics* 5.339.

12 De Selincourt claims that this version was discarded by the time Wordsworth sent a new version in a letter to Coleridge from Goslar. The original passage in the discarded rendering reads: "And let me see thee sink into a dream / Of gentle thoughts, protracted till thine eye / Be calm as water when the winds are gone / And no one can tell whither" (*WPW*, 2:505).

13 *WPW*, 2:28. I have omitted the third stanza and restored the second, which Wordsworth dropped from his editions of 1845 and 1849.

14 Wordsworth's revisions of the Lucy group tend to further this process. The final stanza of the 1798 "Strange Fits of Passion" with its description of Lucy's ringing laughter allows Lucy an insistently human and independent

character which was withdrawn in later versions. The poem "The Glow Worm," dropped from the collected editions, clearly belongs to the same Racedown setting as "Strange Fits of Passion" and the Lucy group, but the incident was probably too particularized to serve Wordsworth's purposes. Lucy may be spirit, but it must be admitted that she is certainly less than spirited, and Wordsworth suppressed the poem and those passages which depicted her otherwise.

15 Geoffrey Hartman, *Wordsworth's Poetry 1787–1814* (New Haven: Yale University Press 1964), 158. Hartman hints at the nature of the figure who is the focus of my inquiry: "She reminds us of the traditional mythical person who lives, ontologically, an intermediate life, or mediates various realms of existence. Nymphs, both watery and human, are an example; heroes in so far as both human and divine, another." Hartman foregoes the pursuit of nymphs or heroes.

Speculations on Lucy's origin and character are legion, and often run afoul of whatever the "true" relation of brother and sister might have been. My own feeling is that it was simply an extraordinarily moving one. R.E. Matlock has proposed a speculative "psychobiographical" reading which substitutes for the canard of sublimated incest a sublimated death wish for Dorothy on Wordsworth's part. Matlock provides no evidence, however, that Wordsworth regarded his sister as "a ball and chain" to his freedom. Such repressed resentment apparently lies far beneath the threshold of biographical and literary evidence, and Wordsworth's frequent and moving tributes to his sister and his confessions of his dependence upon her hardly suggest suspect protestations on his part. Matlock derives a triangular scenario from the Lucy poems, placing undue emphasis on the latest and least satisfying "I Travelled among Unknown Men." He proposes that, torn between his attraction to the absent Coleridge and his burdensome responsibilities to his sister, Wordsworth imagines her death during the Goslar winter, and two years later "his ego is now free to transfer its love to England, the new object of its choice." Wordsworth, Matlock would have us believe, resolved the family drama by finding solace in the arms of Britannia. R.E. Matlock, "Wordsworth's Lucy Poems in Psychobiographical Context," *PMLA*, 93 (1978): 46–66. Paul Magnuson, *Coleridge and Wordsworth: A Lyrical Dialogue* (Princeton: Princeton University Press 1988), 200 identifies Wordsworth's fears as anxiety over being cut off from his past, since Dorothy functions as an image of his past in "Tintern." She does, but she is considerably more than that: his eyes, his ears, his thought, and his inspiration and joy, as "The Sparrow's Nest" declares.

16 Such places continued to haunt Wordsworth for a lifetime. His reaction to the Fountain of Vaucluse, recorded in the notes to *Memorials of a Tour in Italy, 1837*, revives verbal echoes of the "Nutting" poem written thirty-eight years earlier. The spring of Petrarch's inspiration was holy ground for

Wordsworth, even though he concludes his unbridled account with a touching scepticism owing to his sixty-seven years: "Then there was Vaucluse, with its fountain, its Petrarch, its rocks of all seasons, its small plots of lawn ... the beauty of the stream also called forcibly for the expression of sympathy from one who from his childhood had studied the brooks and torrents of his native mountains. Between two and three hours did I run about climbing the steep and rugged crags from whose base the water of Vaucluse breaks forth. 'Has Laura's Lover', often said I to myself, 'ever sat down upon this stone? or has his foot ever pressed that turf? ... my answer was (impute it to my years), 'I fear not' " (WPW, 3:489–90). The passage indicates Wordsworth's awareness that Petrarch's Rime sparse repeatedly seal the image of his muse, Madonna Laura, with the fountains of Vaucluse and their issue, the River Sorgue, both before and after her purported death.

17 WPW, 2:211.

18 C.G. Jung, Psychology and Alchemy in The Collected Works of C.G. Jung, 20 vols. (Princeton: Princeton University Press 1953), 12:52, 83–6. Jung identifies the personification of the unconscious with anima, the archetype who fosters male imaginal understanding by making possible our experiencing and our expression through images. For Jung this is essentially the activity of personifying, the means by which we personalize the external world. Cf. James Hillman, Re-Visioning Psychology (New York: Harper and Row 1975), 42–4. Wordsworth's portrayal of the feminine has troubled some of his readers. Marlon Ross, "Naturalizing Gender: A Woman's Place in Wordsworth's Ideological Landscapes, "ELH, 53 (Spring 1986): 391–440 sees women in a "marginal role" (not to be confused with Hartman's liminal creatures), in which they serve as mediators in the maturation or individuation of the male, an instance of the "colonization of the feminine." Wordsworth does indeed, as Ross points out, ignore the issue of Lucy's personal needs and desires, and the words "colonization" and "handmaiden" have probably earned their current disrepute. Wordsworth's defence may lie with the fact that his males fare no better. Are there any wholly authentic, autonomous characterizations to be found in the Wordsworth canon? Robert Langbaum, "Wordsworth's Lyrical Characterizations, "SIR, 21 (Fall 1982): 319–39 describes Wordsworth's habit of portraying the inner life through characters who represent "a quality of soul or imagination. This is achieved not through action or dialogue but visual impressions and impressions that often include the figure's setting in a landscape." See also Jean Hagstrum, The Romantic Body: Love and Sexuality in Keats, Wordsworth, and Blake (Knoxville: University of Tennessee Press 1985), 93, and "the insinuating of Dorothy into nature and of nature into her."

19 I refer to the chronology established by Mark Reed, Wordsworth: The Chronology of the Early Years (Cambridge: Harvard University Press 1967), 256–60.

20 The Goslar archives contain no record that *Lucia-nacht* was observed in the Hartz in Wordsworth's day, although the custom did survive the middle ages in many rural areas of Germany. Wordsworth probably had no need of a local observation to jog memories of "Lucy night, shortest day and longest night," or of Donne's "A Nocturnal Upon St. Lucy's Day; Being the Shortest Day."

21 The pathos of Dorothy's later life is evoked in her own lines of 1835 written in confinement: "When shall I wander, free as air, / And track the foaming rill?" Quoted in Susan M. Levin, *Dorothy Wordsworth and Romanticism* (New Brunswick and London: Rutgers, The State University 1987), 137.

22 William Blake, *The Marriage of Heaven and Hell*, in G. Keynes, ed., *The Complete Writings of William Blake* (London: Nonesuch 1966), 153.

CHAPTER FOUR

1 *WPW*, 1:263–4.

2 W.J. Bate, *Coleridge* (London: Weidenfeld and Nicolson 1969), 42.

3 Pliny, *Natural History* 35.133. Pliny also notes Nicias's celebrity for producing female portraits of a three-dimensional effect.

4 G. Louis Joughin, "Coleridge's 'Lewti', The Biography of a Poem," *Texas Studies in English*, 143:23 (1943): 66–93. J.L. Lowes, *The Road to Xanadu* (Boston: Houghton Mifflin 1927). Lowes rejected a suspected ascription to Wordsworth by arguing that Coleridge took the scenery and details for his poem from Bartram: "No one who reads the three or four consecutive pages in Bartram can well doubt that they inspired the setting of Lewti" (514). Lowes's "sources" should always be approached with caution. His case for the primacy of Bruce's account of Ethiopia as a source for "Kubla Khan," despite "verbal echoes," is also less than convincing. If the poem channelled Coleridge's recollections of Bruce, the poet repressed the explorer's low opinion of Ethiopian women. The impression garnered from Bruce's description of a luxurious banquet with the court ladies entertaining their lords *sub mensa*, beneath the groaning board, is that Abyssinian maids were a rarity that escaped the explorer's notice.

   Lowes's magisterial authority dies hard. Geoffrey Yarlott in *The Abyssinian Maid* (1966) is unaware of de Selincourt's revelation some twenty years earlier and continues to insist, as did Lowes, that the Mary in the first version of "Lewti" (Wordsworth's) is Coleridge's Mary Evans and conclusive evidence of his authorship.

5 Lowes, *The Road to Xanadu*, 177n, 178n.

6 *EHC*, 2:1052.

7 Mario D'Avanzo relates the spectre woman to "the great whore that sitteth upon the waters" of the book of Revelation. D'Avanzo, "Her Looks Were Free: The Ancient Mariner and the Harlot," *ELN*, 17 (March 1980): 185–9.

8 "Religious Musings," *EHC*, 1:115, 171; *Zapolya*, *EHC*, 2:892, 277; "The Will of the Wisp," *EHC*, 2:980, 2; "Introduction to the Tale of the Dark Ladie," variant reading *EHC*, 2:1059n. But see Coleridge's note to "Ode to the Departing Year" on Catherine the Great: "I rejoice – not over the deceased Woman (I never dared figure the Russian Sovereign to my imagination under the dear and venerable Character of WOMAN – WOMAN, that complex term for Mother, Sister, Wife!) I rejoice, as at the disenshrining of a Daemon! I rejoice, as at the extinction of the evil Principle impersonated." *EHC*, 1:162n. Sarah Coleridge is described as "Beloved woman" in "Lines Written at Shurton Bars," and as "O Beloved woman and heart honoured maid" in "The Aeolian Harp" written in the same happy year, when "Beloved" and "maid" seem to exonerate the "woman."
9 Sarah's biographer, Molly Lefebure, has undertaken a more sympathetic appraisal than Dorothy's. Sarah's addiction to a private punning language, however, probably tried her husband as sorely as Leigh Hunt's "eternal puns" plagued both Keats and Shelley. Molly Lefebure, *Bondage of Love* (New York: Stein and Day 1974).
10 *EHC*, 1:253n.
11 *CN*, 3:4088.
12 *Paradise Lost*, 4.281-3. Milton entertains the claims of the "feigned paradises" but chose Mesopotamia and the Assyrian garden as the primal seat. There is a long tradition connecting Ethiopia with paradise, however. The Ethiopians, who were characterized as a beautiful and virtuous race, at least until Bruce's narrative challenged such notions, were accounted by the ancients as the first of men, the *autochthones*, sprung from the soil by the action of the sun (Diodorus Siculus 3:2). The Abyssinian Mount Abora was among the foremost claimants to the paradisal mount.
13 *The Prelude*, 1805, 11.273-5.
14 *CN* 2:224. Dated October 1804.
15 George Whalley, *Coleridge and Sara Hutchinson and the Asra Poems* (London: Routledge and Kegan Paul 1955), 120.
16 E. de Selincourt, *Journals of Dorothy Wordsworth*, 2 vols. (London: Macmillan 1952), 1:137.
17 E. Curtius, *European Literature and the Latin Middle Ages* (New York: Pantheon 1953), 195.
18 Ibid., 192.
19 Ibid., 195.
20 *EHC*, 1:369n. Kathleen Coburn notes EHC's attribution but unaccountably questions its validity. Only Fruman elaborates on the nature of Coleridge's indebtedness: he "adopted large blocks of language from Gessner's forty-five line poem." Fruman's "blocks" are evasive, his estimate misleading, and *Der Feste Vorsatz* is not a poem. Norman Fruman, *Coleridge, The Damaged Archangel* (London: Allen and Unwin 1971), 510n. "The Picture" has

received little critical attention. Most recent is Marc Porée, "Pour une topique du corps ou l'image-corps en (tous) ses lieux," *Romantisme*, 49 (1985): 77–93.

21 *STC Letters*, 2:808n.

22 Ibid., 2:813. Coleridge likens Gessner to a "Boarding School Miss whose *Imagination*, to say no worse, had been somewhat stirred & heated by the perusal of French or German pastorals." *STC Letters*, 2:810.

23 The notebooks indicate that Coleridge was reading the *Thebaid* in April and May 1802. *CN*, 1:1179.

24 *CN*, 1:1153.

25 Section the Second, Essay 11, "Essays on the Principles of Method," in Barbara Rooke, ed., *The Friend*, 2 vols. (Princeton: Princeton University Press 1969), 1:509.

26 Miguel de Unamuno, *Tragic Sense of Life*, trans. J.E.C. Flitch (New York: Dover 1954), 139.

27 *STC Letters*, 2:865.

28 R.A. Armour and R.F. Howes, eds., *Coleridge the Talker* (New York: Johnson Reprint 1969), 108, 133, 188, 227, 115, 235, 317.

29 *STC Letters*, 1:51. John Beer has observed that "Both Wordsworth and Coleridge had the fortune to be brought up in landscapes which were honeycombed by springs and streams. One could not grow up in the Lake District without being aware of water flowing and pouring on all sides – often from inexhaustible sources." John Beer, "Coleridge and Wordsworth: Influence and Confluence," in Donald Sultana, ed., *New Approaches to Coleridge: Biographical and Critical Essays* (London and Totowa, NJ: Vision and Barnes and Noble 1981), 197. Beer also notes that the poet's Devon and Somerset are comparable to the Lake District in this respect.

30 *STC Letters*, 2:456–7.

31 *CN*, 1:412.

32 *STC Letters*, 1:51.

33 *EHC*, 1:58–9.

34 The lines are among metrical experiments recorded in the notebooks, possibly written in October 1804. *CN*, 2:2224f84.

35 *STC Letters*, 1:301.

36 Horace, *Satires* 2.6.2–3.

37 Lowes, *The Road to Xanadu*, 207.

38 George Watson, ed., *Biographia Literaria* (London: Dent 1950), 108.

39 *WPW*, 1:363.

40 H.P. L'Orange, "Expressions of Cosmic Kingship in the Ancients" in *The Sacral Kingship: Contributions to the Central Theme of the VIIIth International Congress for the History of Religions*, 1955 (Leiden: E.J. Brill 1959), 481. John Beer identifies Xanadu as a circular earthly paradise sacred to the

sun, claiming Coleridge derived his solar mythology from Bryant. J.B. Beer, *Coleridge the Visionary* (London: Chatto and Windus 1970), 218.

41 To venture an opinion on Xanadu is to take on the obligations of a medieval exegete: legions have been there before. Of these I mention only a few with whom I take issue, and the nature of the issues involved. First, a poem whose subject is the creative imagination can hardly be accounted for by unravelling the "hooks and crochets" of Coleridge's literary recollections. Fancy is always operative, but secondary, and its "fixities and definites" mere paving stones on the road to Xanadu. Their disposition, orientation, and character, and the direction of that road would seem more pertinent. Secondly, I disagree with the contention that Xanadu is a false paradise, a deceptive bower of bliss, product of a false creator, or Kubla's "fussy little Paradise," as Geoffrey Yarlott and others would have it, blameworthy because of its "exclusiveness and separation." G. Yarlott, *Coleridge and the Abyssinian Maid* (London: Methuen 1967), 132–3. Xanadu is an earthly paradise sharing the character of such places and, as such, as ineluctable for the reader as for the poet who, having once seen it, desires nothing more from life than the power to recreate it.

42 Yarlott finds such words fork-tongued and pejoratively sensual, although it is never made clear why the speaker should play the serpent in this Eden. George Watson argues that the fault lies as much with the creator as his creation: Kubla is "something of a barbarous fop," a "tyrannical aristocrat." Are we then to identify the pleasure dome with Brighton Pavilion? G. Wilson Knight sees Kubla not as the Regent, but as God, an "intimation of mountainous power" rather than girth. Elizabeth Schneider condemns the goings-on beneath the dome, its ancestral voices prophesying war, as "out of key with other images," another fault in Coleridge's fissured poem. If the dome, too, is faulty, a culpable creation, then the designation "stately" is inappropriate. Denigrators of Xanadu have invariably smelt a rat, if not under the dome, then beneath its incense-bearing trees, although the fragrance of paradise has been regularly celebrated for at least fourteen centuries since the *de Paradiso* of Saint Syrus Ephraem. George Watson, *Coleridge the Poet* (London: Routledge and Kegan Paul 1966), 126–7. Elizabeth Schneider, *Coleridge, Opium and Kubla Khan* (New York: Octagon 1970), 248. G. Wilson Knight, *The Starlit Dome* (London: Oxford 1941), 93.

43 Quoted from the first edition by E.M. Clark in "Milton's Abyssinian Paradise," *University of Texas Studies in English*, 29 (1950): 140.

44 *Paradise Lost*, 4.158–63. "Religious Musings," variant reading, *EHC*, 1:123n. E.S. Shaffer, *Kubla Khan and the Fall of Jerusalem: The Mythological School in Biblical Criticism and Secular Literature, 1770–1880* (Cambridge: Cambridge University Press 1975) extends the provenance of Xanadu's imagery from Genesis to the book of Revelation.

45 Mircea Eliade, *Images and Symbols*, trans. Philip Mairet (New York: Sheed and Ward 1969), 38.
46 Ibid., 39–40.
47 *CN*, 1:7.
48 Ibid., 1:220.
49 *STC Letters*, 1:238 (to George Coleridge).
50 Nai-Tung Ting, "From Shangtu to Xanadu," *SIR*, 23 (Summer 1984): 205–22 is informative concerning Kubla's historic capital. If Coleridge were privy to such information, it is indeed striking that he should choose to transform Chublai's "busy and cosmopolitan capital of some 200,000 inhabitants" into the unpeopled fastness of his Xanadu. Jerome McGann has called Xanadu "the dream of a truly human civilization." But Xanadu is empty as an echo of all save the great Khan himself. Jerome McGann, *Romantic Ideology: A Critical Investigation* (Chicago and London: University of Chicago Press 1983), 98.
51 *STC Letters*, 1:350.
52 Nor, I might add, Napoleon to Josephine. For an identification of Kubla with Bonaparte see Norman Rudich, "Kubla Khan, a Political Poem," *Romantisme*, 8 (1977): 52,3. McGann cites Rudich sympathetically. McGann, *Romantic Ideology*, 101.
53 A.B. Giamatti, *The Earthly Paradise and the Renaissance Epic* (Princeton: Princeton University Press 1966), 11.
54 W.B. Yeats, *Explorations* (London: Macmillan 1962), 306. Yeats was reading Coleridge at this time (May-June 1930) and mentions him frequently in his diary.
55 E. Rochedieu, "Le Caractère Sacré de la Souveraineté à la Lumière de la Psychologie Collective" in *The Sacral Kingship*, 51.
56 Harold Bloom, *A Map of Misreading* (New York: Oxford University Press 1975).
57 I find no fault with Yeats's "Sailing to Byzantium" here, only with those readings of the poem that fail to take into account Yeats's deliberate irony in his choice of the golden bird, which, it must be admitted, is a drollery and an amusement when compared with the other artifacts mentioned, the great golden mosaics of Byzantium with their sages "standing in God's holy fire."
58 *CN*, 2:2915.
59 I am unable to read the close of "Kubla Khan" as "a dramatic representation of imagination's own self-renovating powers with its promise of renewal," as McGann does (*Romantic Ideology*, 90).

CHAPTER FIVE

1 John D. Baird and C. Ryskamp, eds., *The Poems of William Cowper*, 1 – vols. (Oxford: Clarendon Press 1980–) 1:44, 10–12.

2 Ibid., 19, 23–4.

3 H.B. Wright and M.K. Spears, eds., *Matthew Prior: Literary Works*, 3 vols. (Oxford: Clarendon Press 1959), 1:414, 7–10.

4 Harold Williams, ed., *The Poems of Jonathan Swift*, 3 vols. (Oxford: Clarendon Press 1958), 2:589,163–70.

5 Horace, *Epistles* 1.19.1–3.

6 *WPW*, 3:504.

7 John Armstrong, MD, *The Art of Preserving Health* (Dublin 1765), 21.

8 Launcelot Temple (Dr John Armstrong), *A Short Ramble through Some Parts of France and of Italy* (London 1771), 23–5.

9 H.W. Garrod, ed., *The Poetical Works of John Keats* (London: Oxford University Press 1956), 399.

10 K.N. Cameron, ed., *Shelley and His Circle: 1773–1822*, 8 vols. (Cambridge, Mass.: Harvard University Press 1973), 6:610.

11 Edmund Blunden, "The Keats-Shelley Poetry Contests," *Notes and Queries 199* (December 1954): 546.

12 Edmund Blunden, Leigh Hunt: A Biography (London: Cobden-Sanderson 1930), 134. *Shelley and His Circle*, 6:530.

13 Blunden, *Leigh Hunt*, 134.

14 Leigh Hunt, *Foliage: or Poems Original and Translated* (London: Ollier 1818), vi.

15 Ibid., xv.

16 Ibid., xxvii.

17 ibid., lxxi.

18 Hyder Rollins, ed., *The Letters of John Keats*, 2 vols. (Cambridge, Mass.: Harvard University Press 1972), 1:139.

19 Frederick L. Jones, ed., *The Letters of Percy Bysshe Shelley*, 2 vols. (Oxford: Clarendon Press 1964), 2:152.

20 Ibid., 2:2.

21 Thomas Hutchinson, ed., *The Complete Poetical Works of Percy Bysshe Shelley* (London: Oxford University Press 1956), 368.

22 Keats, *Letters*, 2:11.

23 Shelley, *Letters*, 2:475.

24 *Frazer's Magazine*, 61 (March 1860): 304.

25 *Shelley and His Circle*, 8:463.

26 Carl Dawson, *His Fine Wit: A Study of Thomas Love Peacock* (London: Routledge and Kegan Paul 1970), 55.

27 Thomas Love Peacock, *Memoirs of Shelley and Other Essays and Reviews*, ed. Howard Mills (New York: New York University Press 1970), 128.

28 Leonidas M. Jones, ed., *Selected Prose of John Hamilton Reynolds* (Cambridge: Harvard University Press 1966), 46.

29 Leonidas Jones, ed., *The Letters of John Hamilton Reynolds* (Lincoln: University of Nebraska 1973), 5.

30 E. de Selincourt, ed., *The Letters of William and Dorothy Wordsworth*, revised by Mary Moorman and S. Hill (Oxford: Clarendon Press 1970), 345–6.

31 Shelley, *Poetical Works*, 369, 247–50.

32 Horace Smith, *Amarynthus the Nympholept: A Pastoral Drama in Three Acts, with other Poems* (London 1821), v.

33 Ibid., 20.

34 Shelley, *Letters*, 2:44.

35 *WPW*, 3:229.

36 Richard Chandler, *Travels in Asia Minor and Greece* (Oxford 1825), 2:191. (*Travels in Greece* was first published in 1776 as a separate volume.) Chandler's may have been the first englishing of "nympholepsy," but Shelley and Peacock would have been familiar with the Greek word in *Phaedrus* 238D used by Socrates to designate rapture and frenzy. The Greek means literally "seized by the nymphs," although it is likely that by Plato's day it had become a buried metaphor.

CHAPTER SIX

1 A long tradition of Neoplatonic allegorizing of *Endymion* extends from Colvin (1887) to Sperry (1962), including, inadvertently, Earl Wasserman's reading in 1953. More germane to this account is Dorothy Van Ghent's exploration of "The Goddess of Many Names" in *Keats: The Myth of the Hero*, edited posthumously by J.C. Robinson (Princeton: Princeton University Press 1983). Charles I. Patterson Jr, "The Monomyth in the Structure of Keats's Endymion," *KSJ*, 31 (1982): 64–81 relates the poem to the triplex goddess as she is described in Joseph Campbell's *The Hero with a Thousand Faces* (Cleveland: Meridian 1965). Patterson muses on how Keats anticipated Campbell so accurately. He does not explore the context of syncretic mythologies with which Keats was familiar.

2 J. Lemprière, *A Classical Dictionary* (London 1815), no pag. Entry under "Diana."

3 Michael Drayton, *Endimion and Phoebe*, in J.W. Hebel, ed., *The Works of Michael Drayton*, 5 vols. (Oxford: Clarendon Press 1931), 1:150.

4 Artemis's attributes have been identified variously as breasts, eggs, or ripe figs. Any of these would serve to announce unambiguously her association with fertility. James Frazer, *The Golden Bough: The Magic Art* (New York: Macmillan 1935), 1:37. Her association with chastity is a late Hellenistic development. Artemis seems to have been traumatized in infancy by witnessing her mother's terrible labour and enjoined celibacy upon her followers.

5 Horace, *Odes* 1.21.5.

6 Catullus 24.9–12.

7 Plutarch, *Moralia* 367.41.

8 Jane Harrison, *Themis* (Cambridge: Cambridge University Press 1912), 173, 190.

9 Keats's specificity as to the celebrants' sport and the subject of their story-telling indicates that he knew the mythic connections between Hyacinthus, Artemis, and her brother Apollo. Apollo's leman was brought up by Artemis, who was revered at Cnidos as *Hiakynthotrophos*, the nurse. Walter Otto, *Dionysus: Myth and Cult* (Bloomington: Indiana University Press 1965), 204. The story of Niobe is equally appropriate, since her children were destroyed by the archers Artemis and Apollo for having slighted their mother, Latona.

10 Keats knew from his Lemprière that dittany is sacred to Dictynna, the Cretan Artemis. The poppy is soporific.

11 Thomas Gray, "The Progress of Poetry," lines 86–7.

CHAPTER SEVEN

1 Homer, *Hymn to Aphrodite* 257.

2 Nonnus, *Dionysiaca* 40.558–63. Nonnus would appear to be an arcane witness to such matters, but he was a favourite of Peacock and his friends, who delighted in championing the byways of classical tradition.

3 Callimachus, *Hymns* 3.13–15.

4 Compare Wordsworth's description of the moonlit waters of Lake Como: "From high, the sullen water underneath, / On which a dull red image of the moon / Lay bedded, changing oftentimes its form / Like an uneasy snake" (*The Prelude*, 1805, 6.635–8).

5 Hesiod, *Catalogues of Women* 26. Eliade has related the moon and its goddess to the snake, "the animal that changes," by citing familiar effigies of Mediterranean goddesses bearing serpents. They were an attribute of the Great Goddess and appear with her avatars, the Arcadian Artemis, Hecate, and Persephone. The serpent possesses the lunar quality of periodic regeneration as well as telluric properties. Mircea Eliade, *Patterns in Comparative Religion*, trans. Rosemary Sheed (New York: Meridian 1965), 168–9.

6 Plutarch, "De pythiae oraculis," *Moralia* 398C.

7 Jacob Bryant, *A New System; or, An Analysis of Ancient Mythology* (London: J. Walker 1807), 2:272. Bryant denied the existence of Troy and the Trojan expedition and argued the authenticity of Thomas Rowley and Holy Scripture.

8 The worship of Artemis was particularly associated with low-lying land and reed-covered marshes, hence her attribute, the willow. See W.O.E. Oesterley, *The Sacred Dance* (Cambridge: Cambridge University Press 1923), 67.

9 Strabo, *Geography* 8.6.20.

10 Alciphron the Rhetor, *Letters of Courtesans* 5.2.

11 *Republic* 3.404D. 1 Corinthians 5:1, 6:16.

12 Philostratus, *The Life of Apollonius of Tyana* 4.25.

13 Bernice Slote, "La Belle Dame as Naiad," *JEGP*, 60 (1961): 22–30 has made such an identification. Barbara Fass, *La Belle Dame Sans Merci and the Aesthetics of Romanticism* (Detroit: Wayne State University Press 1974), 47 relates Lamia to the water sprite or Undine and cites Keats's reading of De La Motte Fouqué's romance in 1818, but does not inquire into the two creatures' common element or amphibious character.

14 "Nymphidia, The Court of Fayrie," lines 70–2 in J.W. Hebel, ed., *The Works of Michael Drayton*, 5 vols. (Oxford: Shakespeare Head 1932), 3:127.

15 Letter to Murray of October 1820. Leslie Marchand, ed., *Byron's Letters and Journals*, 11 vols. (Cambridge: Belknap Press 1977), 7:200.

16 Heraclitus 74.

17 Kathleen Raine and G.M. Harper, eds., *Thomas Taylor the Platonist* (Princeton: Princeton University Press 1969), 303.

18 Michael Psellus, *De damonium operatione*, Migne *PG* 112.866.

19 Cornelius Agrippa, *De occulta philosophia* 3.19.

20 James I, *Daemonologie* (Edinburgh 1597: reprinted Edinburgh: Edinburgh University Press 1966), 73–4.

21 Bruce Clarke, "Fabulous Monsters of Conscience: Anthropomorphoses in Keats' *Lamia*," *SIR*, 24 (Spring 1985): 555 identifies Hermes' trickster character and his hoodwinking of Jove, but does not explore the implications of these circumstances. Clarke identifies Apollonius with the basilisk, the fabulous slayer of serpents, and Keats's "penanced lady elf" with a Freudian/Derridean association of penned, pen, and penis.

22 Lamia's "death breath" need not imply the end of her infamy or her career. The disappearance of a corpse suggests a sequel: that, true to type, she will pursue further commissions elsewhere. Dorothy Van Ghent describes the "*sparagmos* at the end of the poem when Lamia is changed back hideously into a snake." This representation might serve the ends of narrative symmetry, but there is no textual evidence for it. *The Myth of the Hero*, 117.

23 Plutarch, "De garrulitate," *Moralia* 502F. Erasmus, *Adagia* 4.4.91. Attributing a conversational lull to Hermes' intercession was probably commonplace at gatherings of the Peacock – Leigh Hunt circle as a classicist's protest against the god's demeaning transmogrification into a passing angel.

24 Douglas Bush, "Keats," in *Mythology and the Romantic Tradition in English Poetry* (New York: Norton 1963), 101.

25 From the *Quarterly Review* of 6 October 1818. Quoted in Leonidas M. Jones, ed., *Selected Prose of John Hamilton Reynolds* (Cambridge: Harvard University Press 1966), 266.

26 W. Smith, *Dictionary of Greek and Roman Geography*, 2 vols. (London: Walton and Maberly 1854–7), 1:682.

27 Richard Chandler, *Travels in Asia Minor and Greece*, 2 vols. (Oxford 1825), 2:292. The temple is also described in E. Dodwell, *A Classical and Topographical Tour through Greece, During the Years 1801, 1805, and 1806*, 2 vols. (London 1819), 2:195.

28 Ovid, *Metamorphoses* 2.737ff. Apollodorus 3.14. Hyginus, *Fab.* 146.

29 Hazlitt's review of the 1814 British Institution show in the *Morning Chronicle* of 5 February 1814. P.P. Howe, ed., *The Complete Works of William Hazlitt*, 21 vols. (London and Toronto: Dent 1930–4), 18:14.

30 Ian Jack, *Keats and the Mirror of Art* (Oxford: Clarendon Press 1967).

CHAPTER EIGHT

1 Earl Wasserman established the practice by maintaining that the narrator and his hero represent sharply discriminated perspectives reflecting Shelley's own polarized impulses. E.R. Wasserman, *Shelley: A Critical Reading* (Baltimore: Johns Hopkins University Press 1971), 11. In 1975 Norman Thurston asserted that "We are obliged to read *Alastor* with the constant awareness that the hero of the poem (who reveals himself in his actions) is not at all the same as the narrator ... and that neither narrator nor hero is at all the same as the author (who, except for a dangerously misleading Preface, reveals himself hardly at all)." Norman Thurston, "Author, Narrator, and Hero in Shelley's *Alastor*," *SIR*, 14 (Spring 1975): 119. Thurston overlooks the fact that the poet-hero is his narrator's creation, and he describes the poet as "left without hope and without despair (128)." But the narrator too is left without hope, as if he, like Coleridge's wedding guest, were experiencing the tale for the first time and were stunned by its self-revelation. Jean Hall, *The Transforming Image: A Study of Shelley's Major Poetry* (Urban, Chicago, London: University of Illinois Press 1980), 32 maintains that Shelley "adopted the strategy of his narrator, which is writing about his torment in order to distance it." Most recently, Ronald Tetreault, *The Poetry of Life: Shelley and Literary Form* (Toronto, Buffalo, London: University of Toronto Press 1987), 46 has followed Wasserman in maintaining that narrator and poet "represent different ways of being a poet. The narrator comes to see the Visionary as his fatal counterpart; a sort of double who dares to enact his most deeply repressed desires."

2 The most recent investigation of *Alastor* as a response to Wordsworth is G. Kim Blank's *Wordsworth's Influence on Shelley* (London: Macmillan 1988).

3 Donald H. Reiman, *Percy Bysshe Shelley* (New York: Twayne 1969), 35.

4 Harold Hoffman, *An Odyssey of the Soul* (New York: Columbia University Press 1933), 43–6. Hoffman argued a deliberate deployment on Shelley's part of the Narcissus myth. Barbara Shapiro, armed with object relations theory and the hypothesis of the narcissistic wound, sees it as an unconscious strategy and the poem as symptomatic of the "schizoid narcissistic personality of

Shelley, trapped in regressive and escapist fantasies." Barbara Shapiro, *The Romantic Mother: Narcissistic Patterns in Romantic Poetry* (Baltimore and London: Johns Hopkins University Press 1983), 15.

5 Mary Shelley, *Frankenstein* (London: J.M. Dent 1961), 45.

6 G. Wilson Knight, *The Starlit Dome* (Oxford: Oxford University Press 1941), 186. There is no indication, other than the title Peacock gave the poem, that its hero is Greek and that his quest begins in that country or in Asia Minor. In terms of my own argument concerning the literary sources and the nature of the journey, it is, however, an attractive speculation. Edward Strictland, "Transfigured Night: The Visionary Inversions of *Alastor*," *KSJ*, 33 (1984): 148–60 raises the crucial question about the ancient mariner's voyage, Childe Harold's and the *Alastor* hero's quest: "Where is he going?" Strictland sees *Alastor* following the Coleridgean precedent in divorcing the protagonist from the real world and moving him into a world of myth. Ronald Tetreault is more specific concerning the *Alastor* hero's rambles: "The geography of his voyage clearly symbolizes a journey toward a source, but a source that lies outside the limits of time and space" (50).

7 Donald Cameron, *Shelley: The Golden Years* (Cambridge: Harvard University Press 1974), 223.

8 E.E. Bostetter, *The Romantic Ventriloquists* (Seattle: University of Washington Press 1963), 199. Bostetter writes: "Once again, Shelley is quick to have it both ways," and finds his confusion of the sensual and ideal a muddle. Wasserman points out the passage's autoerotic nature, and Byron's castigation of Keats "self-pollutings" suggests that autoeroticism was endemic among young Romantics.

9 I have made use of the Platonic terms *pothos* and *himeros* with which Shelley was familiar. See Shelley's note to his "Hymn of Apollo," in which he considers *himeros*. Two of Coleridge's notebook entries of 1810 indicate that he too was concerned with the significance of these terms deriving from *Cratylus* 420a. *CN* 3:3777: "General kindly Affection, or fervent benevolence – Attachment – Love – The object absent it is ποθος – Desire." *CN* 3:4335: "ποθος, for the Past: Ἱμερος, for the Present: Ερος, for the Future."

10 Joseph Campbell, *The Hero with a Thousand Faces* (Cleveland: Meridian 1965), 110–11.

11 C.G. Jung, *Collected Works*, 20 vols. (Princeton: Princeton University Press 1953), 5:205.

12 Shelley elaborated the eagle and the serpent image in *Laon and Cythna* two years later, and again as vulture and snake in *Prometheus Unbound*, 3.2.

13 Herodotus, *History* 3.93. Cameron has answered Reiman's mistaken contention that the hero has travelled to the Aral Sea to meet his destiny in the Indian mountain range by appealing to the facts of eastern geography. The westward direction of the final journey supports Cameron's argument. Reiman, *Perry Bysshe Shelley*, 38; Cameron, *Shelley*, 611.

14 F.L. Jones, ed., *Mary Shelley's Journals* (Norman: University of Oklahoma Press 1947), 220–4.

15 Ibid., 218.

16 Mircea Eliade, *Patterns in Comparative Religion*, trans. Rosemary Sheed (New York: Meridian 1965), 433.

17 Victor Ehrenberg, "*Pothos* in Alexander the Great," in G.T. Griffith, ed., *Alexander the Great: The Main Problems* (Cambridge: Heffer 1966), 52–61.

18 Roger Ingpen and W.E. Peck, eds., *The Complete Works of Percy Bysshe Shelley*, 10 vols. (New York: Gordian Press 1965), 1:243.

19 Ibid., 9:180.

20 "Speculations on Metaphysics," ibid., 7:59–60.

21 Hoffman, *An Odyssey of the Soul*, 129. "In a role borrowed from the ark it rests on the topmost ridge of the mountain." Hoffman's explanation is bizarre, although he is unwittingly on the scent of the river's location.

22 Strabo 11.14.13; 11.4.2. Virgil, *Aeneid* 8.728.

23 J. Lemprière, *A Classical Dictionary* (London 1815), no pag.

24 Herodotus, *History* 4.40.

25 J. Hastings, *A Dictionary of the Bible* (Edinburgh: Clark 1898–1906), 1:643. The texts pertaining to the Alexandrine episode are reproduced in Lawton P.G. Peckham and Milan S. La Du, eds., *La Prise de Defur and Le Voyage D'Alexandre au Paradis Terrestre* (Princeton: Princeton University Press 1935).

26 Shelley's account of the passage of the river of life in *Laon and Cythna* suggests a rerun of *Alastor*'s voyage, but, like the poem itself, it is less effective and less resonant because Shelley's commitment to an overly elaborate narrative renders it disconcertingly external: "We know not where we go, or what sweet dream / May pilot us through caverns strange and fair / Of far and pathless passion, while the stream / Of life, our bark doth on its whirlpools bear, / Spreading swift wings as sails to the dim air" (*Laon and Cythna* 6.29).

27 Harold Bloom, *The Visionary Company* (London: Faber and Faber 1961), 280; Reiman repeats Bloom's contention without cavil.

CHAPTER NINE

1 T.S. Eliot, *The Use of Poetry and the Use of Criticism* (London: Faber 1933), 84.

2 Harold Bloom, *Shelley's Mythmaking* (New Haven: Yale University Press 1959), 165. The most detailed readings of the poem to have appeared since this chapter was first published in *ELH* in its original form are those of J.E. Hogle, "Metamorphoses in Shelley's 'The Witch of Atlas,' " *SIR*, 19 (Fall 1980): 327–53 and Brian Nellest, "Shelley's Narratives and 'The Witch of

Atlas,' " in *Essays on Shelley*, ed. Miriam Allott (Totowa, NJ: Barnes and Noble 1982).

3 Major James Rennell, *The Geographical System of Herodotus Examined and Explained* (London 1800), 433.

4 Herodotus, *History* 2.31.

5 Ibid., 2.32.

6 Pliny, *Natural History* 5.10.51–2.

7 J.G. Frazer, *Pausanias' Description of Greece* (London: Macmillan 1898), 1:33.4.

8 Ibid., 1.33.6–7.

9 Carlos Baker, "Literary Sources of Shelley's 'The Witch of Atlas,' " *PMLA*, 56 (1941): 472–9. D.L. Clark, "What Was Shelley's Indebtedness to Keats?" *PMLA*, 56 (1941): 479–94.

10 Bloom, *Shelley's Mythmaking*, 165.

11 J. Lemprière, *A Classical Dictionary* (London 1815), no pag. Entry under "Atlantides."

12 Homer, *Odyssey* 6.123; 12.318.

13 Plutarch, *De defectu oraculorum* 11.

14 F.L. Jones, ed., *The Letters of Percy Bysshe Shelley*, 2 vols. (Oxford: Clarendon Press 1964), 2:87–8.

15 Clark, "What Was Shelley's Indebtedness," 487.

16 Herodotus 4.184. Herodotus is indecisive concerning their pastoral nature, which is asserted in 4.174, but elsewhere he describes them as hunting the swift-footed Troglodytes who feed on serpents and lizards and screech-bats. Such discrepancies prompted Lucian in his *True History* to consign Herodotus to the worst of sinners in Hades. Apollo was associated with the area described by Herodotus. The founding rulers of the Garamantes and the Nasamoneans were his grandchildren.

17 Herodotus 4.191.

18 Ibid., 3.24.

19 Ibid., 4.185.

20 Pliny 5.57.

21 Mary Shelley, "Note on *Alastor*," in Thomas Hutchinson, ed., *The Complete Poetical Works of Percy Bysshe Shelley* (London: Oxford University Press 1956), 31.

22 Carlos Baker, *Shelley's Major Poetry* (Princeton: Princeton University Press 1948), 211; Bloom, *Shelley's Mythmaking*, 200.

23 F.A.C. Wilson, *W.B. Yeats and Tradition* (London: Methuen 1958), 217.

24 G. Wilson Knight, *The Starlit Dome* (Oxford: Oxford University Press 1941), 228–9.

25 F. Sherwood Taylor, *The Alchemists* (St Albans: Paladin 1976), 118.

26 Herodotus 4.185.

27 Brian Nellest, "Shelley's Narratives," 190, note 33, questions my assumption and that of readers since Carlos Baker that Shelley's Thamondocana can be identified with Timbuctoo. Nellest identifies this as somewhat of a crux in the poem and confesses that he can find no reference to Thamondocana anywhere, proposing that Shelley may have garbled the name from a misremembering of a schoolboy translation of Pliny's Ochema. In fact, Shelley's early editors, Locock among them, made this same identification. And they were right: so was Shelley. Θαμονδοκανα lives, or did live, in the mind of Ptolemy, who placed it on the south bank of the Niger (*Geography* 4.6.10). Paulys's *Real Encyclopädie der Classischen Altertums Wissenschaft* notes that the site has traditionally been associated with Timbuctoo and Timkala, although those cities were of later foundation. Shelley's Thamondocana smacks of the classical arcana bandied about by members of the Peacock circle, who, despite their drollery, knew, like Shelley, what they were talking about.

28 Robert Adams, *Narrative of Robert Adams* (London 1816). Shelley read Mungo Park, *Journal of a Mission to the Interior of Africa* (1805) in 1815 and 1816, and his *Travels in Africa* (1799) in 1814. The author died near Timbuctoo.

29 Bloom, *Shelley's Mythmaking*, 200.

30 A large lake is mentioned in Ptolemy's *Geography*, which recounts the voyage and inland trek of Diogenes to what seems to have been Victoria Nyanza. Ptolemy located the lake much farther south than it is. The legend was kept alive by Arab traders until the rediscovery of the lake by Speke in 1853.

31 Herodotus 2.24.

32 Ibid., 2.148.

33 Douglas Bush, *Mythology and the Romantic Tradition in English Poetry* (New York: Norton 1963), Baker (*Shelley's Major Poetry*), and Bloom, (*Shelley's Mythmaking*) cite the influence of Shelley's translation of the *ottava rima* "Hymn to Mercury," completed a month before writing *The Witch of Atlas*. Bloom identifies the witch as a female counterpart of the Homeric Hermes. There is undoubtedly a connection between the two poems, but it should be emphasized that the "Hymn" characterizes the infant Hermes only as inventor of the lyre and as a precocious trickster figure, avoiding the issue of his divinity and role as *hermes psychopompos*. Horace's ode to Mercury is indebted to Homer but concludes with an evocation of the god as bearer of souls. Shelley's witch is all of these: immortal, trickster, psychopomp, and more.

34 "How the god Apis was really a bull / And nothing more" (627–8). Shelley, of course, puns with "bull," but the incident may have been suggested by the encounter of the mad Cambyses, conqueror of Egypt, with Apis, the sacred bull of Memphis. In a fit of iconoclasm, Cambyses stabbed the bull-god and

harangued his priests: "Ye blockheads, are there such gods as these, consisting of blood and flesh, and sensible of Steel? This truly, is a god worthy of the Egyptians" (Herodotus 3.29).

35 Herodotus 2.35–6.

36 Letter to Peacock, 25 July 1818, in F.L. Jones, ed., *The Letters of Percy Bysshe Shelley*, 2 vols. (Oxford: Clarendon Press 1964), 2:25–6.

37 F.L. Jones, ed., *Mary Shelley's Journal* (Norman: University of Oklahoma 1957), 222. Shelley seems to have read the *History* as early as 1815, in 1818, on 1 October 1820, and in December 1821.

38 Shelley's sole reference to a historical figure in his poem is to the Pharaoh Amasis. His career is outlined in Herodotus 2.161–3.

39 *The Letters of Percy Bysshe Shelley*, 2:257.

Index